MW01002322

Wood Knocks
and
Tossed Rocks:

*Searching for Sasquatch with the
Bigfoot Field Researchers Organization*

by Blaine McMillan

©Copyright 2014 Blaine J. McMillan CD1 BCrim

ISBN 978-0-9916825-0-8
Publisher prefix ISBN 978-0-9916825

Forward by Christopher Noël
Cover art by Cindy Dosen
Bigfoot - A Primer by Vince Lauria
Bigfoot Researcher's Quick Reference Guide prepared by Charles Lamica

Back cover photo from BFRO Report # 13390
www.bfro.net/GDB/show_report.asp?id=13390

Formatted by The Writer Connection
www.SelfPublishingResources.ca

Disclaimer:
This is a work of non-fiction. The information contained in this book is meant to expose the reader to the thrill of attending a BFRO expedition. The author has tried to recreate events from his memories of them. In order to maintain their anonymity in some instances the author has changed the names of some individuals. The conversations in the book all come from the author's recollections, though they are not written to represent word-for-word transcripts. Rather, the author has retold them in a way that evokes the feeling and meaning of what was said and in all instances, the essence of the dialogue is accurate.

For my Lobster

"And the men who hold high places
Must be the ones who start
To mould the new reality
Closer to the Heart
The Blacksmith and the Artist
Reflect it in their art
Forge their creativity
Closer to the Heart
Philosophers and Ploughmen
Each must know his part
To sow a new reality
Closer to the Heart"

Rush – A Farewell to Kings (1977)

Contents

Acknowledgments

I would like to thank the following people for their contributions and their assistance.

First and foremost, I want to thank Matthew Moneymaker for bringing me onboard as an investigator with the Bigfoot Field Researchers Organization.

To all of the witnesses that I have interviewed I want to extend a thank you for your bravery in the face personal ridicule in reporting something most people deny even exists.

To all of the other investigators, with whom I have conferred over the years, I thank you for your friendship and your assistance.

To the academics, scientists, BFRO members and authors who granted me permission to reference their works, thank you for your guidance.

And finally to my editors; the Mannos, Traudi and Aldo, my wife Irene, and Allan Yeoman, who attended the BFRO North Vancouver Island expedition in 2009, I want to extend my hand in gratitude for providing the much-needed editorial direction in the completion of this book.

Foreword

In September of 2005, I attended my first BFRO expedition, in Whitehall, New York, and my life has never been the same since. No, we didn't experience a sighting, but the one definite wood knock awoke me to the concrete reality of Sasquatch in my own neighborhood, and Matthew Moneymaker's impassioned teaching illuminated for our small group the broader landscape of this field of inquiry. For several days, he filled us in on the long and colorful history of the research effort, and on what we've learned so far about the nature of this creature.

"It's as if," he told us, "you're trying to make contact with a lost tribe. You approach them with great respect, with the attitude that you know they're smart, and that you want to let them *know* that you know. And that you understand you are trespassing on *their* territory. I think they've seen human activity that seemed endearing or sympathetic. You've probably watched people having fun somewhere, from a distance. And you wish you could go and have fun with them too. I think they watch us and probably plenty of times they wish they could just freely walk among us. But they know they *can't.*"

Doubters love to object, "How could there *possibly* be a gigantic apelike creature in our forests and we not *know* about it?" They say this with a kind of self-satisfied smirk, evidently thinking that the question alone should put the matter to rest, that no reasonable explanation can be put forward. "There's this American chauvinism," Moneymaker told us, "this sense that we're well in control of our own country, thank you very much. That *nothing* like this could get away with it...*in our backyard.*"

I say, there are two possibilities and two *only.* Either they don't exist (in which case all of the tens of thousands of sincere, first-hand accounts of sightings throughout North America, over centuries, are false), or else they do exist. If even one of these accounts is accurate, then probably the vast majority of them are, because that would mean the species is real. And if they do exist, they can only have survived alongside *Homo sapiens* (a violently domineering species) by being far more elusive than we can even imagine.

It is this very elusiveness that has allowed the doubters to go on smirking through the eons. Some feel that we should not attempt to study Sasquatch at all but rather just leave them alone, let them go about their business in peace. My response is two-fold:

1) They would not have been so very successful as a species over thousands of years unless they were perfectly capable of avoiding trouble and going about their business without our assistance;

2) Given natural human curiosity, their discovery is inevitable, so the best course of action is to prepare for that day with learning, with responsibly gathered *information* available to the mainstream media, and to the public at large, which can offset the hysteria at the thought of some dangerous and bloodthirsty "monster" in our midst.

Some of us have known for a while that Sasquatch is quite real, and that it is much closer to *person* than to monster. For the rest, the day of discovery is near at hand, and it will shock the world.

Matthew Moneymaker puts it well. "I grew up in the shadow of the Griffith Observatory and was always aware of the old, famous astronomers, especially Copernicus and Galileo, who suffered severe personal hardship for daring to go against the prevailing worldview. So with this whole Sasquatch effort, I look to those early pioneers, who simply observed the available data with a cold, objective eye and concluded that reality is radically different from what everyone had forever assumed."

In writing *Wood Knocks & Tossed Rocks*, Blaine McMillan makes a valuable contribution to the current paradigm shift with regard to our kindred species.

Christopher Noël, author of
Sasquatch Rising 2013: Dead Giants Tell No Tales

Preface

The question as to why I would want to write a book about the sasquatch and by extension my experiences with the Bigfoot Field Researchers Organization (BFRO) has puzzled me for some time. It was not a question of should I write it but more that there was a need to write it. This need began as a cathartic journal and expanded into the desire to help validate the existence of this creature especially to those who do not believe that such an animal does exist. My intention is for you to share in the thrill of being on a series of expeditions with the BFRO.

This book will follow some basic guidelines:

- There will be no precise locations or directions given to any BFRO expedition sites that are not already public knowledge. That is to say, if an expedition had taken place near the town of Comox, B.C. I will write about that area but I will not be giving out directions or clues to guide you, the reader, to a specific BFRO research area. Many of these expedition locations are still very active and members of the BFRO continually return to these places in order to conduct additional studies.
- I will not reveal the names of any expedition attendees or any BFRO members without their prior approval. Due diligence will be used to acquire everyone's permission. In cases where permission is not granted and the individual is publicly known to be involved with sasquatch research I will use a pseudonym.
- All sources used will be cited.

Every topic or subject worthy of an intelligent discussion must have a base line of common knowledge accepted by the public at large. What follows is a great article written by a fellow BFRO investigator. Authored in 1999, it is re-printed here in its original form with the author's permission.

Bigfoot – a Primer
by Vince Lauria

In the dense forested regions of America may live…no, <u>probably</u> lives…a primate animal that looks like a gorilla with long legs. The evidence suggests that the males of this species may weigh in excess of six hundred pounds and stand an average of eight feet tall. The evidence further suggests that this large man-like creature, with brown or black shaggy hair and often a terrible stench, forages and hunts mainly at night. Capable of running at up to 40 miles per hour but preferring stealth, having great strength and agility yet being extremely shy, this animal has not escaped our notice. It has only escaped inclusion in our collective worldview.

What are the limits of our worlds?   We all live in worlds we know from touch, feel and other sensory experience. But we also live in an extended world that is taught to us by TV, movies, books, education and the stories of our teachers. Our combined personal and given worldview is restricted by the amount and the nature of the inputs we have received.

After reading this article, you may want to further research the subject. There is something hidden out there, and you might want to know if it is a hidden reality or a conspired fiction. This long-legged gorilla thing that walks upright like we do; this oversized phantom of the deep woods that we seldom visit… Bigfoot, sasquatch, gigantopithecus, or whatever you prefer to call it, appears to actually exist. But I don't believe that I can convince you in this article. So at the end you will find a link to a good Web site to begin your own research, including Bigfoot sighting reports in your home state. Then make your own decision.

You may have heard of Bigfoot, as the large hairy man-beast of the Pacific Northwest. But there are as many sightings, if not more, of Bigfoots in the Eastern states than in the West. Another image we have is that this is a spooky, lone creature that likes to terrify humans in its domain. Terrified humans really are left in its wake, but Bigfoots (an accepted plural, but Sasquatch may be preferred) probably lives mostly in docile, concealed family groups.

No way. This can't be true. We've mapped and explored everything. That is what you are probably saying. Where's the proof? There actually appears to be proof in the form of fur and fecal samples, highly detailed casts of footprints, eyewitness reports and sound recordings of calls and screams. There are also a few films and videos of the creature. What we don't have, is a living or deceased animal specimen. That's the only missing proof that would put this animal in our textbooks. But solid, clear video evidence from a close encounter would be more desirable. Later with good funding we might trap one with a large and very strong and expensive live trap. Then we could work to protect it from quiet extinction.

There are stories of Bigfoot specimens being captured or killed, only to become carnival attractions or lumber camp curiosities and never to be examined and cataloged by science. Then, of course, there is the attitude of science in general.

The biologists have invested much more than you, in studying the natural world and they consider themselves experts. It is probably harder for them to admit ignorance than for us, yet their worldviews have been blown wide open in the past by the discovery and capture of unlikely creatures. The giant panda, a thought-to-be-extinct fish called the coelacanth and other rumored creatures have all turned up alive and are in zoos or specimen jars now. We even discovered a stone-age tribe in recent times living on a South Seas island, undiscovered until then by civilized humans.

We are smart, but possibly a little too arrogant. There is precious little money being spent to get proof of Bigfoot. Yet with motion detector video cameras with night vision we could probably accomplish it. Did you win the lottery and don't know what to do with all that money?

Why haven't bones been found? Why hasn't a hunter shot one? There are answers to these questions that make a lot of sense. Click the link at the end of this article to read the answers in detail. For now let it suffice to say that few hunters will shoot a creature that looks like a man. Few will even admit it if they saw something as preposterous as an eight foot tall "boogie man".

Dead bears and other large animals are eaten and dissipated in a few weeks in the woods. They return quickly, bones and all, to the soil. Then too it has recently been determined that our extinct brethren, Neanderthal man, buried their dead. Could this not be true also of Bigfoot families? (I often wondered why Bigfoot remains were not found after Mount St. Helens erupted.)

Bigfoots are said to walk more efficiently than we do. They do not lock their knees as we do with each stride, but rather keep them bent. They also appear to be a true creature of the night with eyes that are designed for night vision. This makes them highly reflective and causes them to shine red like demon eyes at night. Reports of seeing such a thing would be quickly laughed off.

It is suspected that Bigfoots pass the day crouched in a hollow in the deepest thickets of swampy, mountainous and rolling terrain. They, like the mountain gorilla can probably subsist on leaves, shoots, grubs and an occasional small animal kill. But there are reports and evidence, especially in southeastern Ohio, of Bigfoots killing deer, and often for the sake of just their livers. We, of course provide fields of corn, milo and other foods for his taking at night. The Skunk Ape, a Bigfoot version in Peninsula Florida, is said to like lima beans.

The creature is certainly known to be crafty and elusive. He vanishes into thickets and blends with the trees, often climbing small hills with impressive speed and power. He will pound on trees with sticks to communicate to others of his kind, howl, grunt and stomp to bluff and scare intruders into his territory, but he has never been known to attack a human except in rage after being shot. For the most part, Bigfoots seem to exist in our rural woodlands with very little sign that they are there (although probably not in any density of population). Yet it is said that thousands must exist. It is my own speculation that most of the ones that are seen are rogue males seeking to start new family groups. They are not so familiar with the terrain and make errors in their movements that cause them to be seen by humans. They also are thought to be possibly nomadic (not migratory) and thereby avoid the few determined hunters that would zero in on them. Most hunters, of course are after a target species (deer, elk, turkey, etc.). They don't have a license to shoot a Bigfoot, nor would they dare shoot at something that looks like a man. If it turned out to be a guy in a gorilla suit, they could be charged with murder.

It is the eyewitness reports that have convinced me that Bigfoots are real. Most Bigfoot reports are conveyed by people who have nothing to gain and plenty to lose by creating a hoax or even reporting the truth. Many are not comfortable with spelling and the art of writing. They are telling something that just has to be told. You need to read these reports for yourself.

With the easy access via the Internet to research groups, reports are being made of encounters with Bigfoots that happened, for instance, in the childhood of a now middle-aged adult. If you have had an encounter please take the time to submit it. Tiny details may be important to understanding this creature and finally getting solid video proof of its reality.

I found a report from the 1950's of a large Bigfoot seen in the East Brewton, Alabama area at night. Two other encounters from Alabama were found on the Internet, one in Washington County and one in Clarke County. I visited all three of these actual locations and discovered that they had two things in common. The proximity of deep, thick and swampy woods and access to sizable rivers bordered by woods. My guess is that these locations offer a variety of plant and animal foods as well as good cover for sleeping.

If you take a look at your fellow humans, you will notice that most of them follow the same routes from a work place to home. We tend to stay in urban and shopping areas. The large expanses of wooded lands in America are seldom visited at all, let alone at night. During the day we make a lot of noise at recreation sites and stay in campgrounds and on lakeshores. The few of us that ever encounter Bigfoots are like the few of us that ever encounter a UFO…they just don't want to talk about it. They are afraid of ridicule.

There are plenty of known animals in the woods that we hardly ever see. Bears, deer, weasels, cougars, bobcats and other animals are there, and some in large numbers, yet we rarely encounter them. The movie The Blair Witch Project reminded us of our primal fear of the woods at night. We are simply day foragers. Bigfoots own the night where they live. They're there, they're big, they're harmless and they don't want anything to do with us if they can help it. Many Indian tribes know of Bigfoots' existence, but we tend to view their knowledge as mystical legends.

The explorer, Thor Heyerdahl, built the balsa raft: Kon Tiki, and sailed it across the Pacific Ocean to prove it could have been done by primitive peoples. Others made the swim across the English Channel and some have hiked across America. If Bigfoot can escape our sight so long and so easily then I see a challenge for a young adventurer: Take a hike across America, do it at night, until just after dawn, and do it without being seen by anyone. Live off the land as much as possible. You will prove that Bigfoots could certainly do it. You might also find a big, hairy traveling companion.

What would I do if I won the lottery? I'd gather some small, remote or robotically- controlled dirigibles loaded with sensing equipment: infrared, olfactory, sound detection, etc. They would be programmed to seek out and record the presence of animals, and Bigfoot would be top of the list. They could fly silently with electric motors, anchor in tree tops and release again at will. Detecting the pattern of a pre-recorded call, they could move in that direction and lurk, unseen (hopefully) above the trees. Locking onto an individual, by heat, sound, smell or photo vision, they would follow it and record the track with GPS, while video taping anything it could get. Is this a fantasy? I believe the soundless propulsion would be the most difficult element to overcome.

A thought provoking book that deals with Bigfoots and other hominids, as well as evidence of our origin that will blow apart your worldview, is aptly named: "Everything You Know Is Wrong" by Lloyd Pye. It can be found at www.amazon.com except at this writing the book is currently out of stock.[1]

Here is the main jumping off place for further research on Bigfoots. Don't forget to check their database for sightings in your state. http://www.bfro.net/. You can write me here: lvince@panhandle.rr.com.

1   Everything You Know is Wrong by Lloyd Pye is available through Amazon.com.

Introduction

In the 1970's and 80's *The Beachcombers* was a popular television series with many Canadian families. The CBC production was centered on the interactions of the residents of Gibsons, a small BC community on the Sunshine Coast. In one particular episode, entitled *The Sasquatch Walks by Night*, Relic sells "Sasquatch Tours" to thrill-seeking tourists after a sasquatch is sighted near the town.[1] This was the first time I had ever heard of a sasquatch. I was fascinated with the idea that a huge unknown creature could be wandering the woods of British Columbia. At the same time I was also terrified at this prospect, especially while walking home alone from a Cub Scout meeting through the forest at night.

The first bigfoot book that I remember reading was entitled "*Sasquatch*", written by Don Hunter and Rene Dahinden (1973). I may have bought it at the local corner store or maybe at a yard sale. I still have it. Cutting across the front cover on an angle is a simulated filmstrip with a close up of the creature Roger Patterson had filmed in October of 1967. The pages are now yellowing with age and the center photos are starting to crack out of the spine which is not surprising since I must have read that book from cover to cover at least a hundred times. Naturally, this book only fuelled a hunger within me for any book that had the word bigfoot, yeti, or sasquatch in the title. I was, and still am, a voracious reader on the subject but I don't think my parents really took any notice of the library I was soon acquiring. In very short order I had purchased books by John Napier, Ivan T. Sanderson, John Green and others. Each book was written from a different perspective but all of them included the reported cases of Baumann, Ostman, Beck and Roe. These four incidents have now been retold so often they have become benchmarks for all other sightings. By the time I had read all of the books that I could find on the subject I was very familiar with each of these stories. I was even able to refer to them from memory and quote them chapter and verse.

One weekend, when I was about 13 years old, my family headed for Hidden Lake to do some camping and fishing. This was one of our favorite lakes since it was close to home and it offered plenty of activity for everyone. On this particular weekend I brought Hunter and Dahinden's book with me. I was leafing through it when I saw a story about a Mr. and Mrs. Bellvue who were "camped at Hidden Lake, a few miles from the town of Enderby in B.C.'s Okanagan Valley."[2] The book described how, one evening, during the Labor Day weekend in 1959, Mrs. Bellvue was gathering some wood for the fire. At one point she felt uncomfortable, as if she were being watched. She looked up and standing nearby was a tall hair covered giant. After staring at each other for some length of time Mrs. Bellvue returned to her campsite. At first she didn't tell her husband because, in her words, "he would think I had lost my marbles."[3] However, as she was trying to go to sleep Mrs. Bellvue suddenly felt that they had overstayed their welcome and that they should leave as soon as possible. It was at that point that she told her husband about her sighting. Surprisingly, during the day Mr. Bellvue had also felt uneasy about being at the lake and, after hearing his wife's tale, they decided to break camp first thing in the morning. As the last tent pole came down the couple heard the "sound of running feet, moving gradually away from them through the bush."[4]

I was ecstatic! We were camping at the very same lake as the Bellvues had their sighting. I wondered if the same creature could still be living there in 1975 and if so, would I have a sighting too? Unfortunately, I had no such luck. Over the next several years my family had camped at least a dozen times at Hidden Lake and as far as I can remember no one had ever reported seeing anything even resembling a sasquatch. Maybe Mr. and Mrs. Bellvue had been mistaken in what they had seen and felt, or maybe not. Little did I know that my own experience with a sasquatch would take place some ten years later.

In the fall of 1986, my father and I planned an extensive hunting trip to the southeastern corner of British Columbia. There were to be five people in the group: my father, my Uncle Bob and myself. Joining us would be Vic and his son Brent, friends whom we had camped with for years. We had two trucks, an ATV and my parents' travel trailer for some deluxe accommodations. A couple of days before the trip I drove from Comox to Salmon Arm to help my Dad load up the trailer with all of the essentials for ten days out in the woods. The five of us had purchased the required game tags for elk, deer and moose. With this collection of licenses we could switch hunting partners and still have the ability to harvest just about anything that we spotted. For armament, I had a 7x57mm Chilean Mauser; Dad brought a 7mm Magnum and his venerable 303 Mk. V Lee Enfield. Bob, being a southpaw, had a Remington model 7600 30-06 pump action. Brent had the same rifle but it was the Model 76, a lower end version of the Model 7600. On this trip Vic would be carrying an 8mm Magnum.

It was a frosty morning when we caravanned out of Salmon Arm, heading east on the Trans-Canada Highway towards Golden. Once there we would refuel before turning south into the Columbia River Valley. It would take us at least three hours to get to Golden but first we had to get past Three Valley Gap, a narrow winding stretch of the Trans-Canada Highway that was notorious for black ice and falling rocks. Originally we were going to hunt in and around the Spillamacheen River valley, which flows eastward to meet the Columbia, but plans are always subject to change. It had taken us six hours to get from Salmon Arm to the general area where we wanted to be and as my dad and I prepared supper, Vic took the quad and his rifle out for a little spin. Vic was gone for quite a while and when he got back he told us that he had found no fresh game sign at all, neither tracks nor dung. After some discussion it was agreed that there was no reason for us to stay here when it appeared that there was no game to be had. Bob told us of a co-worker who had a fair amount of success hunting the Palliser River basin. Since it was only three hours farther to the southeast we decided to head to the Palliser River first thing in the morning.

To enter the Palliser River valley you have to leave the Banff to Radium highway at a nondescript turn off and then follow the Kootenay River southward. Like most of the roads leading deep into BC's backcountry they are often known only by word of mouth and an accurate odometer. The road itself was a typical narrow gravel road that hugged the side of the mountain as it wound its way up to a steppe plateau where it began to cut across the plain towards the towering Rocky Mountains. We set up our camp on the bank of the Kootenay River only a short distance away from where it joined the Palliser River. Near this confluence there was a flood plain meadow on the left with a high hill on the right. There were other hunters camped in the area as well. One group, staying in pair of camper trucks, was across the road from us while near the meadow was a group of professional outfitters who specialized in hunting from horseback. Their encampment was fairly involved with large portable wood stoves pulling double duty for cooking and for heating the canvas walled tents. I don't know how long the other groups had been hunting in this area but I was concerned that none of them appeared to have harvested any game animals as of yet.

During our initial exploration of the local area it was discovered that a flood had washed away the main bridge over the Palliser River. Try as we may the only way to get across the rushing waters would be by aerial vehicle or on horseback. Having neither, our hunting district was effectively reduced by half. The next several days were spent searching the vicinity for signs of game. Every time we went out we would team up in different groups. After breakfast Bob and I would head in one direction while my father, along with Vic and Brent, would search a different area. At lunchtime everyone would meet back at the trailer to compare notes on what had been seen. This would determine which places needed a second look if the game sign had been promising. This was also a good opportunity to switch partners and refuel the vehicles before heading out again.

Several days in Brent and I decided to go over some of the roads that were closer to the trailer site. After we had crossed the creek feeding into the Palliser I spotted an old logging road on our right hand side. This road appeared to climb the hill to a point above our campsite or maybe even higher. It was my hope that from this vantage point we would finally see a way to get across the river. The road circled to the left as it climbed up the hill and it was quite clear that the hill had been logged off a number of years earlier. The tree stumps and the slash had already started to be grown over by alder and aspen trees.

At a point that was almost directly above our camp the road widened out to form another log loading landing. Looking out his window Brent spotted a fresh set of elk tracks in the soft earth so we quickly bailed out of the truck and loaded our weapons but for safety precautions we did not chamber a round. I took a closer look at the tracks and I could see from their shape and depth that they were definitely from a large bull. Brent and I talked over our next course of action. The tracks were very fresh; maybe a couple of hours old and we figured that there might be a chance that we could catch the bull bedded down.

We paced along the elk's track following it as it meandered from one side of the logging road to the other. The sun was high in the sky with little cloud cover and no breeze to speak of. It was shaping up to be a really nice afternoon. Looking downhill to my right I could see our base camp through the tops of the trees. Brent commented that we could have been sitting back at the trailer and an entire herd of elk could have paraded up or down this road and we would never have known it. On our left the hillside was studded with the stumps left behind from the logging operation. They looked like sore thumbs sticking up amongst the quick growing young alder and willows. As I looked to make sure that the elk track was still heading down the road I saw something that would forever change my life.

It was a track. But what a track! It looked like an extra-large bare human footprint and it caught me totally by surprise. How big was it? Okay you got me! But who walks around the forest with a tape measure while on a hunting trip? Nobody! So, I did exactly what every other person has done when finding such an imprint. I stepped beside it and compared it to my own booted foot. The track before me was about four inches longer than and almost twice as wide as my size 9E combat boot. From the configuration of the toes this was clearly from a left foot and looking ahead in the direction that they were pointed I saw another track but it was almost four feet away. Still unafraid, I walked along counting these tracks as they alternated left foot, right foot, left foot. After thirty or so prints Brent stopped and asked me where the elk tracks were since he could no longer spot them. I told him the elk tracks had moved to the right hand side of the road and then went over the embankment some sixty or seventy feet behind us.

"So, what are we following then?"

It was then that I pointed to the 17 x 8 inch human shaped footprint that was directly in front of him. As Brent knelt down to take a closer look he poignantly asked "What the hell made this track?"

"Brent, I believe that this may very well be a sasquatch track", I replied.

At this point I don't know if Brent actually believed me. We decided to backtrack a bit to see if we could find the point where the tracks of this unknown creature had first come down onto the road bed. As we walked down the road

Brent asked me if I knew anything about the sasquatch and so over the next ten or fifteen minutes I gave him a rundown of the limited knowledge that I had, which was based primarily on Don Hunter and Rene Dahinden's book. I told him the tales about Albert Ostman being kidnapped while prospecting the BC coast in 1924 and the all night assault upon Fred Beck's cabin on Mount St. Helens the same year. I also informed Brent about Mr. and Mrs. Bellvue's incident at Hidden Lake in 1959. Brent may not have recognized the first two locations but he certainly knew the third because we had both camped there dozens of times when we were kids.

After ten minutes of back-tracking we found the place where the prints first appeared on the road. Whatever had made them had come down off the logged hillside above us. Atop the ten-foot high embankment I found a partial imprint and halfway down there was a patch of freshly displaced earth. Both of these were in a direct line with the first track on the road. Again, whatever had made these tracks was walking on two legs and it had come down the hill in two strides. The first track on the road was at least two inches deep over its entire length. I thought that if a human had made these marks then I should be able to duplicate them. At the time I weighed 185 pounds and after jumping off a four-foot high tree stump the corner of my boot heel dented the ground by only ¾ of an inch, which was nowhere near the depth of that bare foot impression.

Ape Canyon, 1924.

Fred Beck had personally related to Rene Dahinden how his father-in-law had fired three rounds from a .35 Remington automatic at a sasquatch peeking from behind a tree. The bullets had creased the tree but when the men had reached the site there was no body to be found but a sasquatch was seen running down in the canyon.

Hunter and Dahinden, Sasquatch, pg. 23.

I really don't know what Brent was thinking but personally I was determined to follow these big footprints as far as I could. Un-slinging my rifle I quickly chambered a round and placed the weapon on safe. Brent followed suit by pumping the slide action on his rifle and then placed it on safe as well. Heading in the direction the tracks had taken Brent queried me as to precisely what our course of action would be should we actually see a sasquatch. Now, you must realize that I was much younger then and so my reply at that time was to "shoot for the center of mass".

"Then what do we do?"

His question made me stop and think for a few moments. What would we do if we actually shot and killed a sasquatch? I know that there had been several tales regarding a sasquatch getting up and walking away after being shot even from a relatively close range. With this in mind, I stated that if we had to shoot one and we actually succeeded in dropping it we would cut off its head because there is nothing I knew of that could survive without its head. Brent accepted this position and off we went.

Following the track way was fairly easy. On the left hand side of the road was a fresh footprint. Let me describe what I mean when I say that this track was fresh. The edges of the print were clearly defined in the earth, showing that the forces of erosion had not yet weathered it to any degree. Further evidence to support this was the absence of plant litter or soil on the inside of the shape. The heel, toes, and the ball of the foot were quite obvious and could not be mistaken for anything else. Some might suggest that the track was that of a large bear maybe even a grizzly but there was no evidence of a bear's ever-present claws.

After 200 yards or so the road began to narrow due to the growth of saplings along the edges, with some of them popping up in the center. These deciduous trees are very prolific. Starting in ones and twos they will sprout very quickly until an abandoned roadway is barely distinguishable from any other thicket of alder, willow or poplar trees. If you have ever walked down an old logging road then you know what I am talking about. As Brent and I pressed on in our quest, the tracks were not as visible amongst these small trees but we were able to spot a freshly broken branch where something had passed by. I was in the lead with Brent trailing six or seven paces behind me so any branches I passed would not inadvertently whip against him. By now the bush was thick enough that we had to carry our rifles vertically in front of us as opposed to having them held across our chests. I suppose we could have slung them on our shoulders but in this position they would have been useless to us if an emergency arose.

Brent urgently whispered, "Stop! Listen!"

I paused where I was and cocked one ear to hear what had made him stop. Straining, I heard…. nothing. No birds, no chipmunks, no bugs. It seemed as if even the breeze had stopped blowing. Then we smelled it. It was an overpowering "wet dog, dead seal on the beach for a week" kind of odor that seemed to be all around us. Whatever it was it was really close. That was it! My hackles flew up and I knew that it was time to get the hell out of Dodge City right now. But running hell bent for leather with two loaded weapons would not have been the safest thing to do.

In a low whisper I said to Brent "We are getting out of here right now! What I want you to do is turn around. Pump out the round that you have chambered and put it in your jacket pocket. Leave the magazine in and the breach open so we don't have any accidents. Let me know when you are ready to go, okay? Well, Brent must have been ready because I had barely finished my instructions when Brent called that he was good to go. I also unloaded my rifle by extracting the bolt and pocketing the round.

"Guide us out Brent."

With Brent in the lead and me positioned as a veritable tail gunner we headed out of the thicket in the direction of the bare roadway. Trust me when I say that it didn't take us too long to get into the open where we no longer felt a sense of immediate danger. When we got into the truck we locked the doors and although there was still plenty of daylight available to continue hunting, we both decided to call it a day.

When the rest of our party returned to camp we acted as if nothing out of the ordinary had happened. We asked them where they had been and what they had seen and they asked us the same. For the remainder of the trip Brent and I did not talk about what had happened less than 1000 meters from our camp. I suppose we could have gone up to the landing and taken some pictures of the tracks but we didn't. It was if we were more afraid of being ridiculed by our fathers than by the smelly thing that had left the huge tracks on the road above us.

After joining the BFRO I gained a large amount of expertise by participating in field expeditions and investigating reports of sasquatch encounters. This knowledge has allowed me the ability to take a second look at what had transpired at the Palliser River.

It is strongly believed by some academics that the sasquatch is an unknown species of primate and many of the eyewitnesses have described what they have seen as just that – a large apelike creature. One of the characteristics of a primate is how they are inquisitive of the world around them. I contend that the sasquatch is no different from any other primate in this regard. There are a great many reports that have been investigated by the BFRO where the sasquatch was seen observing people from behind a tree or a large stump and from just inside the edge of a tree line. The logged off area on the hilltop overlooked not only our campsite but also that of the hunters across the road from us and the other side of the creek. This terrain would have provided any inquisitive hairy biped with an excellent location to watch the activity below while remaining concealed from view.

Personally, I believe that as Brent and I drove up the logging road we had caught a sasquatch unaware of our close proximity and with the speed of our advance it was forced to retreat to the safety of the thicket at the end of the road. Later, as an investigator with the BFRO, I confirmed a similar event[5] that took place in the Interior of BC. In that incident a hunter and his party were scouting out a particular area on the opening day of deer season. They left the area to go for lunch and returned a short time later to finish their survey. On their return they discovered a series of impressions that measured some seventeen inches in length and with a stride being close to four feet. The tracks headed across the field in a very orderly fashion but quite suddenly turned 90 degrees to the left after which the stride increased to almost seven feet. During the course of my investigation I asked the witness about the landscape. He said that whatever had created the track way was originally headed towards the tree line on the opposite side of the muddy field but after turning left it was quickly able to gain the security of some nearby scrub brush. When he and his party got out of the vehicle to take a closer look at the tracks they had experienced an uneasy feeling as if they were being watched and a pungent odor akin to burnt bone was reported.

The similarities between these two cases are uncanny. The discovery of large human-like tracks, a foul smell in the air and having the sense of imminent danger may be looked upon as good indicators of the presence of a sasquatch. There are several questions that I have to put forward. How close were we to actually seeing a sasquatch? Was it standing just around the next corner or watching from behind the nearest clump of bushes? Could it have seen us while remaining screened from our view? Would Brent and I have actually had the nerve to shoot at such a creature if it had suddenly appeared in our sights? I think that if we had been physically threatened we would have had to act in self-defense but fortunately, we never had to find out if our rifles had been powerful enough to kill a sasquatch.

This little tale does not end here. When Brent and I got back to camp we told no one about what had taken place almost within sight of our camp and we held our silence for several more days until the hunting trip was over. This is typical in a lot of sasquatch encounters. By the end of the trip everyone was extremely tired. We had placed over seven hundred miles on our vehicles and in the end we had only one deer for our combined efforts. I spent a couple of days at my parents' home before heading back to Comox and I remember my mom asking me if there was anything interesting that had happened on the hunting trip. It was only then that I told my parents what had taken place. My father chastised me for not taking him up onto the hillside with his camera so he could have taken a picture of the tracks Brent and I had discovered. As far as I know Brent has never told his father.

I have never been back to the Palliser River since that trip but since becoming a BFRO investigator I have researched and completed a number of reports from this same geographical area. In the spring of 2001 a man was driving from Radium to Banff on Highway 93. He had just left Radium and had only traveled for about twenty minutes when he saw a large upright bipedal creature coming out of the trees beside the road[6]. Then, in the winter of 2002, a series of large footprints was discovered crossing a frozen lake[7]. Most recently, in the same watershed where we had hunted in 1986, a lone elk hunter stopped to take a rest and have a snack. While sitting on a tree stump he suddenly smelled and then saw a large hairy animal standing upright, staring directly at him from only sixty feet away. For just a split second he glanced down to steady his rifle resting against his leg and when he looked up, it was gone.[8]

What I find significant about this report is that the odor the witness described to me was the same overpowering stench that had stopped Brent and me dead in our tracks. It had been a "wet dog, dead seal on the beach at low tide for a week" smell that had put us instantly into the fight or flight mode. In the course of completing investigations with the BFRO and in doing research for this book I found a paper on the Bigfoot Encounters website entitled Sasquatch Smell / Aroma / Odor / Scent written by Dr. W. H. Fahrenbach in 1997.[9]

In his paper, Dr. Fahrenbach correlated observations on the odors produced by mountain gorillas, as reported by the late Dian Fossey, with that of humans and the sasquatch. Dr. Fahrenbach went on to say that a strong smell was associated with only about 10% or so of the reported sasquatch sightings in John Green's substantial sasquatch sighting database. I do not know if this percentage is representative of the total number of recorded sightings or only from those witnesses who were actually close enough to the subject where some sort of odor may have been detectable. It has been suggested that the smell can be "turned on", on demand and that is why an odor is not detected in a larger number of close observations. Dian Fossey had said that male gorillas, when in a stressful situation such as confronting another male gorilla or when fleeing enemies, could produce an overpowering, gagging odor that was intense at a distance of 80 feet. This scent, when detected by humans, instilled a sense of fear. In regards to the odors associated with the sasquatch, Dr. Fahrenbach goes on to state that there are "repeated reports of people feeling like they are being observed, being overcome by unreasonable fear, abruptly retreating from the forest without obvious cause may conceivably be due to a hormonal component of sasquatch sweat, perceived below conscious level, although it elicits an immediate emotional response."[10]

After reading this paper and investigating numerous reports sent into the BFRO, I agree with Dr. Fahrenbach's conclusion that the sasquatch, as a primate, may have the ability to exude or produce a scent or an odor when under stressful situations much like gorillas and, to a much lesser extent, humans. If the sasquatch does have this physiological ability, then it would certainly account for the incident that had taken place on the Palliser River in 1986. It had been my first contact with what I strongly believe was a sasquatch.

But it would not be my last.

Chapter One
BFRO Sunshine Coast Expedition, 2005

The objective of a BFRO expedition is to "identify habitat areas - areas where longer term projects will take place in the future, involving local academic institutions."[11] The task of identifying possible sasquatch habitats is carried out by members of the BFRO, who investigate the reports submitted to the organization by those who have witnessed a sighting, have found tracks or who have heard odd vocalizations out in the woods. After sifting through the mountains of data collected, research locations having a higher probability to hold a population of sasquatches may then be identified. Naturally, the BFRO centers its expeditions near these locations of higher probability. It only stands to reason that if you wanted to watch the Bulls play basketball you would have a greater chance of seeing them in Chicago, Illinois as opposed to Flin Flon, Manitoba. Therefore, if you want to see a sasquatch you should go to a place where they have reportedly been seen before. This doesn't mean you will see one, but it does increase the odds that you will.

Wednesday...New friends

In 2005 the Bigfoot Field Research Organization (BFRO) held an expedition on British Columbia's Sunshine Coast. It was to be the organization's first foray into Canada, which is surprising since Canada has always been a center for a great amount of purported sasquatch activity. The expedition was to last from Thursday to Sunday. I decided to get a jump on things and with my wife's blessing; I arrived in Sechelt a day early.

Before departing for an expedition participants have the opportunity to introduce themselves through an online forum site that is dedicated to the expedition. The BFRO administrators use the same website to pass on important information to those who would be attending an expedition. As eager participants we used the forum to discuss a host of topics ranging from personal information to the types of equipment that we would be bringing to the field. This was an important topic because although some of the people attending had been on an expedition before, there were some who had never been beyond their own city limits. I had spent plenty of time in the woods camping with my parents and with the Canadian Forces so that particular portion of the adventure was going to be pretty much of a routine for me.

Upon reaching the base camp location, I noted that there were already some tents set up but there were not too many people hanging around. As I started to unpack my gear, some of the other attendees began to arrive from a foray out in the woods and it wasn't long before the introductions got started. It was a lot of "Hi I'm …" and "Yeah, I read your messages on the expedition site". It was at this point that I first met John and his son, Philip as well as Roger, Dave and Matt Moneymaker. It felt great to finally talk with these people face to face and hear of their experiences with a creature that most of the population jokes about or whose existence is often flatly denied.

I was in my tent getting changed into my expedition gear when I heard another vehicle pull up. The car doors opened and then closed. To my surprise I heard Matt's voice say, "Well Mr. Green? How was your trip?" My heart skipped a beat. Could it be? Nah couldn't be him. I struggled to get out of my tent as quickly as I could, almost tripping on my bootlaces as I went. Once outside, I waited until I had an opportunity to introduce myself. Standing before me was a tall thin man, casually dressed, age somewhere between late fifties to mid-sixties. I was on pins and needles because I was going to meet John Green, the long-time sasquatch investigator. He had been one of the first people to catalogue sasquatch sightings from all over the West Coast. He had worked with Rene Dahinden and Dr. Grover Krantz and he had personally investigated the Bluff Creek sighting.

I waited patiently and at long last there was a break in the conversation. "Hi", I said. "I'm Blaine McMillan from Courtenay, BC".

And as he shook my hand, John said "Hi Blaine, I'm Michael Greene from Pennsylvania."

With those very words my heart sank like a rock tossed into a beaver pond. I felt like such a fool. All was not lost though; later on Mike and I had the opportunity to have some interesting discussions from which our friendship grew. Since that first meeting Mike and I have been on several other expeditions together and have kept in regular contact.

Each new arrival meant wandering over to a campsite and saying hi to someone whose name I would probably forget in a matter of minutes. Of all the people who were in attendance there was one person who did look kind of familiar to me. Now I will be the first person to admit that I am rather bad when it comes to matching up faces and names of people especially if I am in contact with them for only a short period of time. This gentleman approached me and asked if I had been in the military. Maybe my short haircut was what gave me away. I don't know. I told him that I had recently retired after 22 years of active service. He then asked if I had been stationed in Winnipeg as a Safety Systems technician. I said that I had been stationed in the 'Peg from 1988 through to 2003. When I still did not recognize him he told me his name was Aaron and that he had been one of the young Aerospace Engineering (AERE) officers who had received survival equipment training at my unit. To be honest, in the late 1980's and early 1990's the Canadian military had pumped so many young officers through the training system that we always seemed to have a group of them in the shop. I asked Aaron if he had remembered anything from the training I had given him and if I had treated him fairly. To this he replied yes on both accounts. This made me feel great, since I would hate to be stuck out in the woods with someone whom I had pissed off some fifteen years earlier. Some guys are known for holding a grudge.

While everyone was hanging out around the campsite I was getting itchy to go out in the woods and find this elusive hairy critter. But nothing was happening because Matt wanted us all to just sit tight. Evidently there was some guy named Tony who was coming to talk to us about the area we were going to head into. This was actually going to be a good thing. I had talked toTony several times over the phone before getting to Sechelt and I was anxious to finally meet him in person. It wasn't long before I heard someone call out "Hi Tony". I looked up and saw a disheveled man walking across the parking lot. He was wearing baggy shorts and a dirty T-shirt, with flip-flops on his feet. It was the sound of his voice confirmed that he was indeed the guy that I had talked to over the phone. What can I say; even yours truly looks better on the phone.

Over the next hour or so a plan was starting to take shape. The maps were hauled out and placed on the nearest picnic table. Most expedition members had purchased the locally produced map frequently used by sightseeing tourists but would it be of little use for our purposes. On the other hand I had a 1/50 000 topographical map of the target area that I had scrounged up at work. As it showed the precise lay of the land it soon became the working map for the group. The only thing that it didn't show was the more recent roads that may have been pushed through to haul logs from a specific area. But for this information we were relying heavily on Tony, since he was the local subject matter expert or SME.

I suggested that it might be of some assistance to everyone if he could mark the topo map all the places where he had his own sightings or where he had heard of sightings. As Tony started to identify recent sighting locations, I was having some difficulty in grasping what he was clearly spelling out. It was hard to fathom but it soon became clear to everyone that there might be as many as four separate sasquatch groups in the Sechelt area.

I know that this sounds crazy especially since most lay people think that there is only one sasquatch, or bigfoot that wanders aimlessly around the countryside for the express purpose of popping out of the forest to scare the hell out of wayward hikers. I started to question Tony more in depth, not that I doubted him but because I wanted to glean as much information from him as possible. Okay, you got me. Of course, there was still a seed of doubt that I had to ferret out, just in case he was attempting to yank my chain. As Tony continued to point out the sighting locations around the Sechelt region he explained that a number of the incidents or sightings had occurred at virtually the same time but at different locations. On one such occasion, Tony had seen a tall hair-covered creature lifting a bag of trash out of his truck, while at roughly the same time a lady driving down the highway, 10 miles away had a 7- foot tall hairy 'something' cross in front of her car, covering the road in just three steps.

As soon as the mapping lesson was completed everyone climbed into their vehicles and then off we went, in a caravan of sorts, back through town and out to a possible location for some interaction. Sounds easy doesn't it? Well it wasn't. Just getting out of town was a problem. I, along with some of the other newbies, didn't know where the hell we were going and as soon as we came to one of Sechelt's three traffic signals, the convoy was split by a red light. To make matters worse, those who were in the lead did not wait for us to get through the light. By the time I got to the radio to ask directions for us poor saps in the rear, the front-end boys had already gone through the second set of lights which were located on the other side of town.

"Car 54, where are you?"

The radio crackled back. "Blaine! Just follow the road out of town!"

Sure enough, on the other side of town, there were a number of vehicles pulled over onto the shoulder of the road with their four-way flashers on, waiting for us slowpokes. A quick headcount confirmed that we were all together, so off we went again. Before long we pulled off the highway and onto a very nondescript gravel road. It was much like most of the forestry roads that inundate the mountains of BC and as we idled up the road I began to have some reservations about what we were doing. This was the place? It was hard to believe that this was where we were going to encounter the elusive sasquatch, especially when you consider that we had driven only about twenty minutes out of town. And, you would think, that in order to find a sasquatch, we would have to travel much deeper into the forest than we had. I doubt very much that we were more than 500 yards from the highway because I could hear every car that passed by.

At a junction point two forestry roads everyone pulled over and got out of their vehicles. There was already a camper truck parked in place. This was Sid Tracey's rig and it looked pretty nice with an oversized sleeper and a dining room slide out. After the standard introductions I asked him if he enjoyed sleeping on the bunk above the cab of his truck.

"It's great!" Sid replied. "These new campers have a lot more head room over the older models."

Light-heartedly, I pointed out the fact that the vent windows of his sleeping bunk were very close to eight feet off the ground, which would be the perfect height for an inquisitive sasquatch to peek in while he was asleep. On that note everyone in the group took a moment to look up and imagine the possibilities of rolling over in bed only to be eyeball to eyeball with an eight-foot tall hairy thing outside the camper window.

As we stood around waiting for the next thing to happen, I was once again thinking that this expedition was starting to resemble a Royal Cluster Fuck. If someone knew what the hell was going on, I wished that he or she would step up to the plate and tell us the game plan so everyone would be in the know.

Anyone? Anyone? Bueller? No takers?

Tony and Dave, along with several others had spent the previous night at or near this site. Early in the morning they had witnessed a 250 lb. black bear come charging out of the woods in their general direction. Fearing for their safety some of the people reached for their bear spray, but it quickly became apparent that the bear was not concerned with the humans as it ran right past the bewildered observers without even a passing glance. It appeared to the men that as it ran by the bear was trying to hide its tail. Now a bear doesn't really have much of a tail to begin with and so watching one that was trying to tuck that little stub under its backside must have been a pretty comical sight. When I asked them about the incident they said that the other thing that really stood out at that particular point in time was the way in which the bear kept looking over its shoulder as if something had been chasing it.

Roughly sixty yards beyond where the guys had been standing was a thicket and they said that the bear had headed straight for the safety that it provided. As the bear reached the bushes something crashed to the edge of the tree line and began to violently shake a thirty-foot fir tree. The witnesses all swore to me that there had been no wind that morning and if there had been, then all of the trees would have been in motion and not just one.

Gauging the Sun.
If you stretch your arm and hold out your hand so that your fingers are extended below the bottom of the sun each finger thickness from the bottom of the sun to the edge of the horizon counts as fifteen minutes. Each whole hand is worth an hour. Try it out. It really works.

Gauging the sun showed that there were about three hours of sunlight left in the day. The consensus was that we would string ourselves along this power and gas line right of way, in order to cover a distance of about a mile or so. We would set up our satellite camps so we could then spend the night sitting and listening for anything that went bump in the night. Everyone was pairing up with people they already knew so I asked to tag along with John and Philip. We were to take up a position on the far left flank, high above a lake that bordered the highway. This lake is a popular place with the locals. Several weeks earlier a group of teenagers had been out for a night of good-natured revelry. They were swimming and clowning around. You know, typical teenage stuff. At one point they had watched what they thought was one of their friends swimming on the far side of the lake. But when it stepped out of the water and walked into the forest, they soon realized that this large black hair-covered biped was certainly not one of their friends from school.

John, Philip and I drove out to the left flank. We perched ourselves onto a large flat rock and immediately they began to set up their tent. Just fucking great! I had no idea that we were planning on staying out all night. I had figured that we would be there until midnight or so and then go back to base camp. I was wrong. John asked if I had brought my tent.

"No, it was set up back at base camp." That was the whole point of a base camp wasn't it? You know, a place to operate out of? But to also return to later on, right?

"Did you bring your sleeping bag? 'Cause if you did, you can bunk with us since we have the room."

Ah yes, my sleeping bag. In my mind I could see it clearly. It was lying on top of my cot, which was inside my tent, which was set up at the blasted base camp that no one was staying at tonight! Never mind. I will figure something out. Improvise, adapt and overcome. Hell, I could crash out in my truck if I had to and as a last resort I had my camp chair to hunker down in.

As the hours marched by we talked about sasquatch stuff. John said that he and his son had been on a couple of trips south to Washington State in search of our elusive quarry. He related some of the incidents that had taken place on their forays; tales of wood knocks and tossed rocks. All pretty exciting stuff really. By now it was pitch-black out. Looking up, the clear sky was filled with more stars than I could ever count. The only other light source was the waxing and waning of headlights along the tops of the trees as vehicles traveled on the highway below our position. But, by 10:30 pm even these lights were rare. Of course, a cloudless sky meant that the ambient air temperature would be dropping as fast as the sun had. Possibly even down to single digits. I pulled the collar of my combat coat up to keep the slight breeze off of my neck. Sitting out on that rock we were exposed to the elements and anything that was headed for the lake would certainly see us from the tree line.

"Thank God! ... Those blasted crickets have finally stopped!"

When facing to the west, the ground directly in front of us fell sharply away. The bottom of the ravine would have been hidden from our view even in daylight. This landform is commonly referred to as dead ground. These two areas contained thick brush that would have been difficult for anything to traverse. This did not mean that that we wouldn't know if something were trying to sneak through the dead ground. All around us was a natural warning system. They were small and they made a hell of a racket. Crickets.

Chirp! Chirp! Chirp!

If you have ever had a cricket hiding somewhere inside your house at night, then you know what it was like sitting on that rock. Their incessant chirping can drive you crazy. But when you try to close in on the little bugger with the intention of squashing the life out of it, the damn thing shuts up!

Chirp! Chirp, chirp!

Chirp, chirp...

We stopped chatting so we could listen more intently to whatever had made the crickets stop their pesky serenade. Philip, who had been sitting inside their tent using a Super Snooper Listening device, whispered that something was walking through the dead ground below us.

Was it a deer or an elk? The deer are plentiful here and there are large herds of elk that roam all over the Sechelt peninsula.

No! It's on two feet. It's bipedal!

Seconds ticked into minutes and the silence was deafening.

"Is it still moving, Philip?"

"Yes."

"Which way?"

"It's going away from the lake." In other words whatever was walking through the brush was heading past us and towards the rest of our group.

Wow! My first night out on an expedition and I might have had a possible contact with a sasquatch! Boy, was I scared!

We were unable to hear anything but Philip assured us that it was still in moving methodically, step by step, through the dead ground. John, who had an ear bud microphone on his GMRS radio, informed the rest of the group that something bipedal had been heard walking in the grass and that it was headed in their direction. Somebody else replied that they were waiting for it at their end of the line.

Once again time seemed to slip by. Philip could no longer hear the mysterious trekker who had strode so boldly through the dead ground and yet the guys farther down the ridge had reported that they had no contact at all. Whatever it was had simply disappeared into the night. In retrospect, if it had been a sasquatch that had walked below us it may not have seen us because of our position on higher ground. But it may have spotted some of the other groups simply because they may have been more out in the open. With this in mind, it may have altered its course to avoid them, which is why they reported having no contact.

It was getting close to midnight and I had been up for nearly 19 hours straight. I was seriously bagged and to be honest, a little bit scared. Without a ready place to put my weary head, I opted to go find my pillow that was with my sleeping bag that was lying on my cot, which was inside my tent back at the base camp where no one would be sleeping. Except me, that is! John informed Matt that I was heading back to town and that I would be in touch in the morning. As I slowly drove down off the mountain and back to the highway I was feeling that maybe I should stay and tough it out. I was thinking that what if, right after I leave, someone from the group has an actual sighting?

Screw it! I was too tired to care. Rounding a corner on the highway I was thinking how I just wanted the warmth of my sleeping bag, the comfort of my cot and the security of my tent when my headlights caught something stepping off the road and into the bush. It looked very much like an outstretched leg but it could have been anything or nothing. I really didn't care because in fifteen minutes I was back at base camp where I discovered that the main gate was locked.

Now what!?! Oh yes, the campsite manager saying that the gate would be locked after a specific time. Any late arrivals would have to park off to the side and walk into their campsite. I took what I needed out of the truck and locked it up. A short stumble later and I was at my tent where I saw that someone new had pitched their tent in the spot next to mine. There was no way of knowing if this new person was another attendee or just another camper. I would most likely find out in the morning and it wasn't long before I was sawing logs.

Thursday…Just hanging out

When I woke up, the sunlight was filtering through the branches and into my tent. I checked my watch. Wow, 8AM! I must have really been tired because normally I could go all day on only five hours of sleep and for me to crash out for a full eight hours is pretty rare. So, with a fresh change of clothes, my shaving kit and some money I wandered off for a shower. The showers at the campground were coin operated, costing one Canadian dollar coin, commonly known as a loonie, for a ten-minute splash. Breakfast would consist of coffee and some IMP's or Individual Meal Packages. These were similar to the American military MRE's or Meals Ready (to) Eat except in my opinion the IMP's taste far better. For my dining pleasure I would have a choice between beans and weenies or a ham and egg omelet. A tough decision if there ever was one.

During breakfast I wondered what may have happened to the group last night after I had them for the comfort of my tent. There was one question that was foremost in my mind: Did someone have a sighting or any other sort of interaction? Another question that came to mind was where the heck was everybody? Should I head out to find them or should I sit tight at base camp? I waited for a while longer and when no one showed up, I headed out to have a look around town.

Sechelt is not that big of a town so the five-cent tour didn't take very long. Once I had located all of the important things in town, like where to get fuel and groceries, I made a run down the highway to the Canadian Tire outlet to buy some extra batteries and odds and sods. For those who haven't experienced it a Canadian Tire outlet is like an all-round sporting goods automotive hardware store. I also took some time to make a personal call on a family friend who lived nearby before heading back to the base camp. Today was supposed to be the actual start of the Sunshine Coast Expedition and there would be new arrivals throughout the day. I wanted to double-check the condition of some of my equipment and possibly grab a power nap since tonight's outing would be a long one. It turned out that with everybody coming and going from the campsite I would have more luck taking a nap in the middle of a logging operation!

By the time I had returned people were filtering into the base camp. Some of them, like myself, were new attendees who were just arriving for the expedition and some were those who had actually spent the entire night out in the woods without tucking tail and running for home, like yours truly. It was now around noon. I was chomping at the bit to get back out to the woods in search of the Big Guy. However, it appeared that everyone who had stayed out last night were now coming back to get some more rest. But instead of crawling into their tents they just sat around base camp in the heat of the afternoon sun. Personally, I was starting to wonder if there was any organization to this operation and as I was mulling this over, Matt came back to camp with some unexpected good news. Matt informed us that Tony had been in touch with a local person who had reported a visual sighting just a couple of months earlier and that he was making arrangements for her to discuss her experience with us.

When Tony arrived back at base camp he said that the witness was going to meet us near the location of last night's operation. Her father was escorting her as she was very nervous speaking about the incident. This was quite understandable since most people who have actually seen a sasquatch don't even tell their immediate family members, their co-workers or their peers for fear of being ridiculed.

An hour later found us assembled at Sid's campsite and a far as I knew nothing had peeked in his camper window. The witness and her father arrived shortly after we did. The witness was a young lady, in her late teens or maybe early twenties. We, the attendees, did not intend to crowd around her but the softness of her voice caused us to push in closer and closer just to hear what she had to say. Of course this simply had a negative effect on the witness resulting in the quieting of her voice even more! Matt quickly saw that this situation was quite detrimental to her ability to recall the events. To correct it, he had the group stand off to one side while he positioned himself in such a way that the witness was not distracted by our presence. From the sidelines we watched as Matt hung on her every word as she retold the details of an incident that had clearly affected her a great deal. Even though it had been several months after it had taken place she was almost quaking as she voiced the images that were stored in her head.

What really impressed me the most was the way in which Matt had interviewed this witness. Once he had been moved us out of her line of sight she only had to talk to one person and with her father standing nearby she was much more at ease. By allowing her to take the lead in telling her story, and at her own pace, Matt had only to ask her the occasional question in order for her to recall details that she may not have otherwise thought to be important. Things like: 'Was it carrying anything?' or 'Did it use its hands in any way as it entered the brush or to climb the hill?" These questions may not sound important but if you think about it, have you ever seen a bear carry an armload of apples or use its hands to pull itself up a steep embankment? Most people who say that they have seen a sasquatch, have said that the sighting lasted less than a minute. Usually it is a case of there it is and there it was. Gone in the blink of an eye. If you ask any professional investigator, such as a police detective, he will tell you that any witness to a crime may not consciously be able to recall all of the details that were observed but subsequent questioning, carried out in the correct manner, may in fact help the witness to bring additional key information to light.

Imagine if the person who was questioning this young lady started berating her and casting doubt as to what she had seen. What do you think would have been the result of this technique? She would have closed up like a proverbial clam at low tide. Never to repeat what had taken place and never to trust anybody who even smelled like an investigator. Needless to say, Matt's experience showed us that you certainly don't have to be heavy handed when you question someone about an incident with a sasquatch. It is better to be patient and observant because if a person is lying he will eventually trap himself in his own web of deceit.

After the meeting broke up there was still time in the day for us to do some exploring before settling in for another night of sitting and listening. Over the next couple of hours Tony lead us through the back roads around the Sechelt Peninsula. These were pretty BC typical logging roads complete with lakes, streams and more mountains. I felt quite at home since I had grown up driving on roads that were very similar to these.

Even though I had labored over my topographical map before arriving in Sechelt, driving around the area had given me a better appreciation for the lay of the land. By piecing together information that was available from reports published on the BFRO website and from Tony's personal experiences, I tried to put together some ideas as to where our elusive quarry may be hanging out and more importantly, why. I suppose that would actually be putting the cart before the horse. However, many successful hunters will tell you that if you know the specific needs of your prey and where those needs are located then you would have a better chance of catching it. You would think that the needs of a sasquatch would be pretty basic: food, water, reproduction and personal security. Sounds simple, but I would need even more knowledge of a sasquatch's daily habits if I were going to be able to formulate any ideas as to where I would actually find one.

After a quick swing back through base camp the decision - yes, an actual decision - was made to go back to the positions that we had held the night before. Well, why not since I had nothing better to do. Roger (not his real name) and I discussed the idea of staying out overnight and if we got too tired to sit up all night, we would just crash out in the cab of my truck. Mike Greene said that he would join us in our all-night vigil and he that he would be bringing along his toys. I had no idea as to what toys Mike was alluding to but from the sounds of things it was going to be an interesting evening. It was going to be a long night so we made ourselves more comfortable with like chairs to sit on and some food to munch on.

The one item that I had not considered taking out to the field was my tent. I had the time to tear it down from base camp and reposition it out at the remote camp much like John and Philip had done but I couldn't be bothered with all that work. Besides, sleeping in the truck wouldn't be so bad, would it? I guess I wouldn't really know until the next morning.

Once we were parked up on the hillside, we set our chairs on top of the big flat rock. The view of the countryside was excellent. As the sun was starting to set we all sat back and contemplated if tonight would yield an interaction of some kind. There had been no other reported incidents from the previous night other than the bipedal footsteps that Philip had heard.

For those of you who have never been out on an expedition with the BFRO it is hard to describe the thrill of sitting out in the woods waiting to hear a mysterious vocalization or the distant reply to your fumbled attempt at a wood knock. Do you remember when you were only five or six years old? Back then the Magic of Christmas was very much alive within you and you had desperately tried to stay awake to catch a glimpse of Santa Claus. Now imagine for a moment that you have just spent the evening with your family watching Jimmy Stewart muddle his way through "It's a Wonderful Life". You have set out a plate of cookies complete with a glass of cold milk to help Santa keep up his strength and your parents have snuggled you into bed. You desperately try to stay awake but you find yourself getting sleepier and sleepier. Then, just as your eyes close and your chin hits your chest…

THUMP!!

EYES WIDE OPEN

THUMP!!

UP ON THE ROOF?

HEART RACING…and then nothing…

Anxiously you wait. Wanting to hear that next sound but it never comes. Was it all a dream? Maybe so. But in the morning you wake up to find presents under the tree and as dad shovels the snow out of the driveway he notices that some snow has been knocked off the roof. Sometimes you just gotta believe.

On this second night on the ridge the sky was just as clear as it was the first night. Not a single cloud anywhere. There was even enough starlight to allow me to safely walk the twenty yards to my truck without the aid of a flashlight. The five of us shared some munchies and chatted about 'squatch stuff. We also talked about our experiences in the field. John and Philip had been down to the United States for an expedition or two and Mike has been chasing after this elusive creature for quite some time so there were plenty of stories to tell. It was around this time that Mike decided to entertain us with his technological toys. The first thing he showed us was a first generation (Gen-1) night vision Starlight scope. It was similar to the type I had used in the military more than twenty years earlier.

"Where the hell did you get that?"

"Oh, you can pick them up just about anywhere back home. Can't you get them here in Canada?"

"No. What would we use them for?"

"Back home we use them for hunting coyotes… at night. Of course, now there aren't that many coyotes in Pennsylvania anymore."

The next item for Mike's Show and Tell was a thermal imager. This piece of equipment was really cool. Where the Starlight scope amplifies any available light source to visually assist the operator the thermography unit actually sees the heat or thermal signature given off by the subject. A warm object, a deer for example, passing through a cooler background, like a forest, will show up quite prominently. Of course both of these units have their own limitations. A sudden flare of light, such as a match or a car's headlights, can temporarily blind a person using a night vision scope and may damage the unit as well. When using the thermal camera, objects that have been warmed by the sun, rocks and the like will retain heat for quite a long time. These items will continue to show up clearly until they have obtained the same temperature as the ambient air and as they cool the shape of their heat signature will change often looking like something that it is not. You also cannot gauge depth very well with the older units. An object such as a bat can be seen flying through the air but you cannot tell if it is twenty feet or twenty yards away from you.[12]

As we sat around on that big flat rock looking up at the stars, the sleeping arrangements were discussed. Not much to discuss really. Philip and his dad had set up their tent in the same spot it had been in last night. Roger and I were planning on crashing out in the truck and Mike would rough it out in the open. If the weather made a sudden turn for the worse, he would pile in with John and Philip. A little while later, the topic of discussion was either global pollution or tying flies for fishing. I don't remember which. By now it was really dark out and not a creature was stirring, not even a 'squatch.'

Matt called on the radio asking if anyone wanted to give a wood knock.

A wood knock? What the hell was a wood knock?

John volunteered his services and proceeded to dig out a large piece of wood, not unlike a bat, from his vehicle. Mike explained to me and to Roger, that it has been suggested that the sasquatch may communicate with one another over great distances by banging rocks or sticks together. In his book, Dr. Bindernagel wrote of a camper on Vancouver Island who had heard a "stick being hit repeatedly against a tree making a rapping sound"[13] and "that aboriginal elders from some British Columbia coastal villages accept slow rhythmic tree-striking as evidence of a Bukwas or Sasquatch."[14] While John picked his way over to a suitable tree or post to beat on, Mike continued to tell us that to his knowledge, this behavior had never been visually observed despite the fact that the wood knock sounds had been reported from across the continent. From what I could gather the game plan was to produce a sound that would elicit a response from a sasquatch in the form of a wood knock, a vocalization or something else.

John was on the radio.

"Okay Matt. I am ready when you are."

Matt replied, "Give me a single knock in ten."

"Copy. A single in ten."

Ten? Ten what? Oh, ten seconds. Like a countdown.

…Eight… nine… ten.

WHACK!!

John's powerful blow echoed along the ridge. I am not sure if everyone could hear it since we were positioned at the far end of the line. However, everyone was listening. Listening with baited breath.

Listening for a reply of some kind.

Listening... nothing. Zip.

About ten minutes or so later Matt asked John for a double tap in ten. John carefully moved back into position and radioed that he would proceed in ten seconds. This countdown was important because it gave everyone time to prepare for what was about to happen next. So, put down anything that may be dropped and ready any recording equipment that may capture a response. Since none of us on the outer edge had any audio recording gear, we just sat back in our camp chairs to listen with our own ears.

...8, 9, 10

WHACK! pause, 2, 3 WHACK!

After the knocks finished echoing across the valley the silence was suddenly deafening. It seemed like everything was being held in place by a huge pause button. No one moved or spoke, as if everyone, even those damned crickets had stopped to listen for some sort of a reply. Once again we heard nothing at our position but the next day it was reported that a possible reply was heard up the hill from those sitting at the other end of the line. An experienced BFRO investigator, who was closer to the source, stated that the sound was a definitely wood knock but he could not identify the precise location.

By now it was closing in on midnight. I was yawning up a storm in a vain attempt to stay awake. It was a losing battle. I told everyone that I was calling it a night and that I would see them in the morning.

"Good idea," said Roger.

After a round of goodnights, reminiscent of the Walton's, Roger and I folded our chairs, picked up our gear and made our way to the truck. The equipment was locked up in the box and we locked ourselves in the cab. I would like to say that even though we had observed no direct evidence of a sasquatch in our vicinity, we still felt the need to physically lock ourselves in for the night. Why? Both Thom Powell and Dr. Bindernagel have stated in their texts that the sasquatch, like other known primates, is both cautious and curious. I could see the need to secure our stuff in the back of the truck to protect it from the elements but there was no rainfall predicted in the weather forecast for at least another two days. Maybe we were afraid that some big hairy thing might just walk off with our twenty-dollar folding Wal-Mart camp chairs and add them to its collection of items purloined from other campers who were reckless in the care of their equipment. Hell, even Albert Ostman had said that his pack had been rummaged through while he had slept nearby so maybe it just might happen to us too!

And another thing ... why lock our doors? It just does not make sense at all. The creature that we were so desperately seeking reportedly had the strength, speed and agility that were far beyond human limitations. When the roadway was first being pushed into Bluff Creek the workers gave an account of finding big footprints and full 45-gallon fuel drums, along with other heavy equipment being tossed about. More recent witnesses have observed sasquatches crossing open fields as fast as a track star and 3 inch diameter trees have been found twisted off like a pretzel. Common sense would then dictate that if anyone in our party were going to be harassed during the night, it would probably be John and

Philip who were in their dome tent, or Mike, since he was planning on sleeping out under the stars. With everyone snuggled in for the night, it was time to get some serious shut eye so it wasn't long before Roger and I were fast asleep.

Friday...Things that go bump in the night

We woke up some six hours later cramped, hungry and still tired. Both of us had neglected to bring any food, other than stuff to munch on during our vigil, and the rest of our food was back at base camp. Personally, I was getting tired of eating the IMP's, which I had purloined from work. Truth is the IMP's are actually pretty good for being a boil-in-the-bag meal. A company called Freddy Chef produces them for the Canadian military and there are all sorts of menus available from Salisbury steak with mushrooms to wild salmon in tarragon and of course there is everybody's favorite - beans and weenies. As with anything else, military personnel must invent their own vernacular so for example the ham and egg omelet is often referred to as a Lung-in-a-Bag. But on this particular morning I was having none of it! Roger and I decided to head off of the ridge and go to the only McDonald's restaurant in town for some reconstituted substitute for our normal breakfast fare. Just as we were leaving, Mike asked if we had room for one more. We shifted some equipment around in the truck and squeezed him in for the short ride into town.

It was a standard small town McDonald's restaurant with the prerequisite tight parking lot and wrap-around drive-through negotiable only by small foreign built vehicles. Inside this particular Golden Arches outlet was the standard issue, hormone-enriched pimply-faced teenaged employee whose attention span that was significantly shorter than the length of the pre-cut fries. Standing behind and slightly to one side of this frontline worker bee was the key individual responsible for this fast food operation. He was a twenty-one year old early morning shift supervising McÖberfuhrer with the degree from highly touted McDonald's Center of Training Excellence, which is also known as Hamburger University or H.U. for short. What happened next was not their fault but believe me when I tell you that the conversation with these service industry people was anything but enlightening.

"Good morning and welcome to McDonald's. Can I take your order?"

"I'll have an orange juice, a couple of your Egg McThings with sausage and a large cup of the stuff that you like to call coffee."

"Do you want fries with that?"

Quickly, the McÖberfuhrer leans forward to remind "Tim the Server" that fries are not served with breakfast. Tim seems confused. There isn't an identifiable pictogram of my order on the rubber coated keypad so he doesn't know which button to push that will direct the order to the food assembly person standing a mere fifteen feet behind him. Frustrated and close to having a meltdown, his finger hung over the machine like the Sword of Damocles, afraid to commit to any option for fear of screwing up in front of the boss. Finally, the McÖberfuhrer steps in and tells him to give me two of the Number 4's without the corrugated cardboard tasting hash browns, which showed up anyway.

As we ate, the three of us talked about the apparent lack of organization that seemed to prevail throughout the expedition. I made up my mind that I would approach Matt and ask what the full game plan was supposed to be because up until now it still appeared that things were taking place in a very haphazard manner.

The other topic of discussion was the question of exactly who were the "Guys from New York". Last night, when we had been sitting out on the ridge, we had heard over the radio net that there were a group of guys, all of them BFRO investigators, who were coming in from New York. They would be flying into Vancouver and then leasing a vehicle for the drive to Sechelt. I don't know what time they had left New York but by the time they got to the base camp it was probably close to being dark. Matt or one of the other organizers must have left instructions at the base camp on how to get out to our location on the ridge because at about 9:30 pm we started hearing these guys over the GMRS radios requesting assistance from any BFRO members who may be in the area. They said that they were sitting at the start of the access road as it turned off of the highway. We could hear them as clear as a bell but due to the terrain I don't think that Matt could.

With them calling out for someone to direct them up the mountain and people asking them to identify themselves or trying to relay messages to Matt, it soon resembled a huge game of Marco Polo. We could have easily helped by leading them up the mountain but without Matt's permission we were not going to move from our position. And so the game went on.

They would call for us ... "Any BFRO members ... any BFRO members in the area ... do you hear us? We are the "Guys from New York".

Marco!

And then someone would answer... "Who are you guys?"

Polo!

Finally, after an hour or so of playing this game, somebody, I don't know who, was dispatched to go down the mountain to the highway turn off and guide them back to the main body. It was actually an easy drive to where we were but I think that they may have been afraid of heading blindly off the beaten path.

As I had mentioned earlier, I am really bad when it comes to remembering names. There is no disrespect intended and even though I was probably formally introduced to all three of them, I have often found it easier for me to refer to people by something that is memorable to myself and identifiable to others. By simply calling them the "Guys from New York" I accomplished both of these tasks. Think of it as when Captains Hawkeye Pierce and Trapper John MacIntyre, played so brilliantly by Donald Sutherland and Elliot Gould in the original M*A*S*H movie, showed up to perform surgery in Tokyo. Calling themselves the "Pro's from Dover", the two surgeons bluff their way into getting whatever they want including chest x-rays, entry to a golf tournament or a date with a pretty nurse.[15]

I only saw the "Guys from New York" three or four times over the course of the expedition. On Friday, while we were interviewing some additional local people who had sighted a sasquatch in their back yard this three-man crew had headed out in their leased vehicle to explore the back roads. With a video camera aimed out the windshield, just in case something strode across in front of them, and a hand-held GPS linked to a laptop, they digitally mapped out just about every logging road in the target area. Thanks.

The next time I saw them was when the bulk of the expedition members were searching for any likely sasquatch habitats along the back roads of the Sechelt Peninsula. I was in the process of turning the truck around on a narrow intersection. This one particular road appeared to be rather narrow and the branches would scratch the hell out of my truck so I was not about to try it out. Also there was some discussion as to exactly where the road went. Tony assured everybody that it would link up with another road that we had already been on. Just as I deftly completed a six-point turn, the "Guys from New York" approached me on the road. They asked me if I knew where this particular road went.

"No, but Tony does."

"Hey Tony! Where does it go?"

"Pretty sure that it meets up with the trail head for the road we were on last night. It's tight but you can make it."

Matt glanced at the vehicle. It was a Ford Explorer Sport Trac. Similar to mine only newer and with more options.

"Did you guys get the extra scratch and dent insurance when you leased this thing?"

"Yes, we did."

And with that, they forged ahead snapping branches and scraping body panels as they went. It was a good thing that I had not gone down that road because I know that my wife would have been pissed at me for sure.

After breakfast we headed back to base camp. I don't know what my passengers were planning on doing once we got there but I was in desperate need of a shower and a change of clothes. If I hurried I would also be able to get a few more hours of sleep before anyone else from the expedition dragged their sorry butts back into camp.

There appeared to be a routine that was quickly developing on the expedition. First we would go out into the field to sit up all night or at least until midnight. Then after catching a few hours of restless sleep, the daylight hours would be spent doing housekeeping chores like taking a shower, if possible, inspecting and repairing equipment, looking over maps, interviewing local witnesses and restocking our consumables. All of this was just the lead in to another night of taking up a position out in the bush.

With a couple of hours of a really deep sleep under my belt I awoke feeling rejuvenated and ready to go. The local shops were now open so I dashed off to restock my supplies. Sechelt is, by and large, a tourist town. There is some resource-based industry but the majority of the economy relies on the tourist trade. In the summer, B.C.'s Sunshine Coast is flooded with visitors from all over the globe who want to experience a holiday at a much slower pace. With mountains, the ocean and the beaches surrounding the Sechelt Peninsula it is like a picture postcard. The town is also small enough that a person can centrally park his vehicle and cover the majority of the shopping district on foot. This was great since I needed the exercise, and it gave me the opportunity to slow down.

Once I was back at base camp, my shopping spree having been completed, there was time to sit and reflect on what had happened so far and to talk to some of the other attendees. I found that the BFRO often utilized people who either live near the site of the expedition or who have an intimate knowledge of the area like a forester or a game warden. Tony and his wife were the primary local experts in the Sechelt area but another local resident was Fred, who assisted the expedition as a local guide. Dressed in jeans, a baggy shirt and a ball cap Fred had a rough, long hair hippy kind of look to him. Sort of like the type of person you would likely see being taken into custody on the television show "Dog the Bounty Hunter". However, in talking to him, I soon found out that he and I shared many likes and had similar beliefs as well. Fred had lived in the Sechelt area for a number of years. Being an avid hunter and fisherman, he was intrigued about the sasquatch/bigfoot phenomena, especially since the expedition was happening in his own backyard.

At noon, with the majority of the attendees back in camp, it was time to mount up and go for a little road trip. Matt and Tony wanted us to meet another family who had several close encounters of the big and hairy kind. Their house was a few miles away from the initial target area but close to where the previous witness had her sighting as well. If my counting is correct, I believe that there were eight of us in total and when we pulled into their yard it was as if a pack of hungry hounds had descended upon this family. After a brief description of events we fanned out across the yard looking for any secondary evidence. We soon discovered that they did indeed have a large heavy biped pass through their property and possibly on more than one occasion. This evidence was in the form of broken brush and tracks on a pathway that a human would have found difficult if not impossible to negotiate. Unfortunately, the tracks that we found were not suitable for casting and from what I was told this situation actually occurs quite frequently. Quite often footprints are recognizable as sasquatch footprints but they may be only partial in nature or they are found in a medium that is difficult cast such as in snow.

After hanging out at the witness's house for several hours it was once again time to head back to base camp and prepare for tonight's round of fun and games. For those who wanted to, there was time for a shower and to digest the day's events thus far. It was also a good time to get some growlies into me and come to think of it a few more hours of sleep would have been nice, too. Wishful thinking though since I had to make sure my gear was ready to go (my backpack, flashlight, etc.). When we got back, Roger, who had been riding around with me all day wandered off to get his stuff together as well.

I was really hoping that there would be some sort of meeting before leaving for the target area. As a former member of the Canadian military, I was used to having an action plan in place so everyone knew what to expect and what their role would be. The apparent lack of any kind of organization was driving me nuts. This situation was gnawing at me but I thought that I had better get a consensus and some backing before I talked to Matt about what was planned for tonight. A short walk brought me to Aaron's campsite. After talking with him about the current situation, we agreed that from our perspective there wasn't a game plan and when we saw Matt we would try our best to get some answers.

It wasn't long before Matt, accompanied by David, Tony and Mike, idled back into base camp. Tony spotted me over at Aaron's camp and called the both of us over to where he had parked. Something was up.

"Have you eaten yet?"

"No, I haven't."

"Well, don't go anywhere 'cause Fred is going to be here soon with some food from the restaurant."

Mmmm, restaurant food! I didn't know what kind of restaurant Fred worked at, but at this point it wouldn't really matter. I had been eating IMP's for several days now and as I mentioned before, they are actually pretty good but when presented with the opportunity to eat some fresh West Coast Fusion Pub fare, the thought of having yet another boil-in-a-bag meal went right out the proverbial window. With free food being brought in to a central point I thought that this would also be a perfect opportunity to pin Matt down as to a possible plan of attack.

A couple of minutes later Matt walked by Aaron's campsite. He looked as if he was on his way to the washroom so I thought that this would be as good a time as any to confront him.

"Hey, Matt. Can we talk to you for a second?"

"Yeah, sure. I'll be back in a couple of minutes."

The afternoon sun continued to beat down as we waited for Matt's return. It had been surprisingly warm on the Sunshine Coast for this time of year. Warm to the point where the lack of a breeze off the ocean was starting to make the heat of the afternoon quite unbearable. The forests were dry from the lack of rain and despite several forest fires burning out of control in other parts of the province; the Sunshine Coast had been spared thus far. If the fire hazard rating got any higher the back roads we were utilizing would no longer be accessible to us.

"So, what's happening guys?"

Cautiously I asked, "Matt, I was wondering if there was an actual game plan for tonight. And the reason why I am asking is that so far it looks as if anyone who is attending can just come and go as they like and do whatever they want to. It appears that there is no coordinated effort to do anything in any concentrated direction. Aaron and I, both being ex-military, are used to a more structured approach and quite frankly the lack of direct leadership is rather disconcerting to us."

THANK GOD THAT'S OUT.

Matt mulled my words over for about twenty seconds. The delay of his response had me worried. Good going Blaine! You have just barked at the Big Dog. Now you're going to get your nose swatted for it. Or worse, your nose rubbed in it.

"It's like this guys. The people who come out on the expeditions, like you, are, for the most part, on vacation. It would be great to be able to totally direct the movements of the attendees but imagine how you would feel if the organizers of the expedition were to tell you where to go and what to do on your vacation?"

I had to agree with him. If someone tried to tell people what to do while they were on their holidays it wouldn't take very long before the attendees would get pissed off with the organizers. I know I wouldn't like it and just maybe that's the reason why I would hate going on an organized holiday tour package.

"Matt, I didn't mean that everyone has to be told what to do every step of the way," I countered.

"… And it would be impossible to co-ordinate everyone since some people want to do their own thing."

"Like the Guys from New York?"

"Yeah… like the Guys from New York."

Aaron, who up until now had been letting me dig my own grave, suddenly interjected with what he believed might be a solution to our impasse.

"Why don't you simply say that there will be an information session held at such and such a time, and at such and such a location? If you can make it, great! And if not, then you may follow along later. By doing this, you know darn well that the newbies will show up and it also lets the more experienced people still go out and do their own thing if they want to."

Fred had brought the food during our chat and he had delivered it to David's campsite. Everyone was heading over there to eat so we filed in as well. When I saw the food, it was quite obvious that Fred had really outdone himself. On a large serving platter there were these fantastic open-faced sandwiches, almost like bruschetta really, with different toppings and melted cheese. To accompany this extravaganza, was a monstrous Caesar salad! By the time we got over to David's, the participants resembled a murder of crows or a flock of gulls, circling and wheeling above the platter before diving in to snatch a piece of bread before some other squawking bird took it. It didn't take long before the only thing left was half the salad. I don't know if the conversation we had with Matt had anything to do with what happened next but I would like to think that it did. With the majority of the expedition members in attendance, except for the Guys from New York of course, and with their attention held in place by the food, it was an opportune time to make an announcement of sorts.

"Okay", Matt began. "I think that tonight we will change our tactics. So far we have learned from interviewing some of the local witnesses and from Tony's experiences that the 'squatches may be moving through a possible corridor from the ocean shoreline back up into the mountains. Tony and I, and some of you have seen some tracks along with other indicators that support this position. For the past couple of days we have been driving the roads looking for possible evidence of sasquatch activity and at night we have been purposely trying to elicit some kind of a response from them in the target area."

"So tonight we are going to play it really low key. I would like everyone to pair up so that no one is camping alone. We will set up in groups of two or three people at most and space ourselves out along the main road in such a way that they will be unafraid to approach us. Remember folks, that despite their size and their reported strength, sasquatches may be curious but they are also timid. They want to see what we are up to without being seen themselves and they will probably not approach people unless they feel safe. So, we want them to feel safe. We want them to feel that it is alright to approach us."

Matt went on to say that he was pretty sure that our group's activities thus far had not gone unnoticed by the resident "*Locals*"[16]. Some members had heard bipedal footsteps and branch breaks out in the forest when everyone was hunkered down for the night while others had even experienced that eerie feeling of being watched which has often been reported by people who have unknowingly been in close proximity to a sasquatch.

"Tonight we want to act just like a group of campers. Outwardly this will be nothing new to them since they have probably watched this kind of human activity before. However, by keeping our noise level down to a minimum, we may actually hear if they do any vocalizations and if they are approaching us."

Crouching down by the picnic table Matt started to draw out a rough diagram on the ground indicating where and how he wanted us to place ourselves. Once we were actually in situ he said that he would physically ensure that we were in the right spot. Watching Matt draw things in the dirt reminded me of Bill Cosby's Street Football[17] sketch where the quarterback gets down on one knee and draws out the football play on the ground using items at hand to represent his team mates:

"Now Shorty, this is you. This is the coke bottle top"

"But, I don't wanna be the coke bottle top."

"Well, waddya wanna be?"

"I wanna be the piece of glass."

"Okay, you're the piece of glass."

"Listen to this. Now Arnie, I want you to go down ten steps and then cut left behind the black Chevy."

This was great. Matt's instructions ensured that everyone not only knew what the game plan was but what role we were to play. The only other thing left to do, was to decide with whom you wanted to camp out in the woods. With the impromptu meeting finished and the food devoured, I went to finish off my own preparations. That's when Fred called out to me.

"Hey Blaine! Who are you hanging out with tonight?"

"No one so far. You want to pair up?"

"Sure."

The time for this evening's kick off wasn't supposed to be for another couple of hours. This gave Fred and I time to sit back and shoot the breeze. Although Fred was up for the adventure of the expedition he was still a little bit skeptical of the existence of the sasquatch. We talked about some of the better-known incidents such as Roe, Ostman and Beck. I had been following the bigfoot phenomena for a number of years more than he and so I told him about some sightings he was unfamiliar with like the Bossburg cripple.

For the past two nights we had been getting out to the target area a little more than an hour before sunset. Since my new position was under the forest canopy, the amount of available daylight would be disappearing even sooner through the branches of the big firs. Because we knew where we were supposed to be for the night, I felt that there was no need for us to hang around base camp any longer than was absolutely necessary, especially since our quarry was out there in the woods and not dining on Fred's bruschetta at base camp. Getting out before the sun went down also meant that a person could at least take his time to acquaint himself with his surroundings. Personally, I have always found myself to be more confident in the dark if I can see things in the daylight beforehand. In other words, I would like to know precisely where the cliff is when I have to visit the l'il camper's room in the middle of the night!

Fred said that he had to swing by his place to pick up a few things and I had to grab a couple of items on my way through town as well. We both knew our way to the target area and getting out there before the other attendees was important to us. We needed to find a parking spot. There were only a few good spots where we could park our vehicles together and still allow any traffic to get past us. Arriving first also meant that we would have the chance to take a quiet look around before anyone else entered the forest. We would also be able to note any changes as the additional attendees began to filter into place.

During one of our discussions Tony had told me that he would often spend a few hours at a location examining the secondary evidence that he had found. Occasionally, another vehicle would enter or pass through the area that Tony was exploring. Up until this point he had found no indication that a sasquatch may be nearby. That is to say, he had heard no vocalizations or bipedal footfalls or detected any pungent odor. But as the vehicle approached, Tony heard a resounding wood knock that was soon answered by another from deeper in the forest. The vehicle's passengers had not noticed it because their windows were often closed or the tunes were cranked up.

Was this just a coincidence? Or, as Tony had suggested to me, did a sasquatch actually warn the rest of its clan or family group about some hairless interlopers encroaching into their territory? Hey, I know that this sounds like I am assigning a level of intelligence to a creature whose existence most people do not want to even acknowledge. But, it is not that much of a stretch to believe that the sasquatch may communicate in this manner for any number of reasons, and a warning signal may just be one of them. Found in the files of the BFRO are reports where wood knocks and replies have been heard under a variety of different situations and Matt had written an article about these signals. Entitled *Deer Kills and Bigfoots* it relates an incident of a property owner who watched a herd of deer from his kitchen window. The following is an excerpt from that article:

> "As the deer browsed quietly, the owner heard a knocking sound coming from a wooded hillside overlooking the field of deer. The knocking sound, which sounded like a piece of wood being hit against a tree, was answered a moment later by a knocking sound coming from a wooded slope that was closer to his house. A moment

after that, from the first hill, he reported hearing a short, loud growling roar. In response the deer herd bolted in panic toward the closer tree line - at the base of the slope from where the answering knock had been heard." [18]

On the following day the landowner found evidence that suggested that a coordinated attack had taken place upon the deer herd. If this was the case then could it be possible that a sasquatch may also inform its neighbors when the tourists were passing through again?

With this in mind Fred and I planned to meet an hour after leaving the base camp. On my way out of town, I stopped and picked up my sundries. I was in no particular hurry since there was still plenty of sunlight left in the day giving me the opportunity to take a good look at my surroundings. Moving slowly up the main road through the target area, I passed by the fork in the road where Sid had parked his camper and where Matt had so successfully interviewed the witness. A little bit further up the road I suddenly stopped the truck when I spotted something that immediately piqued my interest. A mere twenty yards from the edge of the road was an X. For those of you who have been investigating the sasquatch/bigfoot phenomena for any length of time, seeing one of these structures is probably nothing new. But to me this was as exciting as finding a fresh set of pristine tracks.

So what exactly is an X? An X is just that, an X. For some unknown reason sasquatches like to take pieces of trees, logs really, some of which are twenty or thirty feet in length and build an X shaped structure with them. It appears that this is done by placing the first log so that it rests firmly in the crotch of a tree or by weaving it between two trees that happen to be growing close together, in such a manner that it cannot fall out. A second tree trunk, of similar size, is then anchored against the first log in such a way that it will not fall down. The resulting structure created is clearly an X.

I grabbed my camera and bailed out of the truck. I just had to get some shots of this. After taking two or three happy snaps I bashed my way through the brush to get a closer look. Of course in my rush, I had neglected to watch where I was walking. If there had been any footprints in the area at the base of the X, I had probably walked all over them. If I didn't then the passengers from the next couple of vehicles certainly would add to the careless destruction of any possible evidence.

Why had this X been raised? There is no real way of telling but I know that if this structure had been there before this particular day then it would have been spotted. I say this because the seasoned members of the expedition had been up and down the length of this particular road quite a number of times. If anything, the "Guys from New York" should have seen it because they had been over these roads numerous times with their rented mobile road mapping video research vehicle.

I did want to make sure that the others would be able to locate my find so I stacked up a number of stones alongside the road. Little did I realize that my little pile of stones would attract more attention than the X. Sasquatches have also been known to stack stones. In one celebrated incident in 1967, Glen Thomas watched a family of three sasquatches dig through a scree field of large rocks while foraging for hibernating ground squirrels. As they dug out the stones they would sniff them and then stack them out of the way. Both John Green and Dr. John Bindernagel attended to this site and in the photographs taken; the stacks of stones are clearly visible against the skyline.[19] The six inch stack of stones that I had placed on the side of the road was nothing in comparison to the stone towers piled several feet high but later that afternoon just about everybody who drove up the road would stop to photograph this little pile of rocks and then proceed up the road to announce their great discovery!

"Did you hear about the rock pile?" someone would say.

"Yeah, I know 'cause I put them there."

"Blaine, why did you pile some rocks on the road?"

"To mark the location of the X in the woods."

"An X? What X?" one would ask.

"Where is it?" said another.

"Uh, in the bush near where I stacked the stones."

I don't know how Fred had made it to the rendezvous spot before I did, but when I pulled up he was already there waiting for me. After some chit chat and some refreshments we hiked into the dense forest to a point where we would still hear the arrival of the other expedition members and hopefully there would be some indications that there was a 'squatch or two lurking in the woods, too. Everybody was supposed to meet up at the trailhead and when Matt arrived he would then lead the vehicles back down the road in order to position them for the evening. We were to be strung out along the road with each car or truck being parked on a wide spot, in order to not block traffic just in case there was an emergency. Fred and I had secured our spot already. All of the available roadside turnouts all looked the same, so it was felt that each group would have an equal opportunity to experience an interaction.

As we waited to see if there was any validity to Tony's assertions, we listened as the throng of expeditionaries jabbered amongst themselves about work, the kids and of course sasquatch stuff. Suddenly, a loud powerful bang echoed from the ridge above us. It sounded like it was at least four hundred yards behind us. The effect on the attendees was immediate. They all shut up!

The silence was deafening as the seconds ticked by and then, in the distance…

WHACK!

A reply came from the general direction of the beaver pond far below us. I don't believe those who were milling about their vehicles heard the reply because we were higher up than they were and the slope of the embankment may have deflected the sound.

We sat quietly waiting to see what would happen next. With the sound of the wood knock fresh in their minds the people down below us had decided, en masse, to take a walk down the road. It wasn't long after, that Fred motioned toward the ridge above us where the first wood knock had come from.

SNAP.

CRUNCH.

Something was moving above us and it was definitely bipedal.

Something in the back of my mind said "Blaine, this is not the time to be a hero. So, move your ass!" Fred must have heard the same voice shouting in his head because we both stood up and began to make a quick but quiet beeline for the roadway. It sure didn't take us long to get off the hillside. Once we were on the road we retreated in the same direction as the main body. We didn't want to panic everyone nor did we want the group to storm back up the hill in the hopes of seeing something. Since Matt's strategy was to draw an inquisitive sasquatch in close for some greater interactions, we agreed to stick with his plan. Chasing after something in the forest would simply scare off whatever was there. While walking down the road Fred and I discussed what had just happened and we both felt that once it got dark out, things were going to be very exciting.

Over the next hour or so Matt positioned the vehicles where he wanted them and this simple activity was getting the attendees pretty hyped up. Everyone was now stretched out along the roadway and even the "Guys from New York" had appeared for the gathering.

Now, almost every good story that I ever heard almost always started with the catch phrase: "So, there we were..."

All lined up...

On the road...

Everyone's vehicles were parked so each group was just out of sight from the next group. It was postulated that in this manner each group of expeditionaries would appear to be alone but they would be secure in the knowledge that help, if it were needed, was just around the corner. Of course the whole intention of this scheme was to make us appear to be just a group of campers hanging out in the woods.

Imagine for a minute that you are a sasquatch just walking through the woods, minding your own business and then off in the distance you hear a wood knock or a vocalization. What was that? You wonder who is in your territory so you reply back. A little while later and maybe from a different location you hear another response. Well, being the inquisitive sort, you just have to check this guy out and see what the hell he is up to. And so, off you go.

Quietly.

Cautiously.

As you approach the area from which the sounds had emanated, you see a small group of those hairless 'squatches. No big deal. There are only two or three of them, standing about or sitting near their metal rolling boxes. You can see them but they can't see you because you know that, shrouded by the forest in the blackness of the night, you are safe from their primitive spying eyes.

And what's this? There's another knot of these creatures just around the corner. Well then, you think to yourself, I might as well just stay a while, and just in case one of those beams of light stabs through the darkness in my direction, I will watch them from behind this screen of trees.

So we sat through the night discussing the prevailing theories of cars, politics, our jobs and of course bigfoot, occasionally taking note of the sudden sound of a branch being broken in our immediate area. Fred and I had parked our trucks tailgate to tailgate. I was facing downhill with Fred facing the other way. The trucks were separated by about ten or twenty feet and this gave us enough room to sit off of the road in relative security. John, Philip and Mike had set up their camp about a hundred yards or so down the road from us. Going a hundred yards in the other direction and around the corner were Aaron and Roger. Beyond them were the "Guys from New York" holding down the fort at the uppermost end of the line.

On a lower road, directly below John's group, were a young couple from Washington State in one tent and a solo expeditionary in his own. Due to the terrain their camping spot was extremely tight and as a result the tents ended up being only a few feet apart. This group had arrived late, after a long road trip that had taken them through the heavy bustling traffic of BC's lower mainland, and then up along the coast to Sechelt. The sun had not dropped over the horizon for long when the couple radioed to the rest of the group that they were going to crash for the night. I believe the solo member must have felt that there was no reason for him to sit up by himself because he soon crawled into his own sleeping bag too.

All was quiet. Too quiet!

Even the damn crickets had stopped their occasional chirping.

"Is anyone listening?" It was Sarah from Washington State.

"Go ahead Sarah."

John had an ear bud microphone on his radio and with it he could hear someone calling and reply in a much softer voice than the rest of us. After seeing John use it over the weekend I knew that I would be looking to pick up something similar for my radios.

"We have a visitor!"

Everybody was suddenly all ears.

"Whereabouts?"

"Oh, about ten feet directly behind our tent!"

Over the next few minutes Sarah quietly explained that shortly after getting comfortably secured in their tent, they heard the stealthy approach of a decidedly bipedal something that was now sitting close enough for them to hear it breathing. As soon as we heard this information over the radio, Fred and I were immediately on the move to John's location, albeit cautiously, since we didn't want to trip on the gravel in the darkness. As we walked along we listened, as John and Sarah continued to quietly discuss the incident that was unfolding.

"Sarah, is it still there?"

"Yes, John. It is still here!"

"Sarah, is it doing anything?"

"No, nothing. It's just shifting about."

When we arrived at John's campsite, Mike had his thermal imager trained in the direction of Sarah's tent down on the lower road, but the positioning of the trees and the heat bloom from Sarah's tent, prevented a separate target on the other side of the tent from being seen. The Washington couple was in a quandary. The visitor wasn't doing anything threatening. In fact, it wasn't doing anything at all! But we desperately wanted to get it to move into a position so Mike could get a recording of it on the camcorder, which he had slaved into his thermal unit. Suddenly, I hit upon, what I thought, was a great idea!

"Sarah, its Blaine. Can you hear me?"

"Yes, we hear you."

"I want you to try something. Unzip the door to your tent."

"What?"

"Not all the way. Move it only six inches or so. Just to see what it will do and maybe we will be able to record it with Mike's thermal unit."

Although I couldn't see them, I just knew that everybody who was listening in on the conversation, was now standing in the darkness with their mouths agape at the shear lunacy of my idea. However, in my defense, I rationalized that if the thing behind Sarah's tent was a bear, it would not have been sitting quietly. It would have been sniffing and snuffling about looking for food and it would not have hung around if there weren't any. If indeed this was a sasquatch, and if its intention was to harm them in any way, it could have quite easily torn through the fabric of their flimsy dome tent and there wouldn't have been a thing any one of us on the upper road, could have done to prevent it. If anything, I would have been racing back to my truck to retrieve my field first aid kit so I could start attending to the victims. My scheme was hinged on two points that the BFRO have proven to be true, time and time again. The first point being that under the right circumstances, the sasquatch is curious about us and it will approach us only on its terms. The second point is that there has been no reputable recorded incident of a bigfoot attacking or harming a human being. Oh sure, when confronted with people in its territory, a sasquatch has been known to growl, scream, throw stones, shake and even push down trees. These intimidation tactics have been experienced by many members of the BFRO and from what I have been told, they work pretty darn well.

"Alright, I'll do it. Are you ready? Here goes nothing..."

Zzz Zzziiipp!

"Sarah? Did anything happen?"

"IT JUST WALKED PAST MY TENT!"

This was the solo guy whose tent was three feet away from Sarah's.

"Yeah, I heard it stand up and leave," Sarah said.

But it hadn't gone far. After some additional coaxing on our part, Sarah and her partner actually got out of their tent, stood around for a few minutes and then went back to bed. Soon after closing up her tent for the night she called us on the radio to say that the visitor had come back to its original position right behind her tent.

This was just too much for us to handle! With all that had just taken place, Mike was unable to see anything discerning with his thermal unit because of the multitude of trees. After a brief discussion, it was decided that John, Philip and Mike would go and check the situation out, especially since Sarah was concerned about this thing still hanging around her tent. They planned to take the thermal unit along. This meant that one of them would use it while another would carry and monitor the camcorder with a thumb at the ready to record anything that jumped out at them. The third person was going along for moral support. Fred and I opted to stay put and guard the access to the upper road from any seven-foot plus hairy interlopers. By the time the intrepid trio got to Sarah's tent the visitor was long gone and as with a lot of possible opportunities, nothing was recorded either. But, if nothing else, everybody knew that something was definitely intrigued enough to be sneaking around our campsites.

After the guys returned from the lower road we discussed what had taken place over the next half hour. It was all pretty exciting to say the least. A quick check of my watch showed that it was close to midnight. This was now going to be my third night out in the woods and my tent, my beautiful sanctuary, complete with a cot and an air mattress was still set up at base camp. This thought resounded through my head as Fred and I wandered back up the road to our vehicles. As the adrenaline rush drained from our bodies both of us were suddenly dead tired and we knew we wouldn't be staying up any longer than necessary. After securing our gear for the night, Fred climbed into the back of his truck closing the hatch of the cap behind him.

We radioed each other.

"Goodnight, Fred."

"Goodnight, Blaine."

Once again, I was reclining in the passenger seat of my truck, preparing to snuggle into my down sleeping bag. I took my boots off, my socks off, left my pants and T-shirt on, put my Cobra radio nearby, had my hunting knife drawn and resting on the dashboard in front of me and finally locked the doors. There have been reports where a sasquatch has tried to open a vehicle's door handle and I wouldn't want to surprisingly fall out of the truck in the middle of the night only to land at a hairy pair of size 32 ½ GGG feet! Did I close the driver side window? I think I did. I leaned across the cab and passed my arm right through to the outside! Holy Shit! A lot of good locking the doors does me when I left the bloody window wide open!

Damn it! Where are my keys?

Keys are in! Auxiliary power on!

Power windows, don't fail me now!

Although it seemed like it would take forever for me to fall asleep, realistically it probably only took a couple of minutes before I was headed for the Land of Nod. The eighteen or nineteen hour days were starting to add up and as exciting as this evening had been thus far, I just couldn't stay awake any longer. It didn't take long before I was sound asleep.

BANG!

EYES WIDE OPEN!

WHAT WAS THAT!

Something had woken me up! And as I lay there with my eyes now squinched tightly closed, I tried to rationalize the sound that I had just heard. Now, would Fred sleep with his boots on? Doubtful. But, if he did sleep with his boots on, would I hear him if he rolled over and his booted foot banged the side of his truck box? Once again, it was doubtful. Nope! The sound was definitely from something slapping or banging the side, the roof or the back deck of my truck. The passenger window beside my head and the cargo window of the truck were both open about an inch for ventilation, so what I had heard was a crisp bang on my vehicle and not a dull thud from Fred's. Where's the radio? Got it.

Click... click... click. I quickly keyed my radio but there was no reply.

Click... click... click. Come on guys. Somebody, please reply! Anybody?

BAM... BAM... BAM!

Something heavy, and definitely bipedal, walked past my truck!

Click... Click... Click!

SOS... SOS... SOS!

I really didn't want to break radio silence but no one was answering to the distress call that I was keying on the radio! Maybe, if I whispered into the microphone ...

"Is anybody there? Can anyone hear me?"

"Yeah, I hear you." It was Sarah. "What's wrong?"

"Something just slapped my truck and then walked down the road."

Even with the sound of another human's voice on the radio, I was still shit scared! Scared of what was outside on the road! I know that I had heard it walk away from me but I had no way of knowing how far away it was at this point in time.

BAM... BAM... BAM!

Whatever had walked past me was returning! My passenger window had been open only about an inch for ventilation and even though I had been trying to be as quiet as possible it must have heard me talking to Sarah.

BAM… BAM… BAM! My God does it ever sound big.

"Sarah!"

"Yes Blaine."

"It came back!"

"Where is it now?"

"I don't know. It went past me and then stopped. I think it's between my truck and Fred's!"

Scrunched down in my sleeping bag, I was trying desperately to make myself as small and as inconspicuous as possible. Despite trying to make myself invisible to the world outside the cab of my truck, I am sure that it knew that I was inside this rolling box. I couldn't hear it breathing, and I couldn't smell anything out of the ordinary but I could sense that it was out there. Large and looming, in the darkness it was only ten or twelve feet behind me. The seconds ticked by into minutes. Damn it! Why don't you just leave! To check the time, I would have to push the illumination button on my watch but I was scared that this would only attract even more unwanted attention to me. What was it doing out there? What was so intriguing that it came back for a second look?

BAM… BAM… BAM! Once again it walked past me, heading back down the road towards John's campsite.

"Sarah? Sarah? Are you there, Sarah?" There was no reply. After staying up all night worrying about the visitor behind her own tent she must have finally fallen asleep and as a result I was alone. Again!

Desperate for some human contact, I called out over the radio, "Is anyone awake? Is anyone listening to the radio?"

"Blaine? It's John speaking. Are you okay?"

"No, I am not! Something slapped my truck and woke me up. It walked away and then it came back when I was talking to Sarah but now she has fallen asleep. I don't know where it is, so I'm scared to get out of my truck and besides that, I have to take a piss so bad my back teeth are floating!"

I vaguely remember John saying something to the effect that he would be right up as soon as he was dressed. But it really didn't matter how long he took because I wasn't moving out of my truck until an actual human was standing outside in the sunlight. In the meantime I'd just sit tight and hope that my bladder didn't burst! And how embarrassing would that be? Just imagine not only did the Fearless Monster Hunter get trapped in his truck; he also wet himself while waiting for help! After an agonizing ten minutes, John was standing outside my truck but since it wasn't daylight yet, and the big hairy thing might still be lurking about, I was staying put!

It was about this time when Fred woke up. He opened up the cap of his truck to find John standing nearby. As John filled him in on what had transpired, I nervously lowered my window in preparation to exit my safe haven. I took a long sniff of the air. I didn't smell any great beasties about so maybe it was safe to come out now. Several more minutes went by and with a final cry for release from my swollen bladder, I uncoiled myself from the passenger seat. Come to think of it, I don't believe I even put my boots on before I stumbled to the edge of the road to relieve myself. Within a half hour, the sun had climbed over the mountain behind us, its warmth slowly bringing life to my tired bones. It was now bright enough to see farther into the woods all around us, and with the daylight the woods no longer held any unseen monsters. I sat on the tailgate of the truck with John and Fred sitting across from me. I was barely able to hang onto the fresh cup of coffee that Fred had pressed into my hands. Other expeditionaries began to arrive at our campsite. Philip, Mike, Aaron, and Roger all had come to see if I was okay. Hell, even one of the "Guys from New York" may have shown up too but I doubt if I would have noticed him because I was still in a state of shock and disbelief.

Fred, Fred, Fred. Speaking of Fred! Did he hear any of the goings on just a few feet from his vehicle? Did he see anything outside his truck? Did he sense anything lurking in the darkness? No. No. And no! He hadn't noticed a damn thing except when John was trying to pry me out of my truck. Thanks Fred! Thanks for nothing!

After this incident was published on the BFRO website, I have been asked numerous times if I had seen what had slapped the truck. Do you want to know something? Even if my eyes had been open, which they weren't, I couldn't have seen the thing that had walked past me because it was still far too dark outside. Even if it had been looking directly in the window at me I still would not have seen it! It was 4:30 in the morning when the incident had started and the sun wouldn't have shed any light on the roadway for another hour or more.

Saturday…Fitting in

Breakfast consisted of some IMP's and lots of coffee. I was hungry and I still had the shakes. I fully intended that when I got into town I would go and have some McStuff or maybe a sandwich from the local Subway but for now the military rations that I had scrounged from work would suffice. Besides, Fred enjoyed eating these things too.

And the same questions kept being repeated over and over with each person that I bumped into that morning. What happened? Did you see it? Were you scared? The answers to the questions soon became stock. First off, my truck was slapped. Then, it's a No to the former and Yes to the latter. Thank you! Come again! I swear if one more person asks me what happened I'd kick him where it counts! Oh, good morning Matt. Well, I suppose I could tell my tale just one more time.

Over the next several minutes Matt interviewed John and myself. We explained to him what had taken place that morning. Even though my story was starting to sound like a broken record, repeating the same details over and over, I had not yet heard John's side of things. John said that he had woken up at the point where the visitor had returned to my truck and because he had an ear bud microphone still in place he had quietly listened in on the conversation between Sarah and myself. When the creature had left me for the second time, John had heard it walk down the road towards his position only to veer off to the right, making its way through the forest to wherever a sasquatch would go at 4:30ish in the morning. Most importantly, John was able to corroborate my story. He informed Matt that whatever had left my camp and approached his was definitely large and bipedal.

There were several questions that came to mind. One would think that the first would be something along the line of: Was it or was it not a sasquatch? For me this question was moot. There was no doubt in my mind that what was outside my truck early that morning was a large bipedal primate. I mean, what else could it have been? A bear? Another expeditionary? I highly doubt it since bears are not bipedal and there was no one awake at that time of the morning. I think a much more important question was whether or not the visitor I had was the same one that had sat behind Sarah's tent earlier last night? There was no way of knowing this but the incident at the trail head the previous afternoon pointed towards the possibility that it could have been a different individual. Additionally, there was no way of telling, since we were, once again unable to get the pictures for the photo line-up required by so many of the bigfoot non-believers. What was I supposed to do? Have it stand against a tree that was pre-marked in such a way as to gauge its height and then snap a picture while cringing in the bowels of my sleeping bag?

"Okay Mr. Sasquatch, that will be all for now. Thanks for the photo. I'll add it to my collection of Blobsquatch pictures and just remember you are under suspicion of scaring the crap out of some people, so don't leave the confines of this forest!"

Can you imagine this next scenario? The driver of a vehicle meets up with an intrepid BFRO investigator over a coffee in a donut shop. Obviously this would be the most expected place for a meeting of this kind. After talking to the witness about his particular incident the researcher pulls out a binder from his briefcase. And you just know that the conversation would probably be something like this:

"Uh sir? Now, from the fuzzed out photos that you see in front of you, could you please identify which particular crypto-beast had crossed in front of your car on that dark and stormy night, causing you to leave a stain on the front seat?"

After a few moments the driver, who is now in shock from having to re-live the incident, solemnly declares that what he saw was positively the Rorschach Blob #12. Well, that's that. Bob the Bigfoot will be charged with the misdemeanor crimes of 'Scaring a Motorist with Undue Caution' and 'Jaywalking across a major highway'. He really wouldn't be in this pickle if he had listened to his parents and crossed the road after the car had passed by him.[20] Now, if only Bob the Bigfoot could be made to show up for his court appearance.

As Saturday progressed, it was clearly evident that there was going to be a storm later that night. The clouds were starting to gather to the south and the prevailing winds had also changed direction. The weather on Canada's West Coast is predominantly cyclical in nature with bands of storm systems coming off the Pacific Ocean that will first hammer Vancouver Island and then the Sunshine Coast. Beginning in the fall a pattern of several good days or even a week of nice clear skies will be followed by an equal number of rainy days and by winter this cycle reverses itself with precipitation falling almost every day. This being said, a storm that comes directly out of the north or the south is usually a tempest with high winds and quite a bit of rainfall, but it does not last as long as the steady squalls that come in from the ocean. I don't think the attendees had any indication that the change in the weather would be a significant test of their resolve or that they might just find themselves scrambling for shelter if the skies decided to really open up tonight. Personally, I had no idea where I would end up. My tent was still sitting exactly where I had pitched it. Untouched, unused and unloved.

If nothing else the one thing that was great about coming back to this base camp was the ability to take a shower. Sure, I could have rigged up one of those solar camp showers, hung it from a tree and rinsed off the accumulation of dust from my body. But today I needed to wash, to lather, to scrub, to rinse and to soothe my tired aching dirty body and all for the price of a dollar for ten minutes of pure warm liquid heaven. And so with a pocket full of loonies I planned on being in the shower until the hot water tank was begging for mercy. I left a note pinned to my truck stating my intentions just in case there was an emergency like: If the earth blew up or if a sitting American president was named a clown named Ronald McDonald – you know the really remotely possible things in life - then come and retrieve me from my watery hiatus. However, as I was just a new attendee I doubted if anyone would even notice that I was gone for a couple of hours except for the rezident squirrels.

Yes, I said *rezident* and not resident. It was something about their nervous habit of keeping an eye on everyone in the camp and barking out warnings that reminded me of the Cold War Soviet KGB officers who were always keeping tabs on the populace.

Bark! Where do think you are going comrade?

Bark bark! Do you have your identity papers?

Bark bark bark! Just remember comrade, we will be watching you!
Anyways, back to my ablutions.

Have you ever really taken notice of the pure joy of being clean? Not that I am a fastidious clean freak who cannot go without a wash each and every day. But now that the opportunity to really enjoy a peaceful shower had presented itself I was going to take full advantage of it!

I don't know how long I was in the shower facility and I really didn't care. As the steam from the shower turned the place into my own personal sauna all sense of time had escaped me. In fact, there was so much steam it would have been impossible to shave in front of the mirror therefore I wisely elected to scrape the four-day-old beard off of my face while in the shower. Nearly two hours had slipped by and when I emerged I felt like a butterfly leaving its cocoon. Even the stroll back to my campsite was done at a leisurely pace. I was feeling great and nothing could lesson my joy even if I were heading back to my tent wearing the Emperor's new clothes.

By now it was almost noon and most of the expeditionaries had made it back to base camp. They were lounging, eating, napping, comparing notes and waiting forever. Waiting for the other shoe, and for Matt, to drop (in). I really began to wonder what we would be up to for the remainder of the day, this last day and night of the first BFRO expedition in Canada. Towards my end of the campground were Aaron and Roger as well as John and Philip, all puttering around their respective sites, just killing time. There was no way of knowing what we would be doing next as there was no set game plan. We were on Matt's schedule as he was the one driving the proverbial bus. But I had come to accept this fact. What choice did I have? All of this was new to me and to many other attendees as well. There would be some who could not accept this and as a result this expedition would be their first and their last. Oh well, thanks for coming out. It's been a slice. For myself, I didn't care if this was to be my only outing with the BFRO. I had resigned myself to taking this experience one step at a time and one day at a time. This was such a huge learning curve for me that I did not want to miss anything by getting ahead of everything.

There are quite a number of other bigfoot research organizations that can be found online, Cryptomundo and the BFF or Bigfoot Forums to name just a couple of them. But, having read through a number of the diatribes posted on their websites it is quite evident that the members of these groups very rarely go out into the wilderness to investigate reported incidents or actively engage and pursue the sasquatch. It appears that the members of these other groups are quite content to huddle in front of their glowing monitors, content to type away at their keyboard with their beverage of choice at their elbow while perusing through the Internet news groups, looking for any bigfoot activity that can be marginalized on their blog sites. They are quick to slag anyone who dares to be inquisitive and proactive in the study of the sasquatch phenomenon.

Everyone watched Tony and Matt's vehicles pull into the campsite. Okay it was now time to finally see what the game plan was going to be this afternoon. There were several tasks that Matt wanted to do this afternoon, and to accomplish them the topographical maps were once again brought out onto the table. The first task was the exploration of an entirely new area that lay higher up the mountain from where we had been operating. There was some indication that sasquatches were traversing or migrating from some place up in the mountains all the way down to the seashore and then back to a higher elevation. Precisely when they were moving in which direction, up or down the mountain, would be anybody's guess. If there were a couple dozen or more accurate reports from this particular area there should be enough data to formulate a better strategy to find out where and when these great hairy beasties were traveling. The other item on the agenda was that we had to meet with a local press member for an interview and to ensure that we were at the designated location at the precise time was not going to be easy. Even with the storm clouds continuing to slowly build on the horizon there was a still lot of daylight available to complete everything.

While everyone had been hanging around Fred had rejoined us from wherever Fred went when he wasn't at work and when he wasn't hanging with us. I like Fred. If I hadn't followed my career path through the Canadian military I could have been Fred and I would have been just as happy making Panini and wraps, feeling the heat from the grill, slogging through grease traps and shouting out - Order up!

So, with Fred riding shotgun in my truck and everyone else put into various driver/ passenger configurations we once again followed Tony and Matt out of town to spend some time driving down some additional dusty logging roads in the mountains surrounding the picturesque Sechelt peninsula. Just as before, once we had left the highway the spacing between our vehicles was fifty or sixty yards. This procedure kept us from bunching up in the event there was an accident, a mechanical breakdown or if the lead vehicle ran out of road there by causing the entire convoy to turn around on a single lane gravel road bordered by trees, sheer cliffs, embankments, swamps, rocks and stumps in any combination you could imagine. But the primary reason was to allow the lead vehicle enough time to round a corner while leaving the next vehicle still far enough back to be in position to spot a wary sasquatch who might be trying to cross the road behind the preceding vehicle.

The BFRO convoy was now heading towards a lake that rested up on top of the ridge, and I really wanted to be the last vehicle. Fred said that he knew where the group was headed so while enroute down the highway I radioed that we had to stop to get something at a store and that I would catch up. Ten minutes later and after buying a bag of chips, a chocolate bar and two cups of coffee I was now in the position I wanted to be in. Dead last. Go ahead guys. Roar down the road. Make all the noise and raise all the dust you want. And then maybe, just maybe by being the last in the convoy I will capture footage of some big hairy thing crossing the road in front of me. One could only hope. I can tell you that the trek behind the mountain was nice but uneventful. We did see additional secondary signs of sasquatch activity such as tree breaks, arches and X's but in the end the only interesting incident was when the "Guy's from New York" decided to test out the durability of the paint on their leased vehicle.

With the area explored to everyone's satisfaction and time drawing closer to our appointment with the person from the press, we all began to make the return journey of some twenty miles around the mountain which would place us less than two miles from where we had started. That's right folks! Drive twenty to move two. The only thing good about it was that now Fred and I were leading the pack and everyone else … ha ha ha …could eat our dust! Fred wanted to retrieve his truck from base camp but this would have added at least another six miles to the trip so I told him that I would get him to his vehicle after the interview. It had taken longer going in because we had taken the time to explore a number of the spur roads, so getting back to the main highway didn't take as much time as I had thought it would. Once we had pulled back into the main expedition area we again slowed down to a crawl, idling our way back to the trailhead where Fred and I had heard the wood knocks and the bipedal footfalls. I must have made pretty good time getting there because it was at least another ten minutes before anyone else showed up. Roger and Aaron soon pulled up in their respective vehicles and parked near my truck. As the four of us stood about talking, we heard the sound of a vehicle approaching not from the usual direction but from the overgrown road that continued on past the trailhead. The sound of branches brushing and snapping told me that whoever was coming down that goat trail was really doing a number on their vehicle's paint job. When the vehicle burst out onto the trailhead I had thought that it was going to be "The Guys from New York" because I thought that they were the only ones who were zany enough to attempt this route; but I was wrong. It was Tony and his family in their beat up truck.

At that time there were Aaron, Roger, Fred and myself. Tony and his family were just standing around waiting for Matt and the reporter to show up. I don't know where the rest of the group was hiding out. We had all been asked to be at this location for this press and photo op. Personally; I wasn't too keen on the idea of meeting anyone from the local paper. I was just going with the flow. Besides, I had no plans on opening my face and letting my feet fall out. Having been a member of Canada's military, I had seen what happens when the press gets a hold of a straightforward story. By the time those media sharks have finished chewing on it the truth is twisted up worse than a lawyer's small intestine. Can you imagine what a seasoned reporter would do with a tale of a group of people running around the forest looking for big footprints while howling at the moon and whacking trees with a stick?

And so another fifteen or twenty minutes went by.

No big deal really since there was nothing pressing going on, other than the arrival of the media. The sound of another couple of vehicles could be heard coming up the road towards us. It could have been Matt or the reporter, a hiker coming out for a stroll or the "Guys from New York" coming back for another lap. I should have started a betting pool. It turned out to be Matt and following closely behind was the local columnist/photographer/spotlight feature writer person. After glancing at the motley crew hanging out in the forest she was probably wondering what kind of wild goose chase had her editor sent her on.

What the hell is this? A group of weirdoes looking for a sasquatch and right in my own backyard. Yeah, right! Well lady you don't know the half of it. If you wanted some real fun you should have been with us last night when things were going bump in the night.

The reporter quickly started taking notes as Matt began telling her all about the BFRO. She was asking all the right questions or at least I think she was. While the Q&A session was taking place the rest of us were standing twenty feet away, spread out all around the trailhead. I was standing on the driver's side of Tony's truck playing peek-a-boo with his daughter. She was giggling and laughing, simply a young child full of life.

Whack…whack whack …whack …whack!

Immediately everyone froze in place. The series of wood knocks echoed through the forest. They were clearly audible but they were much lighter in strength than the power strikes that Fred and I had heard emanating from this area just yesterday. They almost sounded like a drummer tapping out a rhythm. Matt called out softly to those of us who were in range.

"Where is everybody? Is anyone in the bush behind me?"

After looking around and taking a quick head count I replied, "We are all here Matt except two people who went down the main hiking trail".

"So there is no one in the forest on this side of the road?"

"No."

Crunch…snap! Something was slowly moving behind where Matt was standing. From the sound of the footfalls it had to be some sixty yards deep in the bush but it was so thick and leafy that there was no way to see more than ten yards in its direction.

Matt quickly came up with a game plan. "Let's see if we can get it to stick around and play but first you four take a slow walk down to the road that cuts back up in this direction. Take your time but not too long. Be observant but rely on your peripheral vision as much as you can and radio me when you are at the bottom of the road."

We had our orders. Aaron, Roger, Fred and I moved off at a fairly quick but cautious pace. We had a hundred and fifty yards to go and with the noise of our boots on the packed earth roadway we couldn't hear if our hopefully unsuspecting target was on the move. We had only gone maybe half the distance when Matt warned us over the radio, "Guys, I am going to give a whoop in five." Immediately we stopped where we were so we could clearly hear Matt and a response, if any.

"Whoooopp!"

Crash! Snap! Crack! Something had definitely reacted to Matt's vocalization.

The radio burst into life. "It's on the move. Get up that cut road fast!"

The four of us sprinted to get to the cut road. If we hurried and if we were lucky it may be headed down the hill towards us and we might just be able to head it off at the proverbial pass. Seconds later we were at the junction and without any regard for our safety we scrambled up the cut road for fifty yards or so.

And stopped.

Listening. Listening?

Nothing at first and then…crack! Snap! It was moving again.

"Which way is it headed, Matt?"

"It's going uphill and fast. You guys might as well come back"

Whatever had been playing the sticks had moved extremely quick and in a bipedal fashion, deeper into the forest, away from our position when the four of us charged up the cut road. Before we had heard the wood knocks no one in our group had seen it or even smelled it. But it most certainly had been watching us for whatever reason. Maybe it was attracted to the laughter of Tony and Sarah's kids.

Back at the trailhead I saw that the reporter had a kind of stunned look on her face as if she just could not rationalize what had just taken place. Questions, questions and more questions! While the rest of us stood about trying to wrap our own heads around what had just taken place, Matt began to answer her queries. When she was satisfied with everything, she had us pose for the quick snapshot that would accompany her story. Either Fred or Tony sent me a copy of the article when it was printed. It was actually a pretty nice write-up. It wasn't the New York Times but it wasn't the National Enquirer either. One thing I did notice was that, although the incident had taken place in the presence of the reporter, it did not make the paper. I don't know if she had decided not to write about it, or if her editor had used his magic red editing pencil to eliminate a story that may be just a little too fantastic for his readers to believe.

With the media session now over, the rest of the afternoon was again spent back at base camp verbally going over what had happened back on the trail. Those who had not been in attendance began talking over the possibility of holding a stake out on that last section of road. There was even talk of baiting the area with fruits and vegetables from a local produce market. And why not! At this point anything was worth a try. All I could think about was the weather. To the north the sky was growing darker by the hour and a cold wind had started to come down the coast. We were in for one hell of a storm. Fred had noticed the change in the weather too. He came over to my campsite as I was contemplating whether to pull up stakes and move my tent to wherever hell I was going to end up later on that night.

"There's going to be a storm tonight."

"I know and it will probably be pretty bad."

"You staying out tonight?"

"Not all night. I have to work tomorrow and I'll need the rest. Besides, if the winds get really bad I wouldn't want to be out in the bush if the trees start to drop."

Fred had just made a really good point and I had to agree with him. If the winds were strong enough even the big Douglas fir trees can easily be toppled over. The approaching storm was definitely something to be concerned about and there was no sense risking personal injury by staying out in the woods. I had two ferries to take the next day. I wanted to start my all day journey back home first thing in the morning and if I actually stayed in my tent I could pack my gear as soon as I woke up. To expedite my departure in the morning I quickly went through my equipment, stowing what I didn't need into the back seat of the truck.

I didn't know what the other expedition members were planning on doing or when. They all seemed to be lounging about on their camp chairs, like lizards basking in the sun, peacefully soaking up as much warmth as possible before tonight's sky opened up and pissed rain all over them. Maybe they were waiting for Matt before heading out. I didn't know why they couldn't make their own decisions. But I did know where everyone one going to be parked this evening, more or less. So really, there was no rush this afternoon to get out and drive the roads looking for a likely active location. Everyone knew where the focus of our efforts was going to be. However, their loafing around base camp did give me a window of opportunity to do some final gift shopping for family. One of the important things that I had learned in the military was that when you go away from your loved ones for a temporary deployment trip, it would be extremely hazardous to your health if you did not bring back something that showed them how much I missed them. Fred said that he also had to take off for a while as well. We arranged to meet back at the same place we had been parked the night before in just a couple of hours. This would easily give us all of the time we would need to complete our own personal business and still be able to get into position before the rest of the mob even got their act together. Before heading out I informed the group that Fred and I would meet everyone back at the site later on just so the organizers were aware of our location. As I was climbing into the truck Mike Greene came over to ask me a question.

"Hey Blaine. You wouldn't happen to have a spare sleeping bag that I could borrow would you? I found my bed roll to be a bit inadequate for the weather conditions and I have been getting kinda cold at night."

A good... No, make that an important Rule of Thumb for all you campers is this: It is always better to help those in need because someday you just might be in need yourself. Sounds Biblically reminiscent don't it? There is something about casting your bread upon the water and having it come back to you when you most need it. Well, it's true. I had the outer shell to my military sleeping bag in the back seat of the truck and I didn't even hesitate.

"Here Mike", I said. "You can use this tonight and I will pick it up from you in the morning before I head back home. Okay?"

"Thanks Blaine."

And with that simple gesture, which would cost me nothing except the time it would take to drive up the mountain to retrieve the sleeping bag, I knew that I made a friend who one day would return the favor and assist me in my time of need. Sure, you can be ripped off if you are not careful. But would you actually loan out your gear to someone who looks like they would take off with your stuff? Of course not. And if you did hand over it to some ne'er-do-well then you deserve to have your stuff ripped off for not being a better judge of character. Here endeth the lesson.

After finishing my shopping, I fuelled the truck for the trip home and then stopped in at the local Subway to buy a sandwich. The rain would be falling soon and I felt that it would be better to get a semi-nutritious something to eat while on the go instead of having to spend time cooking up some IMP's in my flying kitchen. I don't know what the rest of the guys were planning on eating but I hoped that whatever it was going to be, it had better be waterproof because it was going to be a wet one. Sure enough, just when I turned off the highway, the first drizzle was starting to fall. I wondered who was already on site. I had seen John and his son Philip leave the Subway as I was pulling in, so I was sure that they were up on the mountain by now. Aaron, Mike and Roger should also be in place but I had no idea when anyone else would arrive.

At the top end of the road I found that a number of people had already set up camp for the evening. Tony was there and to my surprise so were the "Guy's from New York". Everyone's tents were pitched and the camp chairs were positioned for ease of conversing. Some people were eating; some had coffee or soup that they had made. Knowing that I wasn't planning on staying the night I carefully negotiated a five-point turn and backed into a spot onto the side of the road. Ten minutes later Fred pulled up in his truck and seeing where I had parked he pulled off the very same maneuver, but with one less turn. Bloody show off!

By now it was about 5:30 pm. The shadows in the forest had lengthened quite a bit, with the setting sun making our collective imagination focus more intently on sounds emanating from the woods around us. We sat in our chairs, munching our food, drinking our drinks and talking over the experiences from the weekend. Life was good.

The rain was starting to come down at a fairly constant shower and the gusting wind was swaying the tops of the fir trees. My decision to spend my last night in my tent was a wise one. These guys were going to get soaked to the bone and then they would have to break camp in the morning. Re-organizing and packing your equipment after a week out in the woods is one thing, but doing it after a stormy night when you are tired and cold with your kit all soaking wet makes for a miserable trip home. I sincerely doubted that with present weather conditions there would be any sasquatch activity. Let's think about it logically. If you were a sasquatch would you want to be out wandering in the woods trying to sneak-a-peek at some unsuspecting campers when the wind is threatening to snap trees in half and with the rain coming down so hard that some enterprising individual has started to build an ark? I don't think so. According to the BFRO files that I have read there are much fewer sightings reported during stormy weather which can easily attributed to either a) fewer people being out in the wet to spot a sasquatch or maybe b) the resident sasquatches, like humans, are simply not up to traveling about during inclement weather.

As the evening progressed we stood around trying to stay in the lee of the storm by huddling under some tarps that John had strung from the trees. One of the guys asked if anyone wanted to go and check out the bait pile.

Bait pile? What bait pile?

Evidently some resourceful smarty-pants had stopped off at a local grocery store and either bought or scrounged some apples and melons, along with other fruits and vegetables of various types. He then took this load of produce and went some fifty yards or so past the point where we were knotted out of the rain and randomly pitched all of it into the forest. Some of the melons were broken open when they smashed against the trunks of some forest giants. Now, this rogue crop tosser wanted someone, anyone, to accompany him while he went to see if anything had been interested in his offerings. Personally, I really didn't feel like wandering down the road in the dark. I was getting tired and I was facing a very long drive the next day, but Aaron and Tony were certainly up for it. As the three of them walked away from the group the light from their headlamps could be faintly seen playing along the roadway and through the trees while they looked furtively about. Well, they were not gone for long. It had been a slow cautious approach to the baited location and a hurried retreat to the relative safety of the group.

"You guys are back rather soon aren't you?"

"Yeah, well we ran into a snag."

"And, what would that be?"

"Oh, just the sound of a deep rumbling growl followed by bipedal footsteps!"

It was getting late about 9:30 or 10 pm. The wind was now whipping the tops of the fir trees back and forth like stalks of wheat waving in a summer breeze. The rain was driving down at a 45-degree angle and by all indications this storm was not going to let up any time soon. I had just about enough of the evening's fun and games. Fred was in the same boat too. We both said our goodnights to the rest of the crowd. Fred headed off to his truck while I sought out Mike to remind him that I would be back to pick up my sleeping bag in the morning. As I climbed into my truck Mike said that he would be awake when I came to get it.

Fred again took the lead down to the intersection where we said our good-byes and parted company. Fred had to get back to work the next day. I planned on getting a good night's sleep since I had to be up and packed first thing in the AM. I would have little time to spare because I would first have to drive back up the mountain to retrieve my gear from Mike and then drive like a madman to make sure that I got on the ferry at Earl's Cove. After landing at Saltery Bay, I would have another short drive up the Coastal highway to board another ferry to take me from Powell River, on the mainland, to Little River, on Vancouver Island. I wish they would just build the damn bridge across the Strait of Georgia and be done with it. No more ferries!

When I pulled into the base camp I half expected not to see my tent flattened by the storm. Mother Nature was really putting on a show with the driving rain and violent winds that were howling along the coast. I glanced at some of the other sites nearby and noted how some people had left their gear unattended or unsecured. Their equipment was now just a jumbled soggy pile of stuff that would take a great many days to dry out. The old military adage of "one man, one kit" had certainly paid off. Being responsible for my own gear and for my own well-being meant that I could look forward to having a nice dry tent to crawl into, where I could snuggle up in my sleeping bag and listen to the wind as it tried to rip the trees from the ground around me. By ensuring that my equipment had been put away before leaving, my camp site was not only presentable to those passing by but it would be a hell of a lot easier to pack up come the morning.

Wrapped up in my sleeping bag, I was pretty damn toasty! I decided that before I crashed out, I would call my wife on the cell phone. I had really tried to make sure that I called her at least once a day, usually when things were at a bit of stand still. It was more of a check in to say hi and to see how things were going at home.

"Hi honey. How was your day? Uh huh. Kids okay? Yeah, well we both know that they can be a handful especially when… What's that? Yeah, it's pouring cats and dogs over here, too. Listen Hon, I'm gonna try to make the twelve-thirty ferry but if I don't, the next one will put me into Comox at seven at night. Yeah, I'll watch the roads. Love you and I'll see you when I get home. Oh, and honey? How are your mom and dad doing? Really? Well I hope he's feeling better soon. See you tomorrow. What? Of course I've missed you. Love you. Bye for now."

Drifting off to sleep, I thought about all that had taken place thus far: the people I had met, the friendships that I had made, the opportunity to see the enduring beauty of the British Columbia's Sunshine Coast, the thrill of sitting out in the darkness waiting for a reply to a wood knock, the luck of being able to observe, first hand, the interview of a sighting witness and, of course, the terror of a big hairy something coming to visit me in the darkness. All of these memories were now and forever etched into my consciousness where I would be able to recall them as they had happened. The only thing left to do was to try and get a good night's sleep before hitting the road first thing in the morning.

Sunday…Homeward bound

Did you ever imagine how truly amazing it feels waking up after sleeping prone for one night after spending several nights dozing in a stuffy cramped semi-sitting position? Well, I must say, that on that particular day, it ranked as the fourth or maybe even the third best sensation in my world. Outside my tent, the sun was shining through the fir trees, the air was still. Obviously the storm had blown itself out and I had work to do. But, first things first. Nature was calling to me and it wasn't just the birds chirping in the blackberry bushes.

Coming back from the washroom, I saw that the "Guys from New York" had rolled into camp. They appeared to be in a state of near panic. Gear was being tossed out of the tent, only to be crammed into duffle bags before being piled into their rented Sport Trac. The flurry of their activity could mean only one thing. They needed to grab an early ferry to put them in time for their flight out of Vancouver International back to the Big Apple. As they continued breaking down their campsite, I stopped at their camp to say goodbye to them.

"Hey guys (from New York)! It was sure nice meeting you (whoever you are). This was a great expedition and I hope to see you again someday (even though I probably wouldn't know you from Adam)". Then it was shake hands, shake hands, shake hands and off they went. Total time for them to break camp was ten minutes on the outside. It took me twenty to pack up my gear but then my timing was a little more generous. I had even factored time to have another scrumptious McStuff breakfast.

Driving back up the mountain, after leaving Sechelt, I wondered if anything had happened to those who had maintained the vigil throughout the storm. It was doubtful. I couldn't imagine anyone or anything being out in the downpour last night. When I rolled into the outpost camp to say my goodbyes and collect my sleeping bag only a couple of people were up. John was outside his tent and Tony was out of his truck. Philip was still sleeping in the tent and Roger was still in his truck. And Mike?

Zzzzzz!

"Mike! I hate to do this but you have to get up because I have to get going if I am going to make the 12:30 connection out of Powell River."

"So how was the storm out here in the woods?"

"It was pretty tense with the wind causing the trees to sway", John said. "But, the really interesting things happened after the storm."

"Did something come into camp? Did somebody see something? What? What?"

Over the next few minutes, while I nervously calculated the exponential depletion of my allotted travel time, John, Tony and Mike, who was now out of his tent, thank you very much, told me how the storm had buffeted them even though the trees and a series of well-placed tarps had provided some shelter. The wind and rain had stopped somewhere around 11:30 or so and with that the forest had become eerily quiet save for the water dripping off the branches. John went on to explain that they had heard a distinct wood knock very close to their position followed by the sound of a tree being pushed over. Several minutes went by and then a second tree also came crashing to the ground but on the opposite side of the road from the first.

Could the storm have blown those trees over? I am sure that some trees were uprooted during the night because the highway had been littered with sizable debris. But the time between the end of the storm and the two trees crashing to the ground was a sizable gap. For this reason I think that any windfalls would have remained hung up in the forest canopy until the next big storm forced them down. The other point to remember is that a very distinct wood knock, identified by several seasoned investigators, was heard prior to the first tree falling. With my heartfelt apologies to Bruce Cockburn, all of this conjecture only begs the question – If a tree falls in a forest… was it pushed?

With my loaned sleeping bag tossed onto the back seat I headed off to the ferry terminal at Earls Cove. The tunes were cranked and I was itching to get home. But all the while I kept watching the tree line ahead just in case I caught sight of something waiting to cross the road. I don't think I even had a chance to say goodbye to Matt. I hadn't seen him the night before nor in the morning. He may have been hanging with the "Guy's from New York". I don't know. The rest of the trip back to the Comox Valley was fairly uneventful. I made the connection out of Powell River, which gave me an opportunity to unwind from the expedition while sitting on the ferry.

Several months after returning home I had been diligently watching the BFRO website for some kind of a final report that would encompass the events that had taken place in Sechelt. When nothing appeared I took it upon myself to submit my own report. I wrote, in part, "I would like to thank the BFRO for the excellent outing on the Sunshine Coast [British Columbia, Canada]. I was amazed at the knowledge and the experience that the seasoned investigators had brought to the table."[21]

Chapter Two
BFRO Sunshine Coast Expedition, 2006

Wednesday – Introductory Revelations

I was really looking forward to this year's expedition for several reasons. First, since I was returning to the site of last year's expedition, I would already be familiar with the terrain and second, I was returning as an investigator. By having one expedition already under my belt as well as having completed scores of Class A and B reports, I was feeling much more confident in my 'squatching abilities.

Base camp was to be located at the same campground as the previous year so I had no problem in securing a site. All it took was a quick phone call to the proprietor and everything was all set. My plan was to pitch a tent at base camp and if I was unable to sleep in it, I would have another shelter at the ready. Someone once said that necessity is the mother of invention. The idea of sleeping in the cab of the truck was not something I relished so I came up with a plan to convert the back of the truck into a more suitable accommodation.

I was still driving a Ford Explorer Sport Trac. A unique accessory on this vehicle is the divided hard deck that turns the box of the truck into a locked strong box. I thought that if I removed the deck maybe I could rig up some sort of a temporary shelter that would cover the truck box while protecting me from any inclement weather and any prying eyes. There is an aftermarket product called a truck tent that is designed precisely for this application but the price charged by the Ford Motor Company was, as with most of its vehicle accessories, quite exorbitant. By removing the deck and crisscrossing a pair of fiberglass tent poles through the tie down anchors, which ring the outside of the box, I now had a framework for a mobile shelter. All I needed was something like a tarp or a large rain fly to drape over the poles and tie it down.

When I arrived in Sechelt the weather was warm and sunny with a few clouds scudding along by a light breeze. As with the previous year I was able to get to the base camp a day before the start of the expedition. I gladly paid for a camp site confident that by using my improvised truck tent in the field I would still have my regular tent for the down time in the afternoon.

Circling the campground to my assigned spot I recognized a couple of vehicles from last year's expedition but I didn't see anybody hanging around. I knew some of the people who would be attending from the discussions on the expedition forum site. John, Philip, Roger, Mike and Matt would be here along with Fred and Tony. I was really looking forward to seeing them again as well as the Newbies, or new people, who had signed up to participate. I was in the process of setting up my tent when I spotted Roger and Philip walking down the road. Immediately I stopped what I was doing and headed towards them. A year had passed since I last saw them and now Philip was as tall as I was.

"One man, one kit", he said.

"And don't you forget it", I replied.

After some small talk I learned that Roger had arrived just before I had. Philip said that he and his dad, John, had gotten here the day before and had spent the night with Tony parked deep in the bush on some forestry access road. Talking away, we noticed that we had been standing in front of a campsite occupied by a new member. The tent looked very expensive. It was very low to the ground with access doors at each end and a full vestibule. There was someone stirring inside and I felt that there was no time like the present to say hello. So, without further ado, the three of us sat down at the mystery person's picnic table and just as we did so, this likeable sort of fellow emerged from his tent doing up his pants. I jokingly commented that this might not be the only time that he would be caught with his pants down, to which he firmly replied, "Oh yes it will be!"

After the required round of introductory handshakes, Harold said he worked as an independent IT person. Roger hadn't met him before but Philip said that he had on the previous night. I don't know what it was, but I immediately felt that either this guy had no sense of humor or he was just too tightly wrapped. Little did I know that both of these conditions applied to Harold.

Harold told me that he had read a number of the reports that I had completed for the BFRO. I felt flattered by the compliment. Wow! A feather in my cap and it looked pretty good. I thanked him for his kind words and went back to finish setting up my tent.

Beside my site was a small typical two-person dome tent quite similar to one that you would purchase at any Canadian Tire or Wal-Mart. Except for a few cooking utensils on the table, the site was pretty clean. I didn't know if the owners were with our group or if they were camping by themselves. Only time would tell and within a few moments my new neighbors arrived. Todd and Frances had driven all the way to Sechelt from Ontario. They had traveled nearly 3000 miles and had passed through five provinces. We said hi to each other and before another word could be uttered, Todd asked me, if I were to take people out in the woods for a hike or whatever, would I ever threaten to leave them there?

My answer was, "No, I would not!"

Todd began to explain that on the previous evening he and Frances had gone out to a location where Tony had spotted some secondary signs, mainly X's and arches. The road was pretty rough and it was unlikely that their small compact car would have made the trip. So instead, they piled their gear into Harold's truck for the trek up the mountain. Once in place Tony, John and Philip set up their camp some four hundred yards away from their position. All was quiet. Everyone had turned in for the night and then, sometime around two in the morning I was told, something was heard snooping around their camp. It could have been a sasquatch. It could have been a bear. Hell, it could have even been a squirrel but it didn't matter what it was or wasn't because Harold was terrified! However, instead of gaining strength from the fact that there is always safety in numbers and the fact that there have been no known attacks on a human by a sasquatch, Harold fanatically informed his passengers that they should come with him now or he was leaving without them.

The question was, where was he going to go? The gate at the base camp was locked so there was not much sense in heading there unless he were going to park his vehicle on the road and climb over the gate with all his stuff. They were miles from the nearest paved road and besides tear-assing down some logging road in the middle of the night was not the smartest thing in the world to do. With everything piled haphazardly in the back of his truck, Harold drove madly down the road and away from whatever had been scurrying about in the undergrowth.

Tony, who has a tendency to stay up all night, heard Harold's truck approaching fast towards their camp. Tony stood out on the road making him skid to a sudden stop after which Harold told him that they were all scared of something moving around their camp. I later questioned Tony on this point and he confirmed Todd's side of the incident. He also stated that he had attempted to dissuade Harold from driving through the forest at night but nothing could have prevented him from completing his mission. Harold had also distorted the facts. Not everyone was scared to stay at the remote site. Todd and his girlfriend would have remained overnight if they had known that Tony could have given them a ride to base camp in the morning. In fact, he had suggested that they all stay at their site but instead Harold roared off down the road without a second thought.

After hearing Todd's story, and after confirming it with Tony, I made it a point not to be saddled with Harold for the duration of the expedition, which wasn't going to be a problem. Before heading to Sechelt, Fred and I had discussed the possibility of us working together again. It was agreed that in doing so we would protect each other's backs and share in any discoveries, too.

Would I have been scared if I had been in the same position as the three of them? Yes, I probably would have. Especially, since this same scenario had already been played out the previous year. But as scared as I was, I did not blast off back to base camp then, and I certainly wouldn't have threatened to leave any members of my party behind. Maybe it's due to my military training or maybe it is just common sense but I believe that if you take someone out somewhere, you have an ethical responsibility for their safety. Don't think so? I can't imagine the guilt I would feel if I had fled to safety, while leaving someone behind only to find out later that something tragic had happened to them. Faced with the same set of circumstances, I would have had them join me inside my truck with the engine running and the tunes cranked up.

Much like the previous year, the afternoon dragged on. Waiting, always waiting for the time to go out in the bush. Tony showed up, finally, as did John and Matt. The main body of the expedition wasn't due to arrive until Thursday so we would have the opportunity to finalize our plans to approach our big hairy friends. Fred was going to be working late so Tony and I resolved to go back out to where Harold had camped. The "Hurry Up and Wait" game was in full swing and I was anxious to go. By now I had changed into my 'squatching clothes' and had sorted the equipment in the truck for a remote camp operation.

It was nearing 6 pm. The light would be fading quickly in the forest. If we didn't go soon I would be rigging my new shelter in the dark and I sure as hell didn't want to be doing that. So with Tony leading the way, we left the remaining members to their own devices. We turned off the main highway some twenty minutes later enroute to Fred's house. After briefing Fred of our plans, we headed out to our base camp. By seven p.m. we were off the pavement and the light was filtering low through the fir trees. So far the sky was clear, which indicated that the temperature could be dropping down into the single digit range.

The road we were traveling on was the same one that Harold had careened down some eighteen hours earlier and it was definitely no garden path. There were potholes of every shape and size, loose rocks, humps, and dips. The brush scraped down the sides of my truck and downed trees projected out into the roadway threatening to take out a window if I turned the steering wheel the wrong way. We drove for five; ten, nearly fifteen kilometers until Tony finally stopped, threw his truck into reverse and backed into a pullout. I spun my rig around and faced it in the direction of the return path. It was nearly 8pm and far too shadowy to do any exploring in the woods unless I wanted to fall off a cliff or twist an ankle. And besides, I had to set up my camp…in the dark… again!

As I toiled away, Tony let me know that his wife, Sarah, was bringing out a salmon for us to have for supper. This was certainly going to be a treat. The thought of having a nice piece of salmon started my mouth watering. It wasn't long, maybe thirty minutes later, when I heard the rattle bump of Sarah's van coming up the road with its one working headlamp illuminating the road ahead and a single tail light, dimly shining on the opposite side of course. The van turned and stopped with a lurch at which point the kids, a dog, Sarah and her friend, whose name escapes me, bailed out like an infantry section of the Marx Brothers exiting from an armoured personnel carrier.

Dismount! Dismount! Dismount!

Go! Go! Go!

And then, from the mouth of an approaching child came a thunderous mortar barrage of questions to which there is no defense except to answer the very last question of the volley.

"Whatcha doing? Is that a tent? Are you going to sleep in there? We have a tent but not on a truck. Why do you wear army clothes? Are you in the army? What's in the box?"

"All of my camping gear."

"Hi Blaine."

"Hi Sarah. Kids please don't touch that."

"Kids, let Blaine do his work."

"Thanks Sarah." Oh that's just great! The dog just marked my tires and my camp box.

"Tony! Here's the salmon."

"Thanks dear!"

"Wow! It's after nine! C'mon kids. Bye guys. Happy 'squatching!'"

And with a jolt…they were off!

Leaving us in the inky darkness.

It would be almost an hour before they got home.

Thursday – a Night Sighting

Over the next three hours Tony and I sat in the dark with only our red lamps turned on. Our camp chairs were positioned between our trucks in such a way that we could hear in all directions. The temperature was starting to drop but it was not overly cold. It had already been a long day but I wanted to be awake when Fred arrived and so to pass the time Tony filled me in on some of the incidents that had taken place in the local area. It was really good to hear how active the sasquatch action had been during the past year. With any luck there would be at least one Class A sighting on this year's expedition.

A snap and a rustle alerted us to the fact that we were not sitting in the dark alone. The sound had come from some place behind Tony's truck. Was it a squirrel? Perhaps. An inquisitive sasquatch? Maybe. An ambitious bear? Most likely, since the scent of supper cooking on the camp stove had floated through the forest and we still had the carcass of the salmon, triple wrapped with plastic bags, sitting inside Tony's cooler. I know that this was not the smartest thing to do but we were planning to take the carcass out for a walk once Fred arrived. A glance at my watch showed that it was a quarter to two when I heard the sound of a vehicle coming towards us. Yeah, Fred's here! Now we can go for a walk and ditch the salmon remains before some opportunistic bear wanders into camp looking for a late night snack.

As we prepared to go for our walk we turned on our red LED headlamps. The white ones would only ruin our night vision and would give our position away as we stumbled down the road. Fred was carrying the night vision scope that he had purchased from a BFRO member during the 2005 expedition. By amplifying any available starlight it gave us the ability to have a good look at the surrounding forest. All was quiet. There was no wind at all to mask the sound of our footsteps. Well, it wasn't like we were trying to be stealthy but there were certain nighttime protocols that we were trying to adhere to. Before we walked away from camp Tony left his digital voice recorder running on the roof of his truck. Why? Well, you never can tell when something might turn up now can you?

With the aid of Fred's night vision unit we could see that the road before us ran down a small hill to the bottom of a gully. Then it swept up to the left towards an open area of the gas line right of way. We stopped and I heaved the bagged salmon parts as far as humanly possible out into the clearing. It wouldn't be there for long. In a day or two the scent of the decomposing fish would attract a scavenger of some kind who would undoubtedly enjoy the free meal.

High overhead the night sky was alive with millions of twinkling stars. There was absolutely no light pollution this far back in the bush and there was enough starlight that we no longer needed our red lamps to see where we were walking. Shoulder to shoulder to shoulder the three of us sauntered along the road for another fifty yards all the while trying hard not to kick any loose stones along the way. The road made a slight turn to the left and then began to rise sharply under our feet. We all waited as Fred switched on his NVG unit again. He wanted to have a better look around at the terrain and to see if anything else might be lurking in the darkness. It was at this point that things suddenly and quite unexpectedly got very interesting.

"Fred! Look up the road to the top of the hill. There's something up there!"

Tony whispered excitedly.

As Fred scanned up the hill I looked in the direction that Tony had indicated. A tall dark shape, looking like the trunk of a large fir tree that had been topped off, dominated the crest of the hill. The large amount of starlight illuminated the smaller and thinner sapling trees behind the dark void with twinkling stars peeking between the individual branches.

"Holy shit!" Fred was now looking at the object with his night scope.

"What is it Fred?"

"It's a 'squatch!"

Over the next ten minutes, or what seemed like ten minutes and felt like an eternity, we watched the shape on the hill by sharing the starlight scope between us much the three witches from Greek mythology who shared but a single eye between them. Then, quite suddenly, the 'squatch was gone. It hadn't walked away. We would have seen that since it was thick enough to blank out a section of the night sky above us. It was my turn to look through the scope and by tracking the road as it went up the hill it soon became obvious what had happened. I strongly believe that our whispering must have alerted our big hairy friend. However, since we were down at the bottom of the hill it may not have known what we were. Through the scope I saw that it had laid itself prone on the ground right at the crest of the hill and was now intently surveying us below its position.

"I found it!"

"Where is it?"

"It's right there!"

I had raised my arm to indicate where it was and in doing so I had broken a cardinal rule. By pointing with my finger I did something that 'squatches may recognize as being purely a human habit and as a result the show was now over. With the aid of the starlight scope I watched as it stood up to its full height, turn and walk back toward the tree line where it was swallowed up in the darkness. Fred would later say that it was if a seven-foot log rose from the ground on end and then walked away. For a couple of minutes we just stood on the road in silence with each of us contemplating the major event that we had just witnessed. It was late. The sun would be coming over the horizon in four hours so we headed back to our vehicles.

Back at the camp I quickly realized that my makeshift truck tent was woefully inadequate. Maybe I was insecure with the idea that our big friend might come by for a closer look only to find me in the back of the truck desperately trying not to wet the bed in terror. I knew it was going to be uncomfortable but I resigned myself to crashing out in the passenger seat once again. Fred was setting up his bed when Tony decided to check his digital audio recorder. Just after he started to listen to it, he stopped the machine and called us over to listen as well.

As the audio recorder played back, we could distinctly hear the sound of the three of us talking quietly as we had gotten ready to head up the road, followed by the crunch of the gravel as we walked away. For the next couple of minutes the sharp clunk of an errant rock being kicked detailed our movement. Then came a new sound. A heavy muffled thump followed by another. A swish of branches or twigs sliding against Tony's truck and then another quiet thump. The next sound was what could only be described as a deep inhale and an equally deep exhale. This was followed by more soft thuds, another swish of the branches and more distinctive thuds. Then there was nothing for several more minutes. Tony advanced the recording until he reached the time stamp for when we had returned from our sighting. Our voices sounded urgent and excited, getting louder as we had neared our remote camp.

I believe the only plausible explanation for this recording was that as soon as we had left the camp, a heavy bipedal something walked into our camp, had a look around and then walked away. It had approached from behind Tony's truck only to depart in the same direction and the reason I say this is because there was no sound of any stones being moved on the gravel roadway after we had left or before we had returned. Additionally, the only branches close enough to brush the truck were on the sides. There was nothing at the front or at the back. A final point was the fact that the recorder had been placed on the roof of the truck at a point some six feet or greater off of the ground. The sounds of respiration could have been from an elk since an adult elk can stand five and a half feet at the shoulder[22] and most certainly could have stretched its neck up near the roof line of the truck where the audio recorder was sitting. But the footsteps we heard entering and exiting our camp were not those of a hoofed animal. A bear could have stood up beside the truck but again the footfalls were definitely bipedal and not of a quadruped. Besides, I doubt if a bruin would have been able to pass up the culinary mess residing in Tony's cooler and it, along with everything else in the camp had been untouched. If the mystery visitor was a sasquatch, and I think that it was, was it the same one that we had seen on the hill? It may have been. I am sure that a 'squatch could have easily covered the distance from the camp to the hill faster than we could especially if it was going cross-country. Could it have been a separate individual from the one that we had seen? That, too, is a possibility since different sasquatches have been identified on the Sunshine Coast not only by their size but by the variation in their color as well.

As exciting as all of this was, it was now after three am and I had been up for close to twenty-two hours. After a round of goodnights we all retired for the remainder of the evening. Barely four hours had passed when I finally awoke stiff and cramped. I would have been much more comfortable if I had been in my tent which, like the previous year, was sitting unoccupied back at base camp. There was enough light outside to see without the aid of a flashlight so I figured that this was as good a time as any to get up. When I tumbled out of the passenger seat I must have woken up Fred. The canopy of his truck suddenly opened and his head peeked over the tailgate. He looked as if he had just crawled over twenty miles of gravel road.

"Coffee?"

"Great idea!"

We kept our voices low since it was still early and there was no real reason to wake Tony up. Our movements around camp that morning may have looked careful and cautious but it was more from being cold, stiff and tired. Over coffee the small talk covered the usual subjects like work, fishing and, of course, sasquatches. Since last year's expedition Fred had been out 'squatching several times but for the most part he spent most of his time either managing the brigade at the bistro or playing with his daughter during his time off. That adds up to a lot of long hours and late nights.

Seven o'clock. With our coffee finished it was time for a stretch and a walk. We decided to see if any secondary evidence had been left by the looming shape that we had watched only five hours earlier. Specifically, we were looking for footprints, broken or trampled vegetation, scuff marks, or anything that would positively prove to us that what we had witnessed was real and not some fantastic group hallucination brought on by the lack of sleep and wishful thinking.

Walking down the road in daylight was like going for a stroll down the Yellow Brick Road. Every stick, rock and tree was new to me. I knew that the road had lead downhill before turning and climbing up onto the ridge but I had not seen the stream running under the road nor did I see the turnout only twenty yards from our camp. Parked off the road was Matt's leased vehicle. There was a camp box sitting on the roof and the tailgate door was wide open with Matt, snuggled in his sleeping bag, hanging half out of the SUV. It was such a golden opportunity that I couldn't resist taking a photograph of our illustrious leader, especially when he was least expecting it. Gotcha!

We continued on our search until we reached the bottom of the rise. From this point to the top of the hill we cautiously scanned the roadway for any prints or scuffmarks. Let me make this abundantly clear. To avoid destroying any crucial evidence we did not take a single step forward without looking first. Cresting the hill we split up, one of us to either side of the road with our eyes now trained to the center where the dark figure had been standing. We saw nothing out of the ordinary, just some pebbles, rocks, sand, dust and old tire tracks. The road swept to the right and then around some trees to the left only to follow the course of the power lines. Fred remembered that when it was first spotted the figure had looked smaller than when it had walked away from us. His night vision unit does not provide much in the way of depth perception but this difference in size lead us to believe that it must have been standing farther back from the lip of the hill when we first saw it and then closer when it stood up before walking away from us. With this in mind, we tried to retrace the possible steps that the figure had taken. Looking back beyond the bend in the road, there was some vegetation that might hold some signs of a passing sasquatch. Once we knew where to look it wasn't very hard to miss the signs. Just behind a pair of small five-foot trees was an area where the grass had been flattened down. Looking towards the top of the hill we found indistinct scuff marks, something that looked like toe prints and a possible handprint. From this point, the shape had left along the access road where the surface showed some prints but nothing deep enough to be cast. In my opinion, we had found the proof that we had been looking for. Last night, when we were at the bottom the hill, we had spotted a large bipedal creature standing back by the smaller trees and when we had lost sight of it, evidently the sasquatch had crept forward on its stomach until it could look down the hill at us. When I had made the mistake of pointing in its direction it stood upright and walked away.

Our search had taken about an hour and it was now time for some breakfast. Back at the truck park we discovered Tony and Matt were now awake. Tony was pointing out the large number of X's, arches and structures that had been built in the vicinity many of which could easily be spotted from the back of my truck. Of course, I had seen none of them before now because we had pitched our camp in the dark. Go figure.

It was good to sit and talk to Matt without him feeling the pressure of all the new attendees hanging on his every word. I know this is true because just last year I was a new attendee and I had sat listening intently to everything he said. So far I hadn't had much of a chance to discuss what was new with him and the realm of sasquatch investigations. We talked about the cases that I had completed and of those I was currently researching. The three of us then went on to tell Matt about last night's incidents, of the looming shape, the audio recording and the crushed vegetation. All of this was pretty exciting to us and we felt that our chances of obtaining some photographic evidence on this year's expedition were better than ever before.

Finger Trouble.
Are you wondering what happened to the audio recording and why it was never scientifically analyzed for its content? As it turns out, Tony did not download or copy the recording to his computer and because he was so busy playing the recording to everyone who wanted to hear it he naturally pushed the wrong button which accidentally deleted the file.

I also had some questions to ask; questions that only Matt could provide the answers for. I wanted to know what the make-up of the expedition would be; that is, the ratio of BFRO members to new attendees and what the general game plan was going to be. It was now Thursday and the main body of the expedition would be arriving throughout the day. Sometime in the late afternoon there would be a meeting of sorts, followed by a caravan of eager beavers heading out to a deserted logging road just as the last bit of light would be filtering through the treetops. Of course, you know that this is not what will take place.

Matt said that he wanted to have a meeting with everyone at about four pm, which really meant five or maybe six. Matt's concept of time is very fluid and I think the reason for this stems from his having to deal with deadlines so much that once he gets out in the weeds, everything tends to slow way the hell down. Looking back, in retrospect, I think that Tony and I should have informed Matt about how Harold had threatened to leave some attendees stranded in the woods on Tuesday night. I should have also let Matt know that I would not place myself in a position where I would have to depend on Harold for my safety. A BFRO expedition is a pretty safe adventure with an extremely low accident rate but it is always nice to know that you have someone covering your Six if the shit ever does hit the fan. Would my opinion have been of any importance to Matt? Well, despite the fact that opinions are like assholes – and everyone has one - and as such my opinion may not have been important to him.

For now, we all went our separate ways. Fred had to go home to get something and Tony had to do the same. Both of them said that they would be back at base camp sometime in the early afternoon. Matt said that he was going to hang out at the site for another hour or so before he headed back to wherever he goes for his down time. I wandered back to base camp to contemplate my accommodation options. I could try to redesign my truck tent or I could simply fall back on last year's billet, namely the passenger seat of my truck. As cramped and uncomfortable as it was, it may actually be the best option if I found myself getting out into position near or after nightfall. At this point there was no way to plan on being anywhere at a specific time because at the start of an expedition it would be far more beneficial to remain adaptable.

Lunchtime. Time to recharge the batteries and take stock. Right on cue, Fred showed up as I was making some coffee. Now would be the perfect time to fill him in on what had taken place on Tuesday night. I felt that it was important for Fred to know the details of Harold's actions just in case he accidentally had to depend on Harold for support. Hopefully it would never come down to it but a person could never tell how fast these situations may develop. I had just finished going over the incident with Fred when Todd and Frances pulled into their site beside me. After I had introduced them Fred asked if he could hear firsthand of the terrifying tale of Harold's mad dash from the forest. They obliged his request and described the incident once again.

The new attendees began arriving throughout the afternoon and if this year's expedition were anything like last year's we wouldn't be out in the woods until close to dark. Matt wanted me to be at base camp along with Tony sometime around five pm for a meeting with the newbies so this gave Fred and I some time to revisit the areas that I had seen last year especially the spot where my truck was slapped. On our way out of base camp we spotted John and Philip and knowing that they would be monitoring their radio I gave them a quick shout.

"Hey, John. It's Blaine."

"Go ahead, Blaine."

"Listen, Fred and I are headed out for a quick jaunt up to the main road. You know. The road where all the action was last year. We'll see you in a couple of hours at the most."

"Okay then, Blaine. We will see you when you get back."

"I think that Matt wanted us all to be at base camp by five pm."

"Right, five pm."

A couple of hours were all we would need to get out to last year's site and have a look around. Tony had mentioned that some new structures had been constructed and the X that I had spotted on the side of the road had been removed, only to be rebuilt a hundred yards farther back in the woods. Once out at the location I saw that everything else looked pretty much the same as it did last year. The road was hard, dry and dusty. I would hate to be the last vehicle in the caravan as the dust, rising from a dozen cars and trucks idling up the road, would hang in the air just long enough to coat each successive vehicle in turn with fine brown powder. By the end of the expedition the stuff is in your car, your equipment, your sinuses and every place in between. The only real benefit to all of this dust was the possibility of finding some very large fingerprints on the hood of my truck.

With everyone in camp tuned in to their GMRS radios, especially the newbies, I had guarded our destination just in case some of them recognized a place name from a map and decided to join our foray. Was there really a chance that this might happen? Maybe, maybe not. But I really didn't want to be surprised with a novice out wandering in the woods. The first full outing was to take place in a couple of hours and by tomorrow morning I would have a better understanding of the overall make-up of the expedition.

Due to last year's success, the 2006 Sunshine Coast expedition would draw people from the American eastern seaboard, the California coast and from points in between. Those attending from above the 49th Parallel came from Ontario, Alberta as well as BC. One memorable character had traveled all the way from Ireland and had participated in another expedition before showing up in Sechelt. Fred and I both felt that tonight was going to be pretty crazy, what with both the new people and the old hands all vying for a place to settle in for the night. Therefore we decided to get something to eat now as opposed to trying to cook up some food right when we were supposed to be heading out for the night. Once we were parked on the hillside there would be time enough for camp coffee and an IMP to warm us up.

You may have noticed that I have been using "we" and "us" a lot. The explanation is quite simple. Even though I had partnered up with Fred, it could have been anyone; maybe even you! And it was share and share alike. If he made coffee, it was for the both of us and for anyone else visiting our campsite. Camping etiquette is pretty much common sense, really. If you need something, simply ask. If I can spare it or loan it to you because I don't require its use, then help yourself. But, I expect the same consideration in return. Contrary to the rumor mill, I am not a salesman, so don't pay me. All I ask is that you return the item in the same condition or better, and if you break it, then replace it. Once again all of this should be pretty much common dog (sense).

Rolling back into base camp was a bit of a shock. There had been quite a few new arrivals in the past couple of hours. Some of the vehicles were leased and some were not which indicating that some people had driven great distances while some had simply flown into Vancouver and leased a vehicle for the weekend. Due to the weight limitations on personal luggage imposed by the airlines an individual cannot bring a whole lot of equipment other than clothing. Some will pay the exorbitant extra baggage fees just so they can bring along their own equipment while others simply purchase the camping gear needed to provide for their creature comforts. After the expedition they will sell the equipment to the local expeditionaries or donate it to a local charity.

After eating the sandwiches we had bought at Subway, Fred wandered off to double check his equipment. He would be taking his own truck out in the field as he normally sleeps in the box. As my gear was pretty much ready to go I decided to walk around and introduce myself to some of the new arrivals.

"Hi! I'm Blaine," I said, reaching to shake the man's hand.

"Hi! I'm Stan and this is my son Chris."

"I'm glad to meet you."

"So Blaine, where's the hotspots?"

"The what?"

"The hotspots. Where's the best place to look for sasquatches?"

Wow! What could I say? It was as if he was asking me for directions to the best bistro in town. How was I supposed to explain to him that, largely due to Tony's hard work, it was suspected that at least four different groups of sasquatch had been identified in the Sechelt area. Stan stood staring at me, waiting for an answer. However, as an investigator, I felt obliged to tell him something and hopefully that something would not make me sound like a smart ass either. I believe I said something like 'Pick a direction Stan. The whole damn place is one giant hotspot.'

It is important to note that all who participated in the 2006 Sunshine Coast expedition brought something with them to be shared with the entire group. They brought their own unique perspective; their thoughts, ideas, theories and inevitably more questions on the sasquatch phenomena. Much like the previous year, the individual names of many of the attendees soon became muddled, so in order to remember who they were, I relied on nicknames and place names. There was North Carolina, Colleen's Bunch and the Orange County Crew, to name but a few.

By now it was five pm or later and everyone was itching to get out in the woods. However, not everyone arrived at base camp. Matt asked for a volunteer to stay behind and lead the stragglers out to the initial target area. The clock was running. The safest bet was to have everyone head out to the location that was most easily accessible, that could accommodate at least 90% of the expedition members and with a good possibility of some kind of interaction taking place. The general consensus among the investigators was that we should head to the location where we had based ourselves last year. Matt agreed that this would be the best option, especially in light of all the activity we had experienced in 2005.

With the destination known, it was time to round everyone up. Something more easily said than done. All that was needed was a simple call on the radios announcing that everyone should be prepared to move out in ten or fifteen minutes. In the military this is known as a warning order and it would sounded something like:

BFRO MEMBERS. ALL BFRO MEMBERS
PLEASE BE PREPARED TO MOVE IN FORMATION IN TEN
MINUTES
THAT'S ONE ZERO MINUTES
LEAD MAN WILL BE SO AND SO IN THE _____ VEHICLE
THE LAST MAN WILL BE WHAT'S HIS NAME DRIVING THE
RED P.O.S.

Simple. Direct. And to the point. But, totally ineffective for this group. Instead, the investigators fanned out across the camp to individually inform everyone that they should be ready to go in about ten minutes. An exercise that required fifteen minutes to complete ended up taking over a half hour by the time we had our vehicles lined up. Was the timing all that important? Not really. Except for the fact that by the time we got everyone into position, it was going to be getting dark out in the woods. I am sure that for the first timers it would have been beneficial to see the terrain around them and, my personal pet peeve, be able to set up their camp without the use of a flashlight.

It was an hour later before everyone was safely parked for the night. With the vehicles spaced out every hundred yards or so, the road was effectively covered. Fred and I were in the exact same place where my truck had been slapped by a suspected sasquatch. Todd and his girlfriend had set up their dome tent down the road from us on what had been John's site the previous year. Roger and Harold had staked out the pull-out above us, since it could accommodate two vehicles. Once parked it was now time to break out the camp chairs, set up the stove and have a quick brew up. For those who were new to the expedition, I can only imagine what was going through their minds.

"Now what?"

"Is this it?"

"Did you hear that?"

Another hour went by. The forest was now inky black. Occasionally a member or two would walk up to a camp with his red lamp on, chat for a while, then proceed on to the next camp or back to his own vehicle. The object of the exercise was to look like we were just a bunch of campers, so if there were any 'squatches in the area they might be enticed to come and take a closer look. This had worked in the past but whether or not it would this time was a crapshoot. It was also time to be a little more proactive. John came on the radio and asked for permission to give a double wood knock. Matt told him to go for it but only after he had briefed everyone on what was going to happen and how we should conduct ourselves. Stop what you're doing. Get into a position where you can listen to the surrounding woods for a reply, which could be either a return knock or a vocalization. Be comfortable and be still. A warning order will be given that a knock or a series of knocks will take place in so many seconds.

Whack! Pause, 2, 3. Whack!

At first there was nothing but then it sounded like a whole troop of sasquatch was running up the road towards us. Fred and I were straining to identify the approaching sound when he spotted a beam of light from a vehicle's headlamp shining through the trees. It was Mike. He was shepherding the last of the attendees out to the field and he must not have heard Matt's explanations over the radio or we didn't hear him announcing that he was on his way up the road. It didn't really matter because they were here and as the three or four vehicles filed past me, I waved to the passengers thinking that this was just peachy. How all this commotion would surely have a negative effect on our attempts to illicit a response and that it would take nearly another hour before these newbies were settled enough for us to try something again. But on the other hand, they were entitled to come out and it would not have been right to hold them at base camp just because they may have been held up by a delayed flight or a missed ferry sailing.

"Let's go for a walk Fred."

Wood Knocks & Tossed Rocks

"Uphill or down?"

"Up, of course. We'll do the down part on the return trip."

Nearing Roger's camp, we saw a cluster of red lamps shining in the dark looking much like reflective eye shine from a troop of sasquatch standing on the road. The new arrivals had parked up the road past Roger's site and Mike had walked them down to see everybody. As soon as Mike introduced everyone their names promptly went in one ear and out the other, leaving behind a residue that I would later rename into something identifiable. Ah yes! You're with the (insert name here) group. I'm sorry folks but by now I was getting tired and inattentive. In fact, His Holiness the Dalai Lama could have attended the expedition and I probably would have referred to him as the Orange Robe Man or something like it.

So, Fred and I bid Roger and his guests a goodnight. It was time to crash out and this was only Thursday night. My second night out. There would be two more full days of searching the countryside for secondary signs and two more nights of stalking the woods. If I was going to be of any use to the rest of the attendees, I knew that I would have to get some serious beauty rest. Of course my rest wasn't going to be comfortable. Once again I found myself sacking out in the cab of my truck while my trusty tent stood guard at base camp. As we secured any unnecessary gear for the night, we heard the sound of a truck engine coming down the hill. It was a pair of newbies. After their long trip to Sechelt, they were totally unprepared to spend the night out in the woods so they were heading back to base camp. Someone asked over the radio if they knew the way home. To which one of the pair said that they had a map. If they wanted to go, there was nothing anyone could do about it. All we could do was wish for them a safe trip and tell them that we would see them in the morning.

Up until now we had heard no wood knocks and no vocalization returns. And was it any wonder? The parade of vehicles up and down the bloody road would surely have had a detrimental effect on our chances of having something take place. I was hoping that tonight was going to be quiet so I would get some quality naptime, despite spending the night reclined in a semi-sitting position. Fred, the lucky dog, could at least stretch out inside the box of his truck just as if he were in a tent. I could have stretched out too, if I had packed my tent with me instead of using it as a placeholder at the base camp.

Friday – The Beaver Pond Operation

Six A.M.

All was calm.

All was quiet.

Streams of sunlight filtered down through the fir trees behind me. I had left a window open about an inch for ventilation and I could hear the birds chirping outside. It looked like it was going to be a great day. At the moment there was no rush to do anything except visit the little boy's tree. Twenty minutes later and with the wafting scent of the freshly brewed coffee woke Fred from his peaceful slumber. His truck canopy suddenly snapped open and the tailgate dropped down with a bang that probably startled anyone within earshot.

While sipping our coffee, a couple of IMP meals simmered in the pressure cooker. Ah, breakfast in a bag. Quick and easy. I was having an omelet while Fred opted for the beans and weenies. Thankfully, I wasn't going to be riding with him until after lunch. We discussed the optional plans that had been proposed for today, the new areas that would be explored and we wondered aloud if anyone had any experiences last night. I assured Fred that when we regrouped at base camp any interesting incidents would certainly come out in the wash. I then asked him what time the local Radio Shack opened up. I was looking for a headset style boom microphone for my Cobra radio. Most GMRS radios are proprietary, meaning parts for one type will not fit another or it will fit but it won't work. The ear bud microphone that came with my radio worked but it didn't quite fit right and unless I was willing to hold it in place with a wad of chewing gum, it was going to keep falling out of my ear at the most inappropriate times. I was hoping that maybe, just maybe, there might be something usable from the store in Sechelt. As it turned out, they had nothing that would fit my radios unless I wanted to purchase a completely new radio system, which was something my budget did not approve of.

By noon I was on my way back to base camp. It was time for another coin-operated shower and some open discussions with the other expedition members about any possible incidents that may have occurred. As far as I knew it had been a pretty uneventful night except for the circus parade of vehicles up and down the road. Approaching my campsite, I could almost hear my tent beckoning to me: "Blaine, you look tired. Come inside and have a rest".

That sounds like a capital idea, Mr. Tent.

But, before I could enjoy the truly exquisite pleasure of stretching out full length on my cot and grabbing a few self-indulgent minutes of rest, Todd called me over to his site to see him.

"Blaine, I think we had a visitor last night!"

"What do you mean by the term - *visitor*?"

"I am saying that something or somethings were poking around our tent last night."

This was truly intriguing. Until now, I had always thought that during an expedition the interactions between humans and the sasquatch were pretty much confined to glimpses of shadowy figures and strange vocalizations from the surrounding forest. I had also believed that when my truck was slapped last year, in all probability by a sasquatch, was a random act. However, it would appear that the sasquatch may actually be much more curious about humans than what I had been lead to believe. If this is so, then many of the reported incidents of rock throwing, tree shaking and some of the vocalizations that had been heard could be categorized as being a display of intimidation.

"And why do you think that something was hanging around your tent?"

"Well, I was sleeping and Frances heard something that sounded like soft whispers coming from both sides of our tent."

"Frances, what did you hear?"

"Well, it was soft but firm. Like someone was coaxing or giving directions to another."

"Do you think that it could have been a couple of raccoons? There are plenty around here. Or do you think it was some other kind of animal?"

"No. I don't think that it was a raccoon. I've heard raccoons before. They have a chitter-chattering sound and they are hardly quiet. This was more of a muted mumbling."

"Then what did you do?"

"Todd was sleeping so I woke him up."

"Yes. It took me a couple of seconds to figure out what was going on and then I started recording the sounds. Listen to this…"

As Todd re-played the recording, more people began to gather at his campsite. Everyone simply found a place to sit and patiently listened to the recorded sounds of Todd and his girlfriend's rhythmic breathing inside their tent. This pattern continued for several minutes when a new sound could be heard. Something was cautiously inching around their campsite and it sounded as if it was moving or possibly inspecting their gear. There was the soft ring of an aluminum cooking pot as it was being handled and containers were being eased about. Obviously, these were neither the sounds of a raccoon rummaging about their campsite nor that of a bear ransacking a cooler.

Although he did not know it until later, Todd had situated their tent at precisely the same location John and Philip had been set up the previous year. You may remember that during the 2005 expedition a young lady named Sarah had been approached on the road directly below this position. As they lay quietly in their little dome tent, Todd and Frances began to hear voices or what could possibly be interpreted as voices. The sounds were soft and garbled as if someone was speaking Japanese with a mouthful of marbles and cotton balls. Frances stated that these voices were coming from two different locations – on the road, by Todd's side of the tent, and from the edge of the embankment, which was on her side of the tent.

Now that Todd was aware of what was going on, there was no need for Frances to stay awake, so she rolled over to go back to sleep. As she did so, she paused to look up through the skylight. With no rainfly on their tent, Frances could see some stars twinkling through the treetops high overhead. That was until she saw something that looked like a large hand with outspread fingers come down over the skylight blocking out the stars from her view. It was only there for a moment or two before the stars reappeared. In response, Frances simply rolled over and went to sleep.

What else could she do? Scream aloud and jump out of her tent? What good would that have done except throw everyone, including the mysterious visitors, into a panic mode and then who knows what would have happened. Instead, she remained calm and got some much needed sleep. She didn't even tell Todd what she had seen until they were comparing notes the following morning.

This was fantastic news! In all probability, at least in my mind, their camp had been approached by one or more sasquatches, a mere one hundred yards from where Fred and I were camped. Fast asleep in our vehicles, we had no clue as to what had been going on at the other tent site. For many of those who had gathered around to listen, the exciting details of this incident were exhilarating. Shortly they had woken up, Todd had radioed for Matt to meet them at their tent site. Once he arrived, Matt listened to their story and thoroughly questioned them about what had happened. Following Matt's directions, Todd left their tent precisely where the incident had taken place. It was hoped that since their site had been approached once already, leaving some of their gear around would provide a familiar sight and maybe a sasquatch would be drawn to it again. I knew that Matt would use this golden opportunity to get some real hard evidence of the existence of the sasquatch.

Matt had arrived back at base camp after Todd and Frances had finished telling their tale of the mysterious visitors. Once the mob had dispersed there were still a couple hours left before we were to leave for the forest. I figured that this would be a perfect time to wash off the dust from the road. The sun was shining brightly as I walked to the bathhouse. In my arms I carried a towel, a complete change of clothes and my shaving kit. Jingling in my pocket was a bunch of loonies bound for the coin-operated shower. Matt was parked at Harold's site and as I approached I could hear that they were embroiled in some technical talk about infrared cameras, battery life and stuff.

"Got a minute Blaine?" It was the boss.

"Sure. What's up?"

"Did you hear what happened to Todd and his girlfriend last night?"

"Yeah, I just finished listening to their story. It was pretty amazing that they were able to remain so calm. I doubt if I would have been able to keep it together with something snooping around outside my tent."

"Listen Blaine, I think that there might be a real good chance that they might be back tonight. We know that the 'squatches in this area are used to seeing people like hikers or teens out partying and they probably approach people on a regular basis. I am going to be busy setting up some equipment around Todd's tent in the hope that I can record something. Todd and his girlfriend are going to be helping me with the gear then they are going to just hang out at their tent.

What I need you to do is to run an operation that is going to keep everyone else occupied for a few hours."

"Sure Matt. What did you have in mind?"

"Well, we know that the elk herd is probably moving through the area by following the hollow at the bottom of the hill…"

Over the next ten minutes Matt went over his idea with me. We knew that a small resident herd of elk had been using the dense cover of a hollow to travel through the area between feeding and watering. It was also felt that at least one sasquatch, if not two, may also be using the protection of the dead ground to lay up during the day and to possibly wait until an elk or a deer presented itself a la carte. The game plan was simple. We would position ourselves in such a manner that anything moving from one end of the hollow to the other would have to slip past some of our members in order to do so. In essence, we would simply act as a human fishing net.

"Sounds great, Matt. Is there anything else that I need to know?"

"Only two things. One, make sure everyone is wearing some kind of camouflage or dark clothing. And two, you're in charge."

"No problem, Matt. After I grab a shower, I'll round everyone up and give them the low-down."

"Thanks, Blaine."

As I headed off to the shower building, I went by the Orange County Crew (I told you that I was bad for remembering names) who, like the rest of the newbies, had been hanging about their campsites waiting for something to happen. They looked bored so I figured that there was no time like the present to test my new authority.

"Hello, ladies! I am Blaine from Vancouver Island. Sorry that I didn't have a chance to properly introduce myself when you got in last night. Matt has asked me to make sure that when we go out tonight, everyone must wear some sort of camouflage or dark-colored clothing."

"Excuse me Blaine, but what do you mean by camouflage?"

"Oh right! I forgot that you're from the States. How about … um… (my brain was now scrambling around looking for a term that would be familiar to these two ladies)…how about fatigues?

"No, we certainly don't have anything like that but we do have some dark clothing. Would that be all right?"

"That would be just fine. I also want to let you know that we are all going to get together a little bit late; around five o'clock. We will go over the plans for tonight's outing."

While in the shower, I started to make a mental list of the Haves, Needs, Wants, Assets, and Liabilities that I was faced with. Falling into both the Have and the Asset columns was the fact that I would have a number of seasoned BFRO members and that there would be almost an equal ratio of members to new attendees. This meant that I could pair these two groups together for safety and security.

Safety. Now there was a whole new point to ponder. Of those who were going to be participating in this little operation, who had first aid training? Unknown. And, who had a first aid kit with them that was substantial enough to cover a major emergency? Insufficient data. These were some of the questions that I desperately needed answered. Not sustaining an injury while sitting perfectly still in some darkened hollow out in the woods was one thing. It would be all too easy for someone, slip or fall while walking through the bush in total darkness. A worst-case scenario would be if someone suddenly panicked and ran blindly through a darkened forest, the potential for an injury to occur and the severity of that injury would certainly rise exponentially. I quickly realized with all of this swirling about in my head that I might just have to adjust the configuration of Matt's plan, depending on the number of first-aid kits and qualified first aiders in the group.

Communication was going to be another issue. If the game plan was to bury ourselves deep into this hollow, to the point that we were out of sight and out of mind with the hope that we would be stepped on by a 'squatch, then we had better be quiet about it. I don't recall who had stressed the point but I am pretty sure that it was Matt who had said that only those who had ear buds for their radios would be allowed to have them turned on, which when you think about it, made a lot of sense. You really wouldn't want be trying to blend into the forest when suddenly your radio starts squawking or even worse, starts ringing out for you to answer it because some other twit hit the damn call button by mistake. The point is that with an ear bud firmly in place, if somebody's fat finger did accidentally hit the wrong button, the residents of the forest probably wouldn't hear anything.

"And, what about Harold?"

"What about Harold?"

I carried out a quiet investigation and from what I had heard; Harold had not caused any problems last night. I don't know where he had camped out but no one had mentioned him having a sudden panic attack or driving off to the security of base camp. I wasn't sure if he was coming out with the group that I was heading up. But if he did, I was confident that Fred and I would be able to keep him in check. Well, at least until the operation was over!

As I finished showering and got dressed all of these details and more were running through my head at break-neck speed. Glancing at my watch, I realized that I would have plenty of time to discuss the plans with the other investigators, sort and pack my gear before having everyone head out to the target area after they had something to eat. Personally, I didn't really care if they had eaten yet or not. Everyone had been hanging around camp all afternoon and if they hadn't eaten by now, that would be too bad. It was far more important to have them in place before it got dark out. Besides, they could always grab something enroute to munch on later. Either way, it was time to get this wagon train on the road.

The meeting with the other members was short and sweet; just the way I like them. Since Matt had already talked to some of them while I was showering; there really wasn't much to go over except the possibility of how everyone was going to line up. Fred was now back at base camp so I borrowed his radio and quickly called for everyone who was going with me to come over to my site.

"Okay folks. We are going to be heading out to the same location where we were last night. If you haven't eaten yet, you have about twenty minutes and then we will be lining up to go. Fred will be in the lead. I will fall in behind him and everyone else can file in behind me. Roger will be the last vehicle to ensure that there are no stragglers. We will proceed to the trailhead where we will go over the finer details of the operation. Any questions? No? Great! I'll see you in twenty minutes."

After everyone had dispersed, Fred asked, "Why do you want me to take the lead?"

I explained that I wanted him to pull into our regular spot in order to reserve it. I would then lead everyone past him and up to the trailhead. After the more detailed briefing, those who were staying the night would then follow me back down the road to find a suitable spot to camp, while everyone else would leave their car there so they would not block the road. I was still concerned about the potential for an accident and I wanted a clear path in the event of an emergency.

What should have taken twenty minutes took more than thirty but finally everyone was lined up in a caravan, with Fred leading and Roger acting as the Tail-End Charlie. Matt had left earlier to set up his gear to monitor Todd's campsite. I had the majority of the group with me and the rest were probably going to search out another area on their own, which was fine because some people would rather operate on their own schedule, much like the "Guys from New York" had done last year.

"Is everybody ready? Off we go!"

It took another twenty minutes to get to the trailhead and surprisingly no one got lost getting there. Fred pulled into our pre-arranged spot and everyone else filed past him with the dust cloud growing larger with each passing car. I had really hoped to give a more detailed operations briefing and have everyone positioned within the next half hour. I know that this was wishful thinking on my part.

Up at the truck park everyone piled out of their vehicles and gathered around me. I eyed the group to make sure that they were wearing dark clothing. The Orange County Crew was fashionably dressed in matching dark pant suits complete with high top hiking boots. Using a stick in the dirt I quickly outlined the operation that Matt had come up with. Any questions? No? Well I have some for you.

Who here has an ear bud for their radio? If you don't have one then pair up with someone who does. Only those who have an ear bud will be allowed to use their radio because we want to be as quiet as possible. Also please ensure that the "roger beep" feature on your radio is turned off and try not to hit your call button.

Now, for the big question. Who here has had first aid training? Hands up, please! Two, three people and myself. Okay. Not great, but not bad either. We can live with that. Who here has a first aid kit with them right now? And that would be... me. Not good at all. It was at this important juncture that I decided that instead of being down in the weeds with everyone else, I would place myself above the whole lot of them in a command and control position.

"Listen folks. It's going to be getting dark soon and the place you are walking into will be even darker. It is advisable that you use your red lamps to select a spot fifty to a hundred yards into the bush from off of the road. (Realistically, I don't know how far everyone had penetrated into the forest but I doubt that it was a hundred yards!) And then turn off your lights! All we are going to do is sit quietly and see, rather, hear if anything is moving through the forest. There is a good chance that you may have contact with the big and hairy kind. If there is any problem, that is to say, if someone gets hurt, I want you to use the phrase - "NO DUFF". This will let me know that the situation is real. At which point, I will have everyone turn on their white lights and I will immediately come to your position to administer first aid."

"Are there any questions? No? Good enough. All of those who are planning on returning to base camp after the operation, please leave your vehicles here, so we don't unnecessarily choke off the road. The remainder can drive back down to find a place to park your unit for the night. Please space yourselves out. A hundred yards or so will do it. Since I am going to be sitting on the hillside above all of you, I need a volunteer to walk everyone down to the lower road. Anyone? Alright Mike, thanks."

> "It's all fun and games until the sun goes down."
> -Sybilla Irwin

Idling my truck down the road, I parked behind Fred's Toyota. I saw that Roger, who had pulled out of the truck park right after me, had snuck back into the same spot he occupied last year. It was obvious that some of us were becoming creatures of habit and were quite comfortable with our surroundings. The remainder of the group rolled past me looking for a good bulge in the road that would accommodate their car for the night. While bringing Fred up to speed on the changes to the game plan, I dug out my first aid kit and clipped it to my backpack. I hoped like hell that I would not have to be called upon to use it. But with people walking through the woods in the dark there would be an element of danger. My greatest fear was a sucking chest wound caused by someone falling down and driving a stick into his or her chest. Looking back I don't even recall if there was a planned evacuation route to the hospital. I know there is a hospital or a medical center of sorts in Sechelt but I'd be damned if I know where it was located.

It was about seven pm. With all of the participants making their way down to the lower road, Fred and I began to select a spot above the lower road from where we could easily provide some sort of oversight. With our packs on our backs, we diverted off the main road and headed directly down through the forest. I estimated that there would only be a couple of hours of sunlight left before the shadows had fully enveloped all of us. We wanted our vantage point to be more or less in the middle of the group. I had six pairs of people, pairs being safer than singles when walking through the woods, as one can lend a hand to steady the other as they climbed their way over logs, around stumps and through the brush. Five of those pairs set out to find a place to hunker down for a couple of hours by slowly and quietly picking their way off the road. Some of them soon radioed back to me that it was already dark in the hollow due to the dense forest canopy high above them. I thought to myself that if they thought it was dark now, wait to see what it will be like in a couple of hours and by then they wouldn't even be able to see if there was a big hairy hand in front of their faces.

It took about fifteen minutes for the five pairs to settle in thirty-by-thirty or thirty yards apart from each other and thirty yards in from the edge of the road. I know that the spacing between the groups was accurate because from my observation point I was able to see them as they walked off the road but I couldn't confirm if they were actually thirty yards off the road or three hundred yards off the road. In the grand scheme of things, the positioning of the teams wasn't that critical because the darkness would cloak them and as long as no one turned on their headlamps, they would remain pretty much hidden from view.

There were two more participants in the operation but they were not paired up nor were they down in the weeds with the rest of the group. Farther down the road there was an opening in the forest where a family of busy beavers had made their home. One expeditionary decided to take up a position just inside the tree line at the head of the pond. From this spot he could observe the forest to the right and all the way to the far end of the pond. The remaining member of our cast was sitting high up on the embankment, much like Fred and myself, and from his vantage point, from left to right, he could see the entire pond as well as the far shore which was bordered by some young bushy fir trees. Over the next hour or so, it was as quiet as a church. Fred radioed each group in turn and asked for a Sit-Rep or situation report. A couple of the pairs had radioed to say that small twigs had been snapped but they didn't believe it had been caused by something big heavy and hairy. Fred told them that due to the absence of any real background noise like vehicles or voices, sounds tend to be interpreted as being louder at night than they really are and most likely the culprit was a mouse or a squirrel foraging for food.

By now it was nine pm and we were sitting in the dark. Well, it wasn't that dark but I knew that for those sitting down in the hollow, it was very dark. You know. The kind of dark where it is pitch black and the strain in your eyes has now caused little spots of light to dance about in your field of vision. It was time to quietly pull my people out of the bush and get them back to the safety of the roadway. Breaking radio silence, I let everyone know my plan.

"Okay everyone. It's time to get you the hell out of Dodge and, just to be safe, we are going to do it in an orderly manner. So, starting with the first group, on the far left, I want you to turn on your red lamps and walk out to the road. Let me know when you are safely on the road."

"Copy that."

Five minutes later, the first group was out and I had the second group on the move. The safety of the participants was still my greatest concern but it was getting darker by the minute. Looking high overhead, I could see that the stars were starting to shine down through the tops of the trees. It was taking far too long to get the participants out of the woods. I realized that despite being cautious, if these people began bashing their way back to the road any self-respecting sasquatch in the area would most certainly know about it and so a red light, white light or no light would not have made a lick of difference. Fred and I quickly discussed the ramifications of my idea and we felt that there was no other option but to go for it.

"Okay, boys and girls. There has been a change in plans. I want you to turn on your white lights. Your white lights, please! And carefully make your way out to the road. Once you are there, let me know that you are safe. Does everyone copy?"

Obviously we had made the right decision because a whole host of 'roger' and 'copy that' came over the radio speaker. Through the trees below us, we could see the head lamps being switched on, their xenon beams and white LED lights stabbing through the darkness, indicating which way the owner was looking. It didn't take long before all five groups had radioed us that they were standing safely on the road. At the far end of the hollow were the two solo guys who had not yet responded. The lay of the land had prevented my message from getting through, so I asked if a couple of the attendees would kindly head down the road to relay a message to them. It was important that everyone participating in this little soirée knew what the hell was going on and that our intention was to terminate the current operation. I also wanted to ensure that everyone was duly accounted for. It would not have looked terribly good if I had lost a couple of newbies. A few moments later I had a pair of volunteers who, quite brazenly, headed off down the darkened road in an attempt to contact the two guys who were sitting down at the end of the line. It wasn't long before Fred and I could hear at least one side of the conversation.

"Randy, do you hear us?"

"Yeah, it's the Orange County Crew."

"What's that?"

"It's getting pretty dark out, so Blaine is asking us to come back up the road."

"What's that?"

"Yes. As soon as you can."

Now, Randy had been sitting, all by himself, just on the inside of this tree line while the other solo member was positioned up on the embankment. After hearing the message from the Orange County Crew that we were ending the operation and wanted to regroup, Randy gathered up his gear in preparation to move out. Not wanting to walk through the dense brush he decided that it would be in his best interest to skirt the edge of the pond in order to get back to the road. Makes sense, really. Why would a person risk personal injury pushing his way through an inky black tangled hollow when it would be much easier to walk where it was more open? Randy broke from the protective cover on the edge of the hollow and had scarcely gone twenty feet when his attention was suddenly drawn to the young fir trees on the right side of the pond. Not all the trees mind you. Just one thirty-foot tree in particular, since it was the only one that was being violently shaken. Randy couldn't see what was shaking the tree but in the fading light the other guy, from atop the embankment, could see that there was a very large dark something taking its frustrations out on that tree. Let me make this perfectly clear. There was no wind blowing through the forest at the time. If there had been a breeze then you would have expected to see at least some of the trees in motion and not just one solitary pine that appeared to be thrashing under its own personal tempest.

Not wanting to aggravate the situation any further, Randy decided that the better part of valor would be to immediately head to the road by skirting back along the edge of the tree line. This was about the time when a rock came soaring out of the darkened hollow and landed in the beaver pond.

Ker-splash!!

"Holy crap! There are two of them!"

Randy was now faced with a dilemma. Should he head back out into the open where something was shaking the living shit out of a thirty foot pine tree or should he try to make a mad dash for the road while having to sneak past some great angry beastie in the woods who was now lobbing large rocks over his head and fifty feet out into the pond? Well, he couldn't go forward and he sure as hell didn't want to go back. Instead, Randy went sideways, vectoring directly through the water. Struggling through the brush on his way to the pond, Randy ripped out his ear bud and because of that he didn't hear his over watch call out as he visually saw the second rock arcing out of the woods.

Ker-sploosh!!

Randy wasted no time in getting back to the road and when he finally got there, he looked like hell. He was muddy, wet and visibly shaking. He had left his mountain bike at the spot where he had walked into the bush. Later that evening someone asked him if he was going back to get it to which he replied, "Once it gets light out."

With Randy and the other newbie back on the lower road, everyone made the long trek back to the junction and then along the upper road. Fred and I thought that we would be smart and simply bushwhack our way straight up the hill to our vehicles. Great idea if there was any daylight! Thirty minutes later and with dozens of scrapes and bruises for my effort, I arrived back at my truck. Fred had faired not much better. In retrospect, we should have simply dropped down to the lower road and trudged along with the rest of the group. It may have taken us a few minutes longer to get back but there would have been less risk of a serious injury. Matt may have had his radio turned on during the whole operation but I don't recall him radioing any directions or asking any questions while we were sitting in the weeds. So, I knew that he would be interested in finding out what all had happened.

"Fred, I'm going to go down to Todd's camp to fill Matt in on what happened. Would you mind brewing up some coffee for us? I'll rustle us up some growlies when I get back."

"Sounds like an idea. It'll be ready in about twenty minutes."

With Fred looking after things at our vehicles, I wandered down to see Matt. The camera equipment he had set up was covering the area immediately surrounding Todd's campsite. The hope was that if there were another approach to their tent site, then maybe, just maybe, proof of the great beastie would be digitally captured for the entire world to see. I found Matt talking to Todd and his girlfriend. He informed me that everything was in place and the only requirement was for our big friend to come out to play. I let Matt know that all of the people were back out of the woods and that there had been no injuries. I also filled him in on what I knew of Randy's fun-filled activities down by the pond. Matt said he had overheard some of the radio transmissions while he was setting up the equipment but he wanted to speak to Randy personally so he could hear the details first-hand.

With my task completed, I headed back up the road to have a nice hot cup of coffee. It would certainly help to take the chill off my bones. It was now pitch black out with only a few stars shining down through the second growth fir trees. As I got close to our trucks, I saw some powerful lights bouncing off the tree trunks. Just great, I thought, some newbie is out with a bloody million-candle power spotlight hoping to see a 'squatch out for a stroll in the forest. Well, I was wrong. As it turned out, it was the Orange County crew and another group of adventurers who had had enough of tonight's festivities so they were going back to base camp before the gates were locked. I guess they weren't quite up to having something rap on their truck window.

So long and thanks for coming out.

It must have been around ten or ten-thirty. I was tired to the point that I was starting to get a little bit punchy. Especially since the sum of waking hours had begun to vastly outweigh the amount of down time. It was a sure bet that by the end of the expedition, we would all be dragging our heels but for the moment it was time to enjoy a great cup of java and some semi-warmed IMP's. Tonight's menu included cabbage rolls with tomato sauce. How yummy is

Sgt. Corbin says:
"Any fool can be miserable when he's out in the field but it takes a smart man to be comfortable."

that? It's pretty damn good when you consider the fact that the only things some of the people were eating were cold chocolate bars and soda pop. Having two or more people at each site meant there was no reason not to have something warm to chow down on.

With some warm food in our bellies and a mug of hot coffee in hand, Fred and I wandered up the road a bit to say goodnight to John and whoever was camped with him. As it turned out, Roger and Mike were there as well. It was good to see them after all the activities that had taken place thus far. I filled them in on how Matt was attempting to possibly get some footage this evening. John said that he would be happy to hear some vocalizations during the night since he had some audio recording equipment set up on his truck.

"Well kiddies, it's damn near midnight! Time for me to turn in and get some beauty rest!"

"Hey, Blaine! You had better sleep till noon 'cause you need to get a lot of beauty rest!"

This little dig was from Philip. Philip and I have had a long running chop fight, which is all in good fun. I like Philip. He's a really good kid who works hard for the things that he wants and is pretty fearless when it comes to looking in the woods for an eight-foot tall hairy primate. I could have retaliated but I was feeling pretty tired. It would be better to withdraw from the never-ending situation of two kids shouting at one another, with me being one of the kids.

"Oh yeah?"

"Yeah!"

"Oh yeah…?"

Once we got back to our vehicles we tidied up our camp by putting chairs away, bagging up any garbage and generally securing things for the night. From what we could tell most of the other expeditionaries were already sacked out and we were the last two people who were still up. Fred climbed into the back of his truck and closed the door to his canopy. As I unlaced my own boots, I could hear him quietly trying to shed his gear in preparation to go to sleep. Before heading out for the night's festivities I had unrolled my sleeping bag and left it on the passenger seat of my truck. I tossed my boots over onto the driver's side and stripped off my bush clothes. I wanted to keep my radio handy so I put it on the dash. The same went for my hunting knife. I know that it would be useless as a weapon against a creature such as the sasquatch but I was comforted in the fact that it was nearby.

It doesn't matter where a camper places things before going to sleep, be it in a vehicle or in a tent, because anything placed in a position where it would be handy always disappears once you are asleep, only to re-appear someplace totally different the next morning. With my keys in the ignition and the widows lowered just far enough for some ventilation but not nearly enough for some inquisitive hairy fingers, I was finally ready to get into bed. The seat was reclined as far as it would go and even then I was still in a semi-sitting position. After struggling into my sleeping bag I called Fred on the radio to say goodnight.

"Hey, Fred? Are you secured for the night?"

"Yeah man. I'll see you in the morning. Wake me up if anything happens."

"Will do, Fred."

With that final radio call, the day was now complete. It was after midnight and once again I found myself lying on the passenger seat regretting my inability to resolve the problem of rigging the temporary shelter in the back of the truck. Still, the other option would have been to tear down my tent at the base camp and then set it up at each new location that we were going to stake out in the evening. As slumber slowly crept up on me I wondered how the weather would be the next day and if there would be any additional activity.

Smash!

I sat up like a shot, instantly awake. My eyes were wide open. The sound had come from no more than thirty yards directly uphill to the right of my position. It was a wood knock and it was as loud as if Babe Ruth, assisted by Hank Aaron and Barry Bonds, had just struck a mighty blow against a tree. Pressing the call button on my headset, I radioed Fred and anyone else who may still have been awake.

"Fred! Did you hear that?"

"Oh yeah!"

"Are you getting up to take a look?"

"Nope. Sounded too close."

"Okay."

I thought that if Fred wasn't going to stick his neck out, then neither was I! So once again, I settled myself down to catch some ZZZ's. If it was that close, then maybe we might be approached. There might even be some handprints on the truck in the morning. How cool would that be; to wake up and see a huge palm print in the dust on the side of my truck? The minutes started to drift into each other and I was almost asleep when it happened.

The scream!

It was both high and low pitched at the same time. Unwavering! Lasting ten seconds or more, denoting a massive amount of lungpower! Cougars scream or snarl while bears roar and elk bugle but this sound was unlike all of them. As much as any who have heard this type of sasquatch vocalization, I can surely attest that it sounded much like a woman who was being killed. There is no mistaking it for what it is and it emanated from the same general location as the wood knock.

"Fred? Did you hear that?"

"Yes."

"Are you getting up?"

"No!"

"I didn't think so."

As you can well imagine, I was now very much awake waiting for the next thing to occur and it never did. There was the wood knock followed by the scream and that was it. The lack of any other activity was rather anti-climactic, I would say. But I began to wonder, if Fred had taken one last look around with his starlight scope before turning in for the night, would he have seen it? I sincerely believe that he would have since it was only thirty yards away and when compared to a flashlight, which literally stabs its way through the darkness, the starlight scope is far more discreet and unobtrusive. Over the years there has been speculation and some indication that the sasquatch may be able to see into the infrared (IR) spectrum. If this is true, then if Fred had utilized the IR booster on his night scope, it would have shone through the woods much like a regular flashlight and a sasquatch may have been able to see this beam. However, if Fred had opted to use the device in the passive mode, it would have simply amplified any available light and as a result he may have been able to spot the big fella spying on us before we had settled in for the night. Once again, it was an opportunity missed.

Saturday – Send in the Clowns

I awoke some six or so hours later, tired and sore with a bladder that was screaming for relief. You would think that if you didn't drink any liquids before bed that you wouldn't have to go so badly in the morning. No explanation is needed because this problem can be chalked up as one of those 'Medical Mysteries of the Human Body' that must simply be accepted as fact.

As I was stumbling about on the road in the vain attempt to get some feeling back into my cramped legs, Fred opened up the back of his truck. Earlier, on the previous day, he had informed me that he would have to head home at about noon on Saturday because he had to work at the restaurant in the evening. This meant I would have to find someone else to hang out with for the last night of the expedition. I really didn't care who it was, as long as I did not have to rely on Harold. This was the mid-point of the expedition. Even though Harold had not exhibited any additional symptoms of the odd behavior he had demonstrated at the beginning, other than looking for an eight-foot tall hairy primate, I still did not feel comfortable enough to be out in the woods with him. Especially, if things suddenly went for shit. Having a healthy margin of safety is always foremost in my mind and therefore I wanted to make sure that I was partnered with someone who was going to be there for me as much as I would for them.

"Can we wait awhile to have breakfast?"

"Sure Fred. Why do you ask?"

"Let's go for a walk up to the cut road and see if we can find any tracks left by last night's screamer."

This was a great idea. It appeared that no one else was awake so we could take our time and look around without the usual questions of 'Where are you going? And, 'Can we come along?' It's not that I didn't want another individual to share in any discoveries that we may find but there was a greater chance to spot tracks or secondary signs when there are only one or two individuals walking carefully along a roadway. Evidence was easily lost when there was a herd of people tramping up a trail. If anything significant was found it is a simple process to mark its location and, if necessary, protect it from the elements for further study by a larger group. For example, if I found a footprint that was in a pristine condition I would cover it with something to protect it from the damaging effects of the elements with a large piece of bark removed from a nearby tree or cedar boughs or even a cardboard box from the back of the truck.

We were headed for a spur road, which was located just up the hill past John and Philip's campsite. As we crept by their tent we saw, rather heard, that they were still fast asleep. There was another attendee's campsite at the junction of the spur and the main road. From the rhythmic sounds coming from his tent, it was quite obvious that he was still fast asleep too. His tent was of a unique design. The tent poles were sewn into the material of the tent in such a manner that it framed the perimeter and the walls with several concentric hoops. These hoops gave the tent the amazing ability to twist down into a small circular shape no more than three feet across. Somebody must have had their thinking cap screwed on tight when they came up with this design. Just think of it, you pull into your campsite and the weather is really shitty outside. As a result you are faced with the option of sleeping all cramped up in your vehicle or getting soaked trying to set up your tent on a dark and rainy night. But then, suddenly to the rescue, comes... The Wonder Tent! Simply remove the securing band and with a flick of the wrist ...*voila* - an instant tent! Now, if a person were really smart, he would pack it up with the tent door unzipped so all he would have to do is toss his gear inside and kick the car door closed before he zipped up the tent behind him. This tent is definitely something that is on my Christmas Wish List.[23]

Fred and I skirted past this slumbering solo camper and headed up the spur. It was a good day for a walk. The sun was starting to climb into the sky chasing the shadows from the forest. All around us there were signs that the forest was slowly starting to awaken. Birds were flitting about hunting for their breakfast and the *rezident* squirrels could be heard barking to see someone's identification papers not too far from our position. Hell, they will bark at anything! A deer, a crow even another squirrel will set them off. This was a natural occurrence and we were not overly concerned about it. It's when the forest suddenly shuts up and becomes as quiet as a tomb; that's when you need to take particular attention to what is going on around you. After inspecting the flora for about a quarter of a mile, Fred and I found some secondary evidence in the form of crushed vegetation, some minor tree breaks and yet another X-shaped marker. All of which was quite interesting but I was really hoping for a clear castable track.

I had had enough tramping about and besides it was time for some breakfast. I couldn't remember what all I had left for IMP's but it didn't really matter, as it is all good food. Well, except for the navarin[24]. I could barely pronounce it and so I sure as hell wasn't going to eat it. Maybe I could talk Fred into trying it? If he got sick later on, it would be in his truck and not mine.

Descending back down the spur we found the solo camper up and about. I don't know what time he had crashed out but he looked as if he had been dragged down ten miles of bad road backwards. All and all he was a friendly sort and I soon found out, very knowledgeable on just about every topic one could imagine. This made for some rather interesting conversation about sasquatches to say the least and, in the course of our discussions; he asked whether or not we had heard anything about a sasquatch having the ability to use infrasound. I replied that I had heard of larger animals such as elephants had the ability to communicate over great distances using ultra low frequencies but I did not know that this phenomenon was also being attributed to the sasquatch. Despite our obvious reservations on the subject he informed us that some witnesses had reported that they have felt the effects of this infrasound whereby they have been awoken in their tent by some unseen bipedal creature only to be overcome by a feeling of sudden paralysis. The effect of this paralysis leaves the witness wide awake but unable to lift an arm or a finger or even cry out. I was rather skeptical about all of this and I told him as much. Having the ability to resonate a low frequency tone in order to communicate is one thing but to be able to freeze a subject in place was something right out of Ripley's Believe it or Not.

I was unconvinced of the effects of infrasound but like a lot of things that have been attributed to the sasquatch just about anything is possible only because there is so little that we actually know about the subject. By Googling *infrasound* I later found that in the animal kingdom infrasound is commonly used as a weapon. Some types of whales are able to stun their prey with powerful blasts of inaudible sounds, and infrasound can affect humans by disrupting the normal functioning of the middle and inner ear, leading to nausea, imbalance, impaired equilibrium and immobilization.[25]

Breakfast was going to be a simple fare. Between the two of us we wrangled up some hot coffee, juice, some fruit and an IMP for each of us. I knew how many meals I had left to eat in Sechelt and so I planned on giving Fred his choice of my left over military rations. He would certainly have more of an opportunity than I would to utilize them while out hunting or 'squatching as the case may be.

"Are you sure you don't want them?"

"No, you can have them. I'll try to get some more for next year."

"Thanks Blaine. Thanks a lot. I'll make good use of it. That's for sure!"

I didn't know if I would be able to get any more IMPs for the following year and it really didn't matter anyways. Being able to share these with Fred, or whomever I may have been paired with, was much more important to me. Later on in the day, when I was looking for something to snack on, I saw that Fred had left me the navarin. Thanks Fred.

After cleaning up our parking area (always pack out your trash) we said our goodbyes and went our separate ways. Fred was heading for home to get ready for work and I was off to Sechelt to visit with some longtime family friends. I had intended to have a shower at base camp first but since I had not seen them since the previous year I felt that I might as well head straight from the woods and make a strong impression. The visit would be a short one, as I wanted to get cleaned up then go to ground for a while before securing my equipment for the final night of the expedition. On Sunday morning I wanted to simply start the truck and head off to the ferry at Earl's Cove. No fuss and no muss. Unless I was planning having a nap this afternoon I would no longer require the use of my tent, so it would be packed away as well. Unlike last year the weather had proved to be excellent for this years' expedition so there was no reason why I couldn't sack out in the truck for one more night.

As I drove down the road I slowed to have a better look at Todd's campsite. There was no indication that either he or his girlfriend was awake yet. I wondered if the *Locals* had visited their camp last night especially given the fact that we had one of them scream at us. I also wondered if either of them had heard it. Someone must have and I was sure that when everyone compared notes at base camp the vocalization would be a topic of discussion. More importantly, if something did come by to check them out was it recorded on Matt's equipment?

Driving through Sechelt I suddenly realized that there wasn't a Tim Horton's in town. For those of you who are unfamiliar with the store, Tim Horton's, known simply as Timmy's, is a Canadian icon. They sell doughnuts, pastries, sandwiches and the ever-popular 'Extra Large Double Double', which is simply an extra-large coffee with two shots of cream and two shots of sugar hence the term 'Double Double'. In the U.S. it may be Starbucks Americano non-fat soy-frothed latte's that fuel the daily commuters but up here in the Great White North, its Timmy's all the way. In fact, the coffee shop chain is so popular with Canadians that there was even a Tim Horton's at the NATO base in Kandahar, Afghanistan and from what I hear it did pretty well... for being in a war zone. What I wouldn't do for a Double Double right about now.

I was hoping to spot one of those little barista stands on the side of the road. They are usually built into a converted travel trailer allowing the owner/operator/janitor to haul it from one location to another providing some caffeine junky suffering from withdrawals with a hot mocha java or a double espresso with a biscotti on the side. It's not a Timmy's and it's twice as expensive but desperate times sometimes call for desperate measures. But not too desperate because when it comes to drinking coffee you know you have hit rock bottom when you think that the stuff served at Mickey D's is good coffee. Personally, I'd rather be drinking Drano than coffee from a fast food joint. Now a hot cup of Joe in a truck stop is a different matter. Long haul truckers live on caffeine and if they could take their coffee intravenously every tractor trailer would probably have an IV drip bag hanging off of the sun visor right next to the fuzzy dice. Fill'er up!

The visit with friends of the family went quite well. When asked what I took in my coffee I had jokingly said Bailey's Irish Cream for which Robbie promptly substituted some Tia Maria . Although I would have preferred the Bailey's, I deferred to his judgment due to the fact that not only is he my senior by a great many years. Robbie asked me what I was doing in Sechelt. There was no getting around the subject now so I was up front with him and told him that the BFRO was investigating sightings of sasquatch in the local area.

"What kinda wacky tabaccy are you guys smoking? Besides, there is no such thing as a sasquatch. Didn't they prove that the movie from the States was a load of BS?"

At first Robbie thought that I was off my rocker. But when I began to describe some of the secondary signs of evidence that have been attributed to the sasquatch he fell silent. Robbie used to be an avid large game hunter but now he only hunts the forest for chanterelle mushrooms growing on the mountain slopes surrounding Sechelt. Maybe the details I was reciting had only served to jog Robbie's memory of something he heard or maybe seen. It was great to visit with some longtime friends and enjoy a breakfast with them but all too soon it was time to head back to base camp. Robbie! Don't let anyone call you a sissy just because you can bake a great carrot bran muffin.

Tonight was going to be our final attempt at getting some additional interactions happening with our hairy friends. So far the expedition had yielded several approaches, a couple of vocalizations, a few shaken trees and some tossed rocks. Little did I know that this same activity would continue throughout the afternoon and on into the evening.

On the way back to base camp I stopped only to re-fill my fuel tank and look for some additional touristy trinkets to take home for my family. Once again the small town of Sechelt did not disappoint me in my search for some special treasures. Most of the expeditionaries would now be hanging around their campsites comparing notes, sharing experiences and going over the plans for the final evening. I still had to pack up all of my equipment for the return trip home and I also wanted to enjoy the pleasure of the coin-operated shower one last time.

Once I had parked and gotten out of my truck I could see that some of the other attendees were around. This was pretty normal since the missing members were probably out shopping for trinkets as I had been or getting something to eat. But of those who were around, they appeared to be pretty animated. So it was my guess that something important had taken place. Maybe it was a sighting? Then again, maybe not? Some of these people were getting worked up over every little twig that snapped underfoot. But whatever was causing the commotion I decided that I would have to find out for myself.

There was a considerable knot of attendees hanging out over at Harold's campsite. Approaching the mob, I could hear a very heated discussion on the subject of infrasound that was once again going round and round. Personally, I have never experienced this effect but I do know of several people who have felt this electrifying sensation. In fact, those who have been hit by a blast of infrasound refer to the experience as being "zapped". After standing there listening to the see-saw conversation, I knew it was better if I didn't enter the fray because there were already enough opinions flying around that picnic table. If nothing else, it should be noted that opinions are like assholes in a federal prison – everyone's got one and they're not afraid to share it.

With half the expedition still somewhere out in the field, and the remainder caught up in the current debate, it was time to take that final refreshing shower. I really didn't know what the amenities were like at some of the other expedition locations but I dare say that this site was pretty sweet; a gated campsite, hot and cold running water and no freakin' media. What else could an up and coming monster hunter ask for?

How about some bloody privacy in the shower?

As I was getting ready to drop a couple of loonies into the slot, I realized that the dude in the next shower stall was not in there by himself. His girlfriend was in there soaping up his back and whatever else needed lathering. Now, I am not opposed to couples showering together. Far from it; in fact, I encourage it because it reduces the demand on our precious water resources.

"Hey buddy?"

There was a pause in the action behind the curtain.

"Yeah?" he replied.

"You've got ten minutes to finish up. Then I'm coming back to take my shower regardless of which part of you still needs to be washed."

"Thanks", she answered.

True to my word I wasted no more than ten minutes listening to the incessant back and forth arguing coming from Harold's campsite over some other possible aspect of sasquatch anatomy. The current feverish debate was whether or not eye-shine is merely a reflection of any available ambient light or was it a biologically produced chemical light and therefore emitted like that of some species of deep sea angler fishes? An interesting topic for sure, but the rational argument being put forward by one side was so overwhelming that the opposition was surrounded. Regardless of being pro or con, a well-planned logical argument is always a wonderful thing to behold.

I should have been a lawyer.

All right kiddies. Your ten minutes are up. Ready or not, I'm coming in!

The facility was now empty, leaving me to shower in peace and tranquility. After twenty minutes of hot soapy bliss I began to feel almost human again. To finish things off I shaved and even brushed my teeth. Now I was ready to go out to meet the world by sitting in the dark and waiting for something to go bump in the night. Yeah, right. As if some big hairy primate would really give a shit if I had bathed or shaved.

Coming out of the showers, I headed back to finish packing up my camp. As I wandered down the road, the sun was brightly shining and the birds were chirping. The one thing missing was the argumentative rabble coming from Harold's campsite. I don't know how the conversation had ended but I am sure that the parties concerned simply agreed to disagree before going to their respective campsites to lick their wounds.

John and Philip pulled into camp and parked down at the end of the road. I hadn't planned on who I was going to be hanging out with tonight but if I had my choice, I would have to say that I would rather hang out with them than anyone else except Fred, of course. And since Fred was stuck working at the restaurant tonight, these guys were going to be an excellent alternate choice; not a second choice, an alternate choice. At least I knew that our conversations would be interesting, the jokes would be funny and if the shit ever did hit the fan I knew that I could count on them just as they could count on me to cover their backs.

"Hey, Blaine."

"Hi, John. Any plans for this evening?"

"Not so far."

"Do you mind if I tag along with you guys tonight?"

"No, I don't mind. You're welcome to come along. Matt hasn't mentioned any definite plans for this evening so I don't really know where we're going to be. Have you seen Matt?"

"I saw him up by Harold's site a few minutes ago. I'm going to break down my camp. I heard a rumor that Matt wants us to head out soon for a 'family' photo shoot. If that's the plan, then could you please let him know that I will be ready to move out in about a half hour?"

"Will do, Blaine".

It wouldn't take me long to get things folded, stuffed and crammed back into the box of the truck. Wherever I ended up tonight, I wasn't planning on setting up my tent. I had slept in the front of the truck so often that I am sure my back was starting to resemble the shape of the passenger seat. Of course, this made walking difficult first thing in the morning. If anyone was watching, they would have thought I resembled some old gnarly troll, bent and hunch-backed as I climbed out of the truck only to head for the nearest bush to relieve the pressure from a twisted bladder.

Finally, everything was secured for the trip home, which meant it was time to find out Matt's game plan for the photo shoot. On the way up to Harold's camp, I passed by Tony telling Philip, who was riding in another member's truck, where the photo op was going to take place and how to get there. Good luck with that.

It took about twenty minutes to organize everyone currently at the base camp into some semblance of a convoy. As Tony was the only one who knew where we were going, he was the designated point man. I, on the other hand, fell into the position of being the tail gunner. This meant Tony's job was to safely lead us to some picture postcard spot while mine was to ensure that no-one slipped behind me and got lost enroute. Matt had positioned himself behind Tony to act as the steering committee.

"In one physical model of the universe, the shortest distance between two points is a straight line...in the opposite direction."[26] That statement pretty much sums up our collective effort in getting to Tony's Squirrel Secret Photo Spot. Every road we took was either temporarily closed or we were denied access. After pissing around for nearly an hour we finally got to the location high above the Sechelt Inlet and I must say that the view of the ocean far below was spectacular. Once in position for the "official" expedition photo, everyone with a camera took a turn snapping a picture. With the 'family' pictures taken for another year, it was time to head back to town. I had ferried a couple of newbies out and I had to bring them back to base camp. Before leaving the mountainside, I arranged with John where we would meet for the final night out. On the way down, I had heard on the radio that the weather was supposed to be clear this evening, which meant our night optics would be at their best as would the 'squatch's night vision.

I still had some time to kill after dropping my passengers off, so I headed over to the Old Boot Eatery to see Fred. The place was packed and Fred was in full command. His kitchen brigade was cranking out starters while he was plating the entrées. If you ever have a chance to observe behind the scenes of a successful restaurant, you will be surprised to see nothing less than a culinary ballet. I knew that Fred would be unable to sit and have lunch with me, so I sat up at the bar area. That way I could at least try to carry on a conversation with him. I ordered a beer and some appies. Fred saw me sitting there and did not fail to disappoint. The beer was cold, the food was delicious and in the end I had to say goodbye to my friend for another year.

I was supposed to rendezvous with John and Philip at the lower end of the main road. This was the same road where my truck had been slapped, the same road where Todd had been approached at his camp and where something in the darkness had screamed at Fred and myself. Only this time we were parked down in the bottomland. Covered with thick brush, it was flanked on either side by higher hills. It was like camping inside a hamster cage or a terrarium where a person could easily be observed, or approached, and there wasn't one thing I could do about it. The place really gave me the creeps but I felt a little safer knowing John and Philip were camping nearby. When I drove in, their tent was up and their camp chairs were set out just as if they were expecting company. Well, hello boys. I'm here. Been waiting long?

From the back of the truck, I retrieved a camp chair plus the gear I needed to cook up supper and more importantly, make some coffee. It was going to be a long night and I would need all the help I could get to stay awake. The local weather report for the Sunshine Coast was once again calling for a clear night with the temperatures dropping down near the low teens. John watched as I tossed my sleeping bag into the front seat of the truck.

"Not setting up your tent, Blaine?"

"No. I won't have time to pack up a tent. As soon as I wake up I have to head for the ferry at Earl's Cove just so I can catch the noon ferry from Powell River back to Comox. By the time you wake up, I'll already be heading down the highway."

Unexpectedly, the radio crackled. It was one of the other attendees.

"Can anyone hear me?"

His voice sounded kind of anxious.

"Hey, can anyone hear me? I'm pretty sure that I am being watched from the ridge above me by something pretty big. Can anyone come over to my location?"

Even though the sun was setting, it did not deter the chorus of "Where are you?" from spilling over the airway. Always up for an adventure, John replied to the lone camper that we would be along shortly. Personally, all I wanted to do was sit back and relax, swap a few tall tales and get a half decent sleep in the cab of the truck. But no! Philip was having none of it and my reluctance to go only provided the ammunition he needed to goad me into motion. It was as if I had personally handed him a stick with which to poke the bear. Poke away Philip! You have to sleep sometime!

And so, off we went. There were just the three of us at first but thankfully another attendee joined us from a nearby campsite as we plodded up the hill in the growing darkness. We only had to go about half a mile. The distance was not all that great but with the fading sunlight it was becoming increasingly difficult to maintain some degree of quiet. Not that it would matter. A sasquatch's eyesight, in all probability, is a hell of a lot better than a human's during the day and vastly superior at night but you can understand that if there was a sasquatch nearby, we certainly didn't want to attract any additional attention by having our feet occasionally sending rocks skittering down this secondary road.

Randy was in the midst of cooking his supper when we arrived at his camp. He had recovered from having several large rocks tossed in his direction while extricating himself at the conclusion of yesterday's Beaver Pond Operation. Now he had placed himself alone on the opposite side of the bowl and away from the rest of the group. Maybe his intention was to garner some sort of solitude from the other expedition members while offering himself up as an object of curiosity. Even if this wasn't his plan, the result was the same.

The crest of the ridge above him must have been at least another hundred or maybe even two hundred feet higher in elevation. The usable timber had already been logged off a number of years ago but there were still some trees standing guard along the crest as sentinels against the forestry industry. I don't know why a logging company must deem it necessary to remove every damn stick of wood from an entire valley or glade except for a few pecker poles along a ridge or in the middle of a bloody hillside. It's not like these leftover trees were used as spar poles during the removal of their neighbors and you would think that as responsible foresters they would recognize the fact that these trees having a very shallow network of roots will likely be taken down during the first big winter storm. I suppose they were left standing just so the loggers could sleep at night, happy with the knowledge that they did not completely clear-cut an entire forest.

"So Randy! What's happening?"

"Something smells good. What are we having?"

"Feeling a little creeped out are we?"

With all of our questions rushing at him, poor Randy couldn't get a word in edgewise and so, with a stern look at the rest of us, John quickly took control of the situation. After a few choice questions we quickly heard the whole story.

"Randy. Why don't you start at the beginning?"

"Well, after parking my truck and taking a look around, I started to set up some of my gear. I was hungry so I began to make myself some supper. It was then that I started to sense that I was being watched. It wasn't a sudden feeling. It was more like a slow growing sense of unease; that something wasn't quite right. I kept on making my supper when I happened to glance out of the corner of my eye and I spotted this very large shape on the hillside above me. It was half way up the slope when I first spotted it and whenever I was facing the hill it would freeze like a statue but if I turned away from it I could watch it with my peripheral vision. Only then would it start to slowly move away."

"Which way was it headed Randy?"

"It was moving up the slope, towards the crest of the ridge."

By now the sun had long since set. It was so dark that we could not make out any of the terrain before us. The hillside looked like a solid darkened mass with a series of spikes guarding the crest of the ridge. We milled about looking up at the inky black of the hill. The odds of spotting something with the use of a MK1-IB were Slim to None, and Slim had left town. But, there were two things that we did have to our benefit. The first was the night sky. There wasn't a cloud in sight and the stars were shining so brightly that the sky looked as if a million sparkling diamonds had been spread across a sheet of obsidian providing us just enough light to identify objects close at hand, and even make out the branches on the trees guarding the ridge above us.

The Mk1-IB
Mark One – Eye Ball

A military term referring to a first generation spotting device - the human eye.

I had said that we had two things to our benefit. The night sky was 'the first and the second was Philip. I don't know if it's the fact that he's younger than the rest of us or but his senses always seemed to be tuned just a little bit finer than anyone else in the group. Nice kid, and I really have a lot of time for him but sometimes his ability and the cockiness that comes with it really pisses me off.

"It's still up there watching us."

"Where Philip?"

"Up on the ridge. I just saw it walk between two trees."

"Which two trees Philip? Can you be a bit more specific?"

Without pointing a finger, Philip guided our eyes over the next several minutes along until we were all looking at the same portion of the ridgeline. All the trees on the rim had been silhouetted but below the point where the tree trunks met the ground everything was black. It was along this thin border of light and dark that Philip had seen something quite large gracefully walk out from behind one tree only to disappear behind another. We were all sure that it was up there but we had no way of seeing it in the black so someone radioed Matt and apprised him of the situation.

"I'll be right there", was the excited reply. Within minutes we could hear Matt's vehicle moving towards us along the gravel roads and as it got close we could see its headlights stabbing brightly through the trees. If it was a sasquatch it would most certainly have been aware that humans were on the move and headed in its direction. I sincerely doubted if whatever had been walking up on the ridgeline would still be there by the time Matt had arrived.

"So what's going on guys?"

Being cold, tired and probably a little grumpy I felt that it would be better if I just kept my mouth shut and let John, Randy and the others fill him in on what we had seen so far. Matt quickly took in all of the details and concluded that in all likelihood it had been the sound of our very un-stealthy approach that had caused it to move farther up the slope.

FN C1A1 with a PVS-502 (Gen 1) Starlight scope

The FN or FN FAL (Fusil Automatique Leger) is a self-loading rifle built by the Belgian arms manufacturing company Fabrique Nationale. It is chambered for a 7.62 x 51mm and comes with a twenty round box magazine. Canada adopted the FN FAL, designated as the FN C1A1, as its primary infantry rifle in 1955.

"But, let's just take a look just to be sure."

Matt reached into the protective case resting on the passenger seat and brought out a piece of equipment. I couldn't see what it was but I overheard Philip say, "Is it a Gen2 or a Gen3?"

To which Matt replied, "It's a Gen3".

Obviously, they were talking about some sort of night vision device. If this device were truly a third generation night vision unit then it would be light years ahead of the Gen1 starlight scope that I had mounted on top of the FN -FAL rifle over twenty years earlier.

As Philip began to look around at the night sky I could hear him whispering things like 'Amazing' and 'Fucking Awesome'. But he cut his expanded view of the heavens short when someone reminded him to take a look at the ridgeline above us. The minutes marched by while Philip trained the Gen 3 on the crest taking the time to watch not only for movement but also for any changes in the shapes of things. It is really important to carry out successive observations because an inquisitive sasquatch may shift its position ever so slightly and what may appear to be a solid tree stump may change shape or even vanish from view all together. After twenty minutes of glassing the hillside Philip concluded that whatever had been up on the ridge was now long gone.

"Yeah, it must have been the noise of you guy's walking up the road that spooked it off."

I'm inclined to agree with Matt's assumption but I would like to add that I believe the roar of his SUV chewing up the road certainly didn't help the situation either. With only a few extra bodies approaching up the road a curious primate may have hung out just a little while longer to see what the hell was going on in its own backyard. But, with the sound of vehicle heading ever closer, with its big shiny headlights stabbing every which way into the darkness, it may have been clear to a sasquatch that this indicated that people may be looking for it and therefore it was time to get the hell out of Dodge City. So for now the show was over.

"Hey Blaine have you ever looked through one of these Gen3's?"

"No I haven't Matt. I have used something similar but not this particular unit."

"Well, before you look through it, I want you to look up at that group of stars over there. When I was a kid I was really into astronomy and I can tell you with certainty that what you are looking at is the Andromeda star system and at 2.2 million light years away it is the closest galaxy to the Milky Way."

As bright as the stars were all I could see was a small group of bright lights that were just beyond the constellation Cassiopeia. It sure didn't appear to be much when I was using the old Mk1-IB, but when I looked through the Gen3 device I was literally dumbfounded. It was as if I were looking up at an entirely new universe. I could now see a hundred if not a thousand times more points of light in the sky, and as for the Andromeda galaxy, I could quite easily make out its squashed oval shape amongst the other constellations.

It was getting late. Like me, John and Philip also decided to call it a night so we said our goodnights to the group. I also said goodbye to Matt and Randy, explaining that I was planning to take the first ferry out of Earl's Cove and since it would be close to an hour's drive north, I wouldn't have an opportunity to say goodbye to them on Sunday. After that, there was nothing left but to head back to our vehicles and prepare to go to ground. For some unknown reason the walk down the hill felt as if the road was rockier than on the way up. Maybe it was because I was so damn tired and all I could do was simply shuffle my feet along the road knocking every loose stone that was in my path.

It didn't take very long for the three of us to return to our site. The chitchat was light as we prepared for bed. My sleeping bag had already been pulled out of its stuff sack and was resting across the gear on the rear passenger seats. A wise old infantry sergeant once told me that because your service sleeping bag is filled with goose down, it is easy to compress. However, if you want to take full advantage of the down's insulating properties you should shake out the sleeping bag at least a half hour before going to bed causing the down to loosen up and capture an extra layer of insulating air. As a gentle reminder the sergeant would growl at us, too. "Make it fluffy or you'll be sorry!" Surprisingly, those who didn't heed his words always complained of being cold.

I was in the midst of brushing my teeth when I heard Philip ask, "Did you hear that?"

"No, what was it?"

"A wood knock. A couple hundred yards east of us."

Since no one had followed the protocol of giving a warning call on the radio net it had to be assumed that it was real. Just to be sure, John quickly asked via radio if anyone had done a wood knock without a warning call. Quickly, everyone called in stating that no one had done so and then one person asked if he could give a response knock. It appeared that John and Philip were going to stay up and monitor this new round of 'wood knock ask and answer'. I would have stayed up too, if I could have kept my eyes open. It was time to shuck off my boots, strip off my grubby duds and snuggle up in the passenger seat for one last night. Once in place, it didn't take long before I was sound asleep.

Sunday – Goodbye…for now

Beep…beep…beep!

The alarm on my watch announced that it was now time to wake up and hit the open road. I had enough time to drive back into Sechelt in order to purchase a scrumptious artery clogging McSomething, which could be eaten one-handed while driving north to Earl's Cove. When asked by the pimply-voiced drive-through attendant as to my choice of beverage, I opted to have the orange juice instead of the coffee because I just wasn't up to drinking some global corporation's carefully disguised reconstituted camel piss at this time of the morning. Once again, I wish Sechelt had a Timmy's!

It wasn't long before I drove past the turn-off leading to where John, Philip and the rest of the expedition were still sleeping. I don't know if anyone heard it but I honked the horn a couple of times as I zoomed by. If anyone had heard my horn I know they wouldn't think anything of it, other than some vehicle cruising down the highway maybe honking at some animal or other on the road. But you never know.

With food in my belly and the tunes blaring from the stereo I was in full highway-cruise mode. As the distance between me and home grew shorter with each passing mile, I began to calculate time and distance ratios to ensure that I would meet not only the ferry from Earl's Cove to Saltery Bay but more importantly the noon ferry that would take me across the Strait of Georgia from Powell River to Comox. If for some unforeseen reason I missed the noon sailing, I would have to wait until five pm for the next one. If you have ever been to Powell River, you can understand that waiting for five hours for a ferry was not an option.

While driving up the Sunshine Coast highway, I took the time to reflect on my experiences during this expedition, of the new people that I had met and to fully appreciate the knowledge that I had gained. All in all I would have to say the expedition was a success and I say this from a specific point of view. Years ago, when I was assigned to 435 Transport and Rescue Squadron in Winnipeg, Manitoba, I worked alongside a guy by the name of Glen Swanson. Glen and I had been on many deployments together, from Thule, Greenland in the far north to Cherry Point, North Carolina in the south. No matter where we went and no matter what the working conditions were, we always seemed to have a good time. The reason for this is very simple. Glen looked upon TD (temporary deployment) with the attitude that all trips are good and some are better than others. With this in mind, I apply the same ethic to my outings with the BFRO in that all expeditions are good and some are better or maybe more productive than others.

After returning home I would learn that there had been three class A sightings that had taken place during the 2006 Sunshine Coast expedition and although most sightings continue to go unreported, the entire area remains a hot bed of sasquatch activity.

Chapter Three
BFRO Vancouver Island Expedition, 2007

It's always… location, location, location

At some point in January 2007, near the middle of the month, I received a phone call from Colleen. Colleen and her family had attended the previous year's Sunshine Coast expedition and had two Class A sightings. Reportedly, one sasquatch was a juvenile and the other one was an adult. The two sasquatches had been observed from a distance of about 60 yards.

"So Blaine, where's your expedition going to be?"

"What expedition?"

"The expedition on the Island?"

"What expedition on the Island?"

"Haven't you been looking at the BFRO web page?"

"No, I haven't seen the web page lately because during the Christmas and New Year's holiday season I have been just a little more focused on doing things with the family than with the BFRO."

Vancouver Island Fun Fact #1
Vancouver Island is 290 miles in length and 60 miles wide at its widest point making it the largest island on the west coast of North America. In total, Vancouver Island covers 12,407 square miles.

"Well, when you have the time, take a look. Matt has posted the general locations for the expeditions this coming year. It appears that there will be two taking place in BC, one on the Sunshine Coast and one on Vancouver Island. Matt has listed you as the organizer for the one on the Island.

"Oh, really?"

"Yes he has. So where is it going to be held?"

That question would prove to be the proverbial $64,000 question and the task of organizing an expedition loomed before me. There is a vast history of sasquatch activity on the Island and I had completed quite a few reports for the BFRO but this operation would be larger than anything I had previously done before. I had planned out a few camping trips for Cub Scouts but Cub Camps do not usually have the Scoutmaster leading his charges down some darkened road in order to purposely elicit a response from an eight-foot hairy primate. That's not to say that Cubs and Scouts haven't encountered a sasquatch in the past. Far from it. In fact, one reported incident took place at a youth camp not far from Nanaimo. According to the Bigfoot Encounters website[27] an un-named individual was attending a summer camp at Camp Morecroft in the summer of 1982 or possibly 1983. The witness wrote that the group had decided to spend a night camping on nearby Gerald Island, which is accessible by a short canoe trip. During the night he and another camper saw a figure moving easily through the darkened tree line. Was it a sasquatch? In the article the witness does not openly state that he saw a sasquatch only that in the dark of night something had incessantly thrown rocks at his group with a great degree of accuracy. The campaign of terror ended when the sun rose over the Strait of Georgia after which the battle-weary campers were able to retreat to the main camp.

At my first opportunity, I called Matt to discuss what was required from an expedition organizer. I was worried that I would not be up to the task because there was a lot riding on conducting a successful expedition. During our conversation, Matt explained the process of how to register the attendees, how to track them through the necessary paperwork and if I had any problems there were people in the organization who would be able to help me sort things out. The one thing that really impressed me was the networking that went on between the various organizers. This is a very important point and I'll tell you why. When a person applies to attend an expedition it is made abundantly clear that in the event that he, she or they cannot attend the expedition there will be no refund of the attendance fees and in reality to try to send back cash, cheques or electronic fund transfers would be a logistical nightmare. However, circumstances such as work constraints, an accident, a death in the family or some other unforeseen reason may prevent a person from attending so the BFRO honors those who have completed the registration process by allowing them to join another expedition when the timing is better suited to their individual circumstances.

Much like when I am completing the investigation on a reported sighting, I try my level best to check out the validity of the witness. If a witness turns out to be unreliable, then the report may still be completed but it will not be published. Instead the completed report would simply reside in the database as reference material. The same criterion applies to those who want to come on an expedition. Every attendee must be phoned and interviewed by the organizer who will discuss topics ranging from physical health, camping experience, the reasons for attending and their expectations of the expedition. This is the golden opportunity for the organizer to weed out or disallow people from participating in the expedition but even after some careful examination the odd duck can and will slip through the cracks. But is this really necessary? In light of what had occurred with Harold on the 2006 Sunshine Coast expedition I would have to emphatically say yes. I distinctly remember at one point of that particular expedition – near the end when Harold's eccentricities really began to be prevalent – I quipped that maybe he should increase his medication to which he replied that he already had. And, he was drop dead serious about it.

Sgt. Trombley says:
"If you fail to plan then you are planning to fail!"

Having a "Harold" on an expedition would be something that I would simply have to plan for and it would be prudent to do so simply because there was too much at risk in regards to the safety of the attendees and the security of the organization's valuable equipment. I knew that I could easily adjust my personal approach in order to successfully deal with just about any personality type that I ran into. Little did I know that on this expedition my abilities would be put to the test.

During the month of January most Vancouver Island's Beaufort mountain range is blanketed with snow so it would be some time before I would be able to head out to any likely sasquatch habitat areas. In order to find a suitable location I would have to drive every highway and logging road on the Island and with the price of fuel there simply had to be a better way to find a location where there had been some recent activity, some place where there were plenty of secondary signs and where I could hold a base camp. By accessing the BFRO's extensive database I soon began to identify several areas on the Island that had a greater history of reported sightings, vocalizations and tracks. Not only did

I look at the reports that had been completed but I also looked at the scores of unfinished reports that had been sitting in, as I call them, the deadwood files as they may reinforce the history of a given area. For example, focusing on the local region I knew that the local K'omoks First Nations band has its own tales of hairy giants who supposedly inhabit Mount Washington and Forbidden Plateau. I have also seen a cast of the track collected by Dr. Bindernagel, found while he was hiking through Paradise Meadows on the western side of Mount Washington. Additionally, one of my first investigations was on a report from two brothers who had experienced something creeping around their campsite near Constitution Hill, which is on the eastern side of Mount Washington. This report was never published in the public database due to the lack of supporting evidence but it did point to one more possible incident from this particular area.

So why wasn't the first Vancouver Island expedition held in the Comox Valley? The answer to that question is: I don't really know. The data certainly showed that there was some activity but it was really slim at best. Maybe it was also too close to my home and I would have been tempted to sneak away on a daily basis for a refreshing shower and a hot meal. It's one thing, while in the field, to take a daily whore's bath, where you wash with one end of a towel and dry with the other, but I know that it wouldn't look very good if I was showing up every day looking all clean and pressed while the rest of the group slowly began to smell like our quarry[28].

The Comox Valley was out of the running for this year's expedition. Another possible location was out near the southern tip of Vancouver Island. There had been a number of reports from the Sooke Hills area. The Sooke Hills are a popular recreation destination for the people of Victoria. However, the location wouldn't work too well, what with us trying to be quiet and observe the forest as a bunch of urbanized hikers noisily galumphed through woods while enroute to the next leg of their personal völksmarche.

The idea of putting the base camp and the entire expedition toward the north end of the Island was an option but surprisingly there had been a lack of reports from this region. This was by no means an indication that there are no sasquatches residing in the area because given the terrain and the ecology of the north end of the Island I am sure that there are. The lack of reports can be traced directly to the number of people living or working in a given area. The northern part of Vancouver Island simply does not have the same human population base of the mid or southern parts of the Island and if a sasquatch were to jaywalk across a logging road, there are far too few people around who would witness it. Of those people who do live up-Island they are largely employed in commercial forestry, mining or the fishing industry. These are real macho men and if one of these guys ever did see a sasquatch, even if it were an extremely close and detailed sighting where there was no question as to what he had witnessed, it is very doubtful that he would tell anyone for fear of being ridiculed. The First Nations people, who inhabit many locations on northern Vancouver Island, have a rich history of folklore with regards to the world around them. When asked about the sasquatch, they are largely non-committal. As far as they are concerned this creature is part of their culture, to be revered and left alone. In other words, they're not talking either.

While wading through the reports submitted to the BFRO from Vancouver Island, I discovered a number of incidents that were emanating from the Cowichan River Valley. This valley is closer to the southern end of Vancouver Island with the city of Duncan being the largest human settlement. The Cowichan Valley has two principal rivers flowing through it, the Cowichan and the Chemainus, and is dominated at the northern border by Mount Prevost and Mount Sicker. Twenty miles west of Duncan is Cowichan Lake, a typical British Columbia fjord-like lake that extends some eighteen miles in roughly an east and west direction. Historically speaking, the Cowichan First Nations has had plenty of contact with the sasquatch but more recently there was a report published in a local paper of a series of large humanoid footprints, measuring fifteen inches in length and sinking three inches into the soil as they marched across a First Nation farmer's strawberry field.[29]

As I continued investigating and finalizing BFRO reports from the four western provinces, I also began to focus more attention on the Cowichan Valley. There was one report from a young adult who recounted how he and his pals had been camping at a remote location along one of the rivers. On previous outings to this location they had heard distant vocalizations and the occasional wood knock. But, on this particular night the witness said they had been sitting around a small campfire, relaxing from the rigors of life, and they could hear something circling them outside their firelight. Knowing that there was safety in numbers, they were unafraid of the sounds that they were hearing. Shortly thereafter, when another friend showed up on his dirt bike, a juvenile-sized sasquatch leapt up from the edge of the darkness, and took off running through the forest. It had been seen by more than half the people present sitting around the campfire.[30]

Much like other primates, including humans, sasquatches are inquisitive and these young campers could have been under the surveillance of a curious hairy biped. With the sound of the crackling fire and the nearby river, it may have been unaware of the approaching dirt bike until it was very close, at which time it beat a hasty retreat to the safety of the surrounding forest. As unlikely as this story sounds, it would appear that the witness and his friends were telling the truth. It was during the investigation that several more reports from the Cowichan Valley came to light. Another sighting took place on a very rainy night when a motorist saw a tall hairy creature walking down the side of a deserted country road. As the driver and his passenger approached from behind the individual, they slowed down thinking that it was someone who might appreciate a ride. However, as they pulled closer, they soon realized that this was not some down and out person plodding his way through a rainstorm but a stooped heavy-set, soaking-wet, hairy biped that was taller than the passing vehicle. As interesting as this was, I could not get to the primary source of the report and so I had to chalk it up as anecdotal at best.

What I was still looking for was one or two more really solid incidents to convince me that the BFRO expedition in British Columbia should be held in the Cowichan Valley and I was soon rewarded with something happening at the other end of the valley. A couple living on the south side of Duncan had filed a report with the BFRO in regards to a number of vocalizations that they had heard outside their home in the evening. I quickly contacted the couple and found that there may be some evidence that a sasquatch may have been trespassing on their property.[31] There were some relatively innocuous objects in their yard had been moved inexplicably from one place to another as if they had been picked up, examined and subsequently dropped for lack of interest. Additionally, the tops of several trees in the woods behind their house were found snapped off six to seven feet off the ground. When added to the vocalizations that had been reported in the initial incident, the whole situation was interesting enough for another BFRO investigator to install an infrared camera system on their property. In order to record any suspicious movements in their yard the witnesses allowed this camera to be hooked to a digital video recorder, which was eventually linked to a computer so it could be remotely viewed via the Internet.

A similar remote viewing experiment was once carried out by the BFRO at a location in Washington State. In that particular incident a family had been having some trouble with food disappearing from their outdoor freezer with items such as a half a pig and a bag of smelt being purloined by the nighttime marauders. The chicken coop and rabbit hutch had also been stealthily raided. Members of the family had even seen a sasquatch on several occasions. In his book *The Locals*, Thom Powell wrote about investigating the incident and of the attempts to remotely capture an image of a sasquatch.[32] Even though there were no clear or definitive photos taken there was a very large shadowy something with a stooped posture and a conical head that walked by the camera. The series of images can still be viewed on the BFRO's website.[33]

I have watched the footage many times and in my honest opinion, the figure in question looks more like a sasquatch than it does anything else. Could the footage have been faked? Sure. Anything is possible. But Thom clearly states that when this footage was captured "all of the human residents had already retired for the night"[34] and quite frankly, I would have to take his word on it. As for the remote camera in Duncan, I believe that the experiment has been discontinued with no remarkable images being recorded. The vocalizations are still being heard, as is the witness's uncanny feeling that something has been passing through their property.

It was sometime in March when I saw that there was a new report on the FLATS from yet another witness in Duncan. This person was reporting that she had found what she believed to be several sets of sasquatch tracks. Now this was really exciting. Duncan is close to where I live and if this recent activity were legitimate it would galvanize the Cowichan Valley as the location for the expedition in British Columbia.

I contacted the witness to find out when it would be convenient to meet with her. During our discussion I learned that she had also found a number of possible tree structures in the Cowichan Valley. The amount of activity described sounded like it was almost too good to be true and had certainly caught my interest. Just for the fun of it, I made arrangements for a buddy of mine from Port Alberni to join me in this little adventure. For at least a dozen years we had served together as military aircraft technicians and I thought that this outing just might provide a little fun for the old bugger.

It didn't take long for me to get all the pieces in place. Several weeks later I would pick up my friend while enroute to Duncan where we were to meet the witness and her husband. Duncan is only a couple of hours away and that's an easy drive by any means. I have always enjoyed driving on Vancouver Island. North, south, east or west. It doesn't really matter in which direction you go because all the roads are in really good shape and if you want to take some real pleasure in a road trip, there are a many places for you to visit along the way. Parksville, Nanaimo and Chemainus all have attractions that can divert your attention, not to mention the dozens of roadside taverns where you can enjoy a hearty meal.

Once in Duncan, Bob and I made for a local restaurant to meet the witness and her husband. Introductions were made. Blaine and Bob meet Cindy and... Bob. I thought to myself that this may get a little confusing trying to keep the Bobs straightened out.

"Hey Bob!"

"Yeah?"

"Sorry, not you."

"Me?"

"No, the other Bob. My Bob."

After a round of coffee and some small talk we headed off to the location that Cindy had designated as Area 1. As we followed them out of town, I began to wonder out loud as to where we were being led.

"Where the hell are we going Bob?"

"Your guess is as good as mine, pal. I'm only along for the ride."

"Hey! They're signaling a turn! Is that a road?"

With a quick brake and a sharp turn, we pulled off the main road onto a skinny-assed, scotch broom-infested cart path which, after going another hundred yards or so, widened out just barely enough room for both trucks to be safely parked together. It appeared as if the road continued on ahead for some distance while another overgrown goat track lead off at a 90-degree right angle to the first. This place looked as if it had been logged off some time ago. Provincial law states that logged areas must be replanted but it appeared that only a small amount of the required new growth saplings had ever been stuck in the ground. This could have been any wood lot to be found either out on the side of a mountain or down in a valley, although in reality it wasn't all that far from town. Several rural houses were clearly visible from where we had parked our vehicles.

"C'mon! The X's are over this way."

And with that, Cindy started to lead us across the field and through the new growth.

"Hold on a second! Where does this road go?"

"It kinda parallels the tree line but it just leads to a dead end. Usually that's where the salal[35] pickers park their vehicles so they're out of sight. But the tree signs that I want to show you are over this way."

"Well, it's been raining for a day and a half so let's take a walk down the road and see if there are any tracks."

I took the lead with Bob, Cindy and her husband, Bob, following from a discrete distance behind. The important point to remember was that on this day we were the first people to be in this particular area. The road was actually just a cart track complete with dips, knolls and with brush growing right along the edge in order to scratch every passing vehicle. Every rut, dip and hollow was filled with water and it was about ten minutes down the road when I found my path blocked by a giant puddle spanning the width of the road. The water in the puddle was crystal clear so I asked everyone hang back while I navigated my way around it. Starting at the six o'clock position I gingerly edged my way clockwise around the puddle all the while looking down into the water. Nine o'clock, twelve o'clock, three o'clock and still nothing when suddenly, at the four o'clock position, I saw an impression in the mud at the bottom of the puddle!

"Hey everybody! Come take a look at this!"

At the bottom of the puddle was a well-defined track measuring roughly 17 inches by 6 inches. All five toes were clearly evident. Unfortunately the sun was at such an angle that taking a photo would have shown nothing and we had no method of casting the track even if we could have drained off the fifty plus gallons water that filled the puddle. We were all amazed at the discovery and it raised our expectations of what was to come.

"Okay, let's go see the tree signs that you found."

I followed Cindy through the replanted trees and down a slope to a point where the ground dropped away sharply to form a catch basin. It was partially filled with water from ground run-off and along the edge of the bowl there appeared to be an innocuous looking mish-mash of downed trees.

"The tracks I found were down in the bowl. There was a larger one and a much smaller one. The larger one was only the front half of the foot and it measured about five inches wide and six inches long. The other track was much smaller in size only three inches wide and four inches long."

I went down into the bowl for a closer inspection. The tracks were still there but not in the bottom in the muck where you would expect them to be. They were on the side of the embankment where something had stepped up and out of the hollow. This was why the larger track only showed the front half of the foot because the toes were used to gain a purchase while the heel was raised clear of the earth. The smaller track was entirely visible from toes to heel. As impressive as this track evidence was, I soon realized that it was the stick or tree structures positioned at the bowl that was even more astounding.

Cindy began to show me what she thought were the X's and arches commonly attributed to the sasquatch. At first she wasn't sure but for interest sake she had taken several photos of the things that she had spotted. On subsequent trips to the site, she took several more photos of the same location. When she reviewed these sequenced pictures she realized that something was manipulating the structure. Logs and branches were being added, structures were being dismantled only to be rewoven in a different order. This one, then the next one and then that one was changed to this one, under that one with the next one over top. There were X's, arches, twists and loops. Pieces of wood the size of my wrist and larger had been, for all intents and purposes, braided together for some unknown purpose. Time and again, week after week, she had returned to this site in order to digitally document the evidence and by taking the photographs from the same positions she was able to clearly identify the changes that were taking place. For all of her dedicated work I wish to thank her and commend her.

Cindy suggested to me that this depression or bowl could have been used as a kind of sasquatch nursery or jungle gym of sorts. A nice, safe place where a baby 'squatch could romp and play amid the woven logs while remaining under the watchful eye of its hairy protective mom. If you think that I am simply leading you down the garden path, I want you to review the following incident before making up your mind.

Located only three miles outside Lake Cowichan, Primate Estates is a private farm that operates as an animal sanctuary housing 52 assorted primates and nine exotic cats, including a serval, a caracal, a lynx and, until recently, Suzy the Siberian tiger. In the spring of 2007, as reported by the CanWest News Service, someone had released the Siberian tiger from its enclosure on purpose.[36] When Suzy escaped from her cage the local press was all over the story, interviewing anyone who cared to comment on the situation. One such person, Corey Bath, had "circulated a petition supporting legislation that would make it illegal to breed, house or import exotic animals for life in a cage."[37] Ms. Bath lives less than a mile from Primate Estates and with all of the ferocious beasts living nearby she was concerned for the safety of her three young children. Ms. Bath also reported that when she was 18 "she saw an orangutan running down the street. "I thought it was a bear and then, 'Oh my God! It was a monkey!" she said."[38]

The owners of Primate Estates refuted her statement by clarifying the fact that they have never housed an orangutan on their property. Therefore, it is my contention that when Ms. Bath was 18 years old, the creature she had observed on the road was, in fact, a juvenile sasquatch. The evidence supporting this position is as follows:

- First, Primate Estates is located near, what has been described as, a possible sasquatch nursery.
- Second, an infant or juvenile sasquatch is often reported to be reddish brown in color, which just happens to be the same color as an orangutan.
- Third, a young sasquatch would be of similar size to an orangutan.

- Lastly, and most importantly, is the fact that Primate Estates has never owned or housed an orangutan.

The rest of the day was spent looking at other areas around the Cowichan Valley where Cindy had seen more X's or arches, and I must say that she had mapped out quite a few. By the end of the day I had decided that there was more than enough evidence supporting the idea of holding the 2007 BFRO expedition right here. What lay ahead would be a veritable mountain of logistics. I would have to locate a suitable base camp, conduct the interview and registration of the attendees, determine the best travel routes to and from the location, field questions from and provide answers to the newbies, repeaters, BFRO members and the organization's administrative staff. As time went by there would be a thousand unforeseen little details just waiting in the wings demanding my immediate attention.

Over the next couple of months, and with the fantastic assistance from the BFRO administration staff, I began to register all those who wanted to attend the expedition. The expedition dates for the Vancouver Island expedition had been set for mid-September so there was plenty of time to lay down the groundwork for a really good outing. I was hoping to have close to twenty-five newbies and a half dozen experienced BFRO investigators. My intention was to assign four or five newbies to each investigator who would loosely watch over them. You know: answer their questions, certify that BFRO protocols are followed, hold their hands when it gets dark, then put them in their jammies and tuck them into bed.

In regards to organizing an expedition, the only things that had been carried out thus far were an analysis of the BFRO database and a cursory drive around the Cowichan Valley. One thing that had to be done was a more in depth exploration of the area and to do that I would need some assistance. I asked John, whom I had met during the previous BFRO expeditions in Sechelt, if he would like to come over to the Island to help me. After checking his schedule John said that he and his son, Philip, would be available the following month. I also phoned Cindy, who had been an immense help to me already, to see if she would want to further her investigation of the sasquatch. It was about a month later when we all met in the Cowichan Valley for a weekend excursion. John and Philip appeared pretty excited about the evidence Cindy had found and after showing them around, we selected a level campsite. It was situated on the turn of a spur road high above a gravel pit. From the perspective of a sasquatch, our choice couldn't have been better. On the inside corner of the landing was a fifteen-foot high embankment. It was covered in second growth balsam fir trees offering an excellent vantage point to observe anything parked down on the road. Below the road's out turn was a deep, dark canyon. Littered with fallen trees, it looked like it could provide a safe place to hide or even a means of escape. The gravel pit itself may also have been a significant feature as well. Maybe the gravel pit presented some kind of an entertainment venue, as humans tend to hang out doing things in gravel pits like shooting rifles, camping, having a campfire and sometimes all of these at once. On the last night of the upcoming expedition these factors would later prove simply too irresistible to, what is suspected to be, an inquisitive sasquatch.

By the end of the weekend we explored the back roads crisscrossing the Cowichan Valley by vehicle and on foot. Nothing untoward took place during the night spent on the spur. Although Cindy is completely at home in the outdoors, I think she was a little unnerved when, around midnight, John suggested that we all go for a stroll up the road.

"Cindy, you won't need to shine your flashlight."

"If I don't have a flashlight on, how am I going to see where I am walking?"

"Well, there's actually enough ambient light to see the roadway. You just have to be careful that you don't trip over anything and besides, if there are any 'squatches around here, shining a flashlight will just keep them away. So, by going for a walk without shining any lights we may just pique a sasquatch's curiosity and if we are lucky, we might get trailed or have one follow us home."

"What do you mean by trailed?"

"Sometimes a sasquatch will wonder just what we are doing or where we're going especially, if we are not acting normal. Most normal people do not go walking down a road, in the middle of the night without using a flashlight. By doing the opposite, by doing something that they are not expecting, sasquatches sometimes become curious enough to come closer. A sasquatch will occasionally follow a hiker from a discrete distance by walking as we walk and stopping when we stop."

"Isn't that a bit dangerous?"

"There have been no known attacks on a human by a sasquatch. And if they were truly dangerous, then people would disappear every time they venture out into the forests and the sasquatch would have to be hunted down."

Our discussion of all things 'squatchy continued in low tones as we walked up the road. The trees crowding near the road blocked out most of the available starlight making it nearly impossible to see where we were going. Later, during the expedition, I would learn a valuable tip on how to walk down a darkened road or pathway from a BFRO member from Washington State (see Chapter 4 – Tips and Tricks). To have a flashlight or at the very least a headlamp with only the red L.E.D. lamps turned on, would have been a godsend and would have prevented some of the tripping that we experienced. We must have walked for about forty-five minutes up the road before turning around and stumbling back downhill. I don't recall hearing or smelling anything untoward on that particular night. From all outward appearances we were just a bunch of friends out camping overnight; other than the topic of conversation, the walk in the dark and the fact that John rigged the roof of his Jeep with his home-built Coleman cooler IR camera trap. The one thing that I distinctly remember was the fact that this was Cindy's first foray into 'squatching and I think she was a little freaked out over the whole thing. Since then, what with the all expeditions she has attended and the incidents she has investigated, Cindy has become one of the best sasquatch investigators I have met.

Notice to move

Fast-forward by several months to the beginning of September 2007. Registration for the 2007 BFRO expedition to Vancouver Island was nearly complete. Cindy and I had coordinated the why's, where's and how's. We had a place for the base camp that was easily accessible, low key to the public at large and would be central to all of the areas we wanted to concentrate on. In case any attendees were really desperate to have a shower and they didn't want to bathe in the river, Cindy contacted the local sports center about their rates and schedule. It seems that they didn't care if you actually used the exercise equipment as long as an individual pays the entrance fee.

I was all set to head down Island on the Tuesday when I received a phone call the night before from Ron Crandall (not his real name), an attendee from some place north of Comox on Vancouver Island. Ron said that he was heading to the base camp at 5 AM.

"Why do you want to go there on Tuesday, Ron? You do realize that the expedition doesn't start until Thursday?"

"Yeah, but I really want to get a jump on things."

"Ron, there won't be anyone there. I'm not going to get there until later in the afternoon and besides, since you're a new attendee you shouldn't really be there until Thursday."

"Yeah, I explained to Matt that I have done video work before and I can bring my cameras with me so the expedition can be documented. He told me that he was getting there on Tuesday and I need to be there so we can talk about how he wants things filmed."

"Tell you what Ron; I'm not saying that you can't get to the base camp early. This is a free country and you can go wherever and whenever you want. But, you really don't have to be there until sometime in the afternoon. I can hear in your voice that you're really pumped so take your time on the drive south and I'll see you there."

This had been one more in a string of strange phone calls from Ron. For the past couple of days I had been receiving calls from this guy, phoning me at all hours of the day and night. Ron kept asking questions about the expedition and about the BFRO. Questions that I simply could not provide answers for because he was not a member of the organization. Sorry Ron, but that's privileged information. At one point he called me, I am sure it was the Saturday before the expedition, to tell me that his truck was broken and he had no way of getting down Island. I knew that I couldn't take him and his gear since my truck would be loaded to the gills with my own equipment. The only solution that I could offer was for him to package up the basics and take the bus down to Duncan. Once there I, or someone else, could collect him and his gear from the bus depot.

"Yeah, that's an idea." Click. The phone went dead.

The following day Ron phoned at 10:45 pm to tell me that he was borrowing a vehicle from a friend and he wouldn't need to be picked up at the bus depot.

Thanks for telling me. Now can I go back to sleep!

Something about this guy told me that he was going to be trouble and I had better bring my concerns to Matt while there was still time to prevent a catastrophe from happening. With all the pressure of organizing my first expedition, the last thing I needed was to have to hold someone's hand and babysit him for the duration of the weekend. I definitely would have to call Matt in the morning.

"Hi Matt. It's Blaine calling."

"What's up? I'm trying to finish packing for the trip north."

"It's about this Ron Crandall guy. Are you sure he's okay to go because I think that he's more than a little on the edge. He could even be over the edge. I'm not sure which but I'm concerned about him attending the expedition."

"I've talked to him a few times and he's going to be filming parts of the expedition for me. I think that he's good to go."

"Okay, if you say so Matt. I'll see you in a couple of days."

"Don't worry Blaine. He'll be fine. See you on Tuesday."

Tuesday arrived soon enough. I took my boys to school and then threw the remainder of my gear into the truck. It would be a short drive; only about three hours down to the base camp. I was excited to go, excited to meet my friends again and to meet the new attendees as well. But in the back of my mind was this nagging concern about Ron and his irrational phone calls. Time would tell how that scenario would play out and three hours was all the time I had.

Before getting to the base camp Cindy and I rendezvoused with Matt and Wally at a nearby hotel. Wally is an older gentleman and he would not be spending the nights out in the woods with us while Matt sometimes rents a hotel room close to the expedition site in order to maintain contact with members of the organization via the Internet. After Matt and Wally had settled their luggage in their rooms we quickly headed out to the expedition area. I didn't know it yet but there were going to be some heavy hitter BFRO members who would be attending and they would be arriving in the coming days.

At base camp we met the park supervisor with whom I had arranged camping sites for the attendees. She inquired as to the nature of our expedition. Our explanation of how expedition members tend to leave late in the day, spend all night out in the bush only to return early in the morning, made it abundantly clear that the activities of the members would probably not be conducive to being positioned next to people out camping for the weekend. Simply put, our vehicular traffic at odd hours of the day would probably piss some people off. As a consolation prize she offered us the use of the group campsite at a lower rate and with our own access point. Truly this was a brass ring so we grabbed on with both hands. A short five-minute drive put us at our exclusive home for the weekend with an expansive view of the Cowichan River.

Ron was there too. He arrived in a small white P.O.S. hatchback packed with almost as much stuff crammed into it as I had in my truck. He picked a site for his tent and began to haul out his stuff. Simply watching him was hard work because he was here, there and everywhere, all at the same time. In a word, I would best describe his behavior as being twitchy. Like a squirrel he was always moving, always looking around, always ...

Base camp was shaping up nicely and soon we rallied in our vehicles to head out to the forest. Cindy and I wanted to show Matt and the crew some of the local areas that we had explored in advance of expedition attendees arriving on Thursday. The primary location that we wanted to show them was the gravel pit and the switchback. Sure, there were other areas that Matt wanted to explore and others that Cindy certainly had more local knowledge of but the gravel pit was the area that I wanted to concentrate on. However, before we could even get close to the spur road our merry little caravan toured the myriad of logging roads throughout the valley. First, down one road and then the next. Over hill, over dale and taking a left after two successive rights found us boxed in at a dead end. I hope that everyone remembers how to do a five-point turn on a single lane road 'cause that's the only way we're getting out of here!

It was getting dark out. So naturally Matt proposed that we now look for a place where we could spread out and occupy some portion of the forest. In other words, "Let's set up camp in the dark!" By the time the decision to park for the night was reached, we were very near the gravel pit, so I radioed Matt suggesting that we could rally there.

"Sounds like a good idea."

In and around this particular gravel pit there are a number of side roads where a vehicle and its occupants can hunker down for the night in the hope that something will vocalize, toss a rock, slap a vehicle or even try to use your door handle. And, if that doesn't leave a stain on the front seat nothing will!

We spaced ourselves out over a half mile area. Cindy and I went back up to the landing on the spur road above the gravel pit. Matt and Wally, along with John and Philip, found a spot on a dead-end road that was wide enough for both of their vehicles. Last, but not least, Ron was positioned at the bottom hill that had been logged off and left littered with slash. Although it's not pretty to look at, a hill such as this quickly becomes overgrown with young deciduous growth that attracts hungry ungulates such as deer and elk, which in turn is food for a hungry sasquatch.

By now the forest was as black as pitch and once again I found myself in the most detested position of setting up my tent in the dark. With use of a headlamp and the truck's headlights I was able to throw it all together in short order. I simply had to unroll my sleeping pad, toss in my sleeping bag and my duffle bag. The next task was to grab a camp chair and get ready to settle in for a night of listening to the sounds in the forest. Cindy had recently purchased a new toy for when she went out 'squatchin. Commonly known as a bionic ear, this sound amplification device would allow her to listen in on anything that moved in the woods. It consists of an amplifying microphone and a stereo headset. To enhance the sound capturing capabilities a parabolic dish is mounted on the amplifier to focus and direct every little sound towards the microphone. I swear that with these units you could hear a mouse break wind from a hundred feet away. The bonus feature on this unit is the audio output where you can plug in an audio recorder of your choice. This allows you to record a nearby whoop, a distance scream or maybe an exchange of wood knocks all of which, depending on the conditions under which its gathered, could be considered as evidence of an unknown North American primate.

We sat in the dark for a couple of hours listening to the forest. There was the sound of mice foraging on the forest floor and the wing beat of an owl chasing after them. There was a deer or two or possibly an elk picking its way over some fallen logs but we could hear nothing bipedal walking amongst the trees. Believe me when I say that with the use of a bionic ear all of these different sounds are quite discernible from one another.

There was very little radio traffic between the three temporary campsites. I'm pretty sure that everyone was tired from traveling to Vancouver Island and from driving all over Hell's half acre. I was concerned about how the daily cycle was starting to take shape. If the other two BC expeditions were any indication, I would really have to try to keep Matt from having us setting up in the dark. So far I was failing miserably at reaching this objective. Tomorrow would be another day where we would explore a few more roads before the main body arrived on Thursday but for now it was time to call it a night.

It must have been near midnight before I was all snuggled in for the night. Cindy's tent was positioned twenty feet away. We were not as much afraid of an inquisitive 'squatch as we were from a hungry bear or an ambitious cougar. Twenty feet seemed like a distance that would provide each of us a modicum of privacy while affording security at the same time.

"Okay folks! Time to say goodnight. I'll see you in the morning."

"Yeah, okay Blaine."

Everyone radioed their 'goodnights' and that should have been the last of the calls until morning. But, radio silence was soon broken when Ron called out in a panic that he had seen a bear outside his vehicle. Big deal. The Cowichan Valley has a large population of resident bruins so it was not surprising that he might spot one.

" Hey Ron!"

"Yeah?"

"Stay inside your car and it can't hurt you. Just make sure your windows are rolled up!"

"Thanks for the advice."

"Any time, Ron."

As I lay in my tent, I sincerely hoped that Ron had the good sense to listen to the guidance offered to him over the radio. However, you never knew what a person's experience level might be. Maybe he's never seen a bear in the wild. Or maybe he has seen bears in the wild but doesn't consider them to be dangerous. Or, maybe he believes that since bears look so darn cute and cuddly, like Winnie the Pooh, they all deserve to have the stuffing hugged out of them. All I knew was that the last thing I wanted was to have to administer first aid on someone foolish enough to try to play with a bear in the middle of the night. Yes, stranger things have happened but this would not be a good start to the expedition.

Wednesday…the full court press

Morning arrived with the sounds of birds chirping and tweeting in the trees bordering the edge of the spur landing. I don't remember what time it was but it had to be early; probably somewhere close to 6 am, I would suspect. It was peaceful. Unless I am forced to get up immediately upon awakening, I like to take this time to gather my thoughts and analyze what had happened the day before. Next, I like to map out the needs and wants for the coming day while taking into account the materials and resources I have on hand to achieve my tasks. And, after a silent nod to the gods, I would climb out of my tent with the hope of having a great day.

"Blaine? Are you awake?"

Cindy was whispering from her tent in a voice that was barely audible even registering under the sounds of the birds. Something had certainly caught her attention and I wondered what it was.

"Yeah, I'm awake. What's up?"

I tried my best to whisper back to her. Unfortunately, I tend to have a rather loud voice. Probably from the years spent having to constantly shout to be heard over the din on a flight line. With this in mind, I have to really focus on the volume and timbre of my voice when I need to enunciate.

"Do you hear the birds?"

"Yes, I can". Of course, I could hear the birds chirping especially since the damn things woke me up.

"Listen closely because something out there has been whistling back and forth from some place up the hill from us. Birds can't whistle 'cause they don't have lips. I think it could be a 'squatch."

There it was! Soft, but distinct. Long with a sharp up-turned note at the end and from over there…a reply. Shorter in length than the first with a demanding attention tone; as if the first was an inquiring call. Something like - 'Is anyone out there?'. With the second being something of a directive – 'Hey! Over here!'

We quietly listened to these whistles ask and answer each other from the hidden security of our tents. This wasn't a woodland game of Marco Polo simply because the sounds repeatedly came from the same two locations. One was on the plateau above the spur to our left and the other from the top of the ravine eighty yards farther up the road. Did we record it? I know I didn't and I don't think that Cindy did either. Looking back, I believe that if these were two sasquatches trying to quietly communicate with one another, it may have had something to do with us camping on the spur and if either one of us had started to rummage about inside a tent in the attempt to employ a digital voice recorder, that activity would have certainly scared them off. Besides, the 'Ask and Answer' show only lasted for a few minutes and then all that was left was the chirping of the birds.

Excitedly, we radioed Matt and told him of the whistling activity. Within minutes he came roaring up to question us about our suspicions. Riding shotgun with him were John and Ron. After we had explained what had taken place Matt drove farther up the spur road while John, Ron and I decided to do a quick inspection of the plateau that overlooked our landing. The chase was on! I was so eager to go I didn't even take the time to put on my socks or boots and instead slipped on a pair of low-cut hikers that nearly resulted my having a sprained ankle. Seriously though, I don't know why we were in such a panic. Did we all believe that we were going to leap into the woods and spot a 'squatch sitting on a stump whistling a tune? Maybe we did. If you have been on an expedition you would understand that it is hard not to get excited when things are happening around you and how dynamically people act or react to a nearby vocalization or even a wood knock. When a person has an actual sighting it has the stunning effect of causing the details of the incident to remain crisp in their memory forever. Details that can be unwaveringly recalled by the witness and withstand the probative inquisition of other expedition members.

So, with Matt grinding his way farther up the mountain and with Cindy holding the fort on the spur landing, the three of us launched ourselves through the dense brush bordering the road. Once we had gained the other side we found the trees well-spaced with a thick carpet of spongy green moss to cushion our footfalls. It was eerily quiet. No birds chirping and no bugs buzzing. It was as if a cone of silence had been dropped over the plateau and the last time I had encountered this situation I had been close enough to smell a 'squatch. Was I just as close this time? Unfortunately, no.

John and I methodically worked our way towards the lip of the embankment that overlooked the spur landing. We were looking for primary and secondary signs of sasquatch activity. Signs like tracks, strands of hair, X's and arches. Such things are usually not blatantly evident and so we were careful in our approach in order not to miss anything. As luck would have it we were successful in our search. We found a number of smaller arches, a pair of well-placed X's and a number of well-defined tracks measuring roughly fifteen inches long and nearly six inches wide. Since I have never been instructed in the art of tracking I was unable to determine the age of the impressions but they sure looked fresh to both John and me.

In the meantime, Ron was loping through the woods like an old hound dog searching for a runaway convict. Weaving his way between the trees, Ron climbed over logs in order to eyeball every bent or broken branch, which he immediately considered as evidence and shouted to tell us about it. Good thing we were trying to be subtle in our approach. I don't know if sasquatches have a sense of humor but if they do, I can imagine the Whistler watching from behind a big fir tree as this mutt scampered about without his leash.

When we heard Matt driving down the mountain the three of us worked our way out to the road in order to rendezvous with him and Cindy at the spur landing. The information of our discoveries was exchanged and dissected amongst ourselves and it was decided that this would be the location that we would occupy this coming evening. After dark we would be more proactive in our methods to attract the resident sasquatches by utilizing call blasters, wood knocking and thermal imagers. To accomplish this we would be joined by half a dozen more, highly-regarded researchers. On the way back to base camp we all had high hopes that there would be more exciting interactions.

Back at base camp everyone dispersed to do his or her own thing. Matt and Wally went back to town, as did Cindy. John and Philip had some personal errands to attend to south of Duncan while Ron headed out to acquaint himself with the area by driving the roads. This gave me time to make myself a late breakfast and catch up on some additional sleep. As the expedition organizer

I would have precious little time for sleep once the main body arrived. On this day, unbeknownst to me, the expedition would be joined by long-time sasquatch enthusiasts Cliff Barackman, Jim "Bobo" Fay and John Callendar. Over the past couple of years I had heard of their amazing experiences on other BFRO expeditions so when they pulled into base camp later in the afternoon I was extremely pleased to welcome them to Vancouver Island.

Since the main body of attendees would not arrive until tomorrow, there was time to come up with a game plan of sorts. When Cindy and I brought the new arrivals up to speed on what had happened thus far, it was generally agreed upon that our attention should continue to be focused on the area around the spur road. And why not! It offered all the requirements that an inquisitive sasquatch would need to spy on some clueless campers. All we had to do is offer ourselves up as bait to bring them in. On this night we would also employ two tools that I hadn't used in my own research: state of the art handheld thermal imagers and a call blaster. With the addition of half a dozen more investigators we would also be able to more effectively cover a larger area.

Today was a lucky day! Lucky in that we were able to gather our small band together and head out from base camp before darkness had fallen. Once out in the forest there was still enough available light for each and every separate group to prepare to set up their meager accommodations for the night, be it a tent or a car camp. I don't know whom to thank for this little gift, but I am eternally grateful for it. And, as things played out over the rest of the expedition, it would be the last time that it would occur, too.

To get the most effective use out of the call blaster Cliff and Bobo took up a position high up the mountain above the spur landing. Matt and Wally placed themselves in the gravel pit with John and his son parking in a likely spot a short distance downhill from it. Cindy and I regained our site on the spur landing while John Callendar, with Ron's help, set up an observation post at a bend in the road beyond the junction with the spur road. Everyone checked their communications within their immediate group and with those out on the perimeters.

"Cliff? It's Matt. How do you read?"

"You're good. John, can you hear me?"

"Which John?"

"Callendar. Which John is this?

"It's John Tarrant, Cliff. I can read you fine."

"Yeah Cliff, John C. here! I can hear you. A little weak. Probably because of all the trees between us. Blaine and Cindy? Are you reading this call?"

"Cindy here. Yes, we can hear everyone."

With the communications check completed and our temporary camp set up, it was time to settle back, make something to eat and possibly brew up some coffee. It was a magical time of the evening. There was no wind to hamper our hearing and the nearby creek was also too far away to bother us. The occasional bird chirped as it flitted past. The darkness began to envelop us as the sun dropped behind the mountain lengthening the shadows of the trees. Before long we were sitting in complete blackness waiting for the games to begin anew.

"Is anyone able to do a wood knock or two?"

It was Matt. Another hour had gone by after the darkness had settled in. We were going to start slow with a couple of knocks, then wait before turning Cliff and Bobo loose with the big guns, the call blaster.

"Yeah Matt, I can give you a couple. Give me a couple of minutes and I'll be ready."

"Don't forget to give us a warning first."

"Copy that."

Standing on the edge of the spur landing was a large western red cedar tree. For thousands of years the First Nations people of the west coast of North America have used the materials from this tree to manufacture everything from ropes to clothes to transportation to shelter. Tonight this majestic tree would serve as my sounding board. By the morning its smooth fibrous bark would be dented and bruised from my attempts to elicit a response from our hairy friends.

"Okay everyone. Double knock in ten."

Nine, eight, seven, six....

Whack! Two, three. Whack!

The sound of the wood knocks, enhanced by the contour of the canyon below the spur, echoed down the hillside and through the woods. Everyone in our little band remained stock-still listening for a reply. Ten minutes went by with no discernible reply. But that did not mean the show was over. Far from it.

The plans for the evening included vocalizations, call blasting and more wood knocks. The application of these techniques was all in the timing. Too little and your efforts may simply go unnoticed. Too much and any 'squatch worth its salt would more than likely recognize our attempts to lure them in; less, as being produced by a human but more as not coming from another sasquatch. There is definitely a fine line between what works and what doesn't and if I knew where that fine line sat, I would be able to whistle up a sasquatch anytime I wanted.

It would be sometime before the next attempt but that did not meant that we were going to sit idly by. Just because I had given two knocks did not mean that a sasquatch would necessarily have to reply nor would it need to. The intention of my knock was to imitate a sasquatch and in essence announce or identify my location to anything within earshot. As such, an inquisitive 'squatch may simply elect to quietly approach my location on the spur landing in order to see who was calling. This is where our passive equipment would come into play.

Earlier in the evening Matt had dropped off a new toy for us to play with. It was a hand-held thermal imager. Built by L3, the Thermal-Eye[39] is similar in concept to the one that Mike Greene had used on previous expeditions but it is much smaller, about the size of a pair of binoculars. When you look through the cupped eyepiece the magic of the built-in software displays the residual heat the rocks and the trees have absorbed from the sun. The unit is so sensitive that if you place your hand on the side of your vehicle or pick up what is seen as a cold rock and hold it, the side of your vehicle will show a warm spot in the shape of your hand and the rock will glow with the heat it has absorbed from your hand. This particular unit only displays the temperature variation in shades of gray with black being cold and white being hot. There are other thermal imaging units that will display the temperature variation with a range of colors; again with black being the coldest and white being the hottest, but shades of red, orange and blue make specific temperature variances easily identifiable. The L3 Thermal-Eye also has a USB video-out connection allowing the user to slave-in a recording device of some kind. So, with Cindy using her bionic ear and with a small digital video camera that I just happened to have coupled onto the thermal unit, we now had the means to detect and record any 'squatches trying to sneak into our camp at night.

By now it was about ten o'clock and, like a high stakes poker player, Matt was about to up the ante.

"Cliff and Bobo?"

"Yes, Matt."

"Are you able to do some call blasting?"

"We sure are. Which call do you want to try first?"

"Let's try the one we used a couple of months ago.[40] We've had really good luck with it whenever we've used it on the Olympic Peninsula. Because the topography here is similar, it might work just as well."

"Sounds like a plan. I'll give you a warning call when we're ready. It won't take long."

And it didn't. Cliff, being an experienced 'squatcher, must have set up his call blaster shortly after finding an opportune place to park high on the ridge above us. After selecting the correct audio recording he then radioed his warning to the rest of us.

"A single call blast in ten."

Vancouver Island Fun Fact #2

Along with not having coyotes, there are no skunks, moose, porcupines or poisonous snakes native to Vancouver Island.

If you have never heard a sasquatch vocalization it is hard to describe the mournful howl emanating from high up on the mountain. It was clear and distinct and certainly not from anything most people would identify as something recognizable. It was not the howl of a wolf or the angry scream of a cougar and it certainly couldn't be a coyote because there are no coyotes on Vancouver Island.

I don't know how much power Cliff's amplifier was pumping out or how far the sound of the recorded vocalization would travel but I did know that there were farm houses within a couple of miles of our location. In fact, I wondered if our call blast would have any effect on the animals residing at Primate Estates or if it would generate any new reports sent to the BFRO website. Suddenly there was a call over the radio from John C.

"Hey guys! Y'all see those lights in the sky?"

"Lights? What lights?"

"There are these lights in the sky off to the east. About five or ten miles away! They seem to come out of nowhere, fall towards the ground and then they disappear!"

John seemed pretty agitated by what he was seeing. His observation skills are very well honed and if he was reporting that he was seeing something, you can bet that there is something to be seen. I decided that I had better walk down the spur road take a look at the eastern night sky.

"How many are there, John?"

"Hey, Blaine! There've been two sets of four and the last set had only three!"

I had an idea as to what the mysterious lights were so I kept walking down the hill. Through a break in the trees, I saw them for myself. Sure enough there were one, two, three, and finally, four very bright white lights slowly falling from the sky and then disappearing from sight. Within ten minutes another string of lights suddenly lit up the sky east of us. It was then that I realized what these mysterious lights were.

Flares.

They were great big flares being dropped from an aircraft. When I was in the air force I was lucky enough to be assigned to 442 Search and Rescue (SAR) Squadron. During my posting I was cross-trained to handle armament on the aircraft, which meant I was responsible for loading the pyrotechnics prior to launching the search aircraft. One of type of flare was the LUU-2A/B.[41] A three-foot long thirty-pound mechanically actuated parachute stabilized magnesium flare generating two million-candle power of illumination. They are used to turn night into day within a search area or they could be dropped to light up a target area. As in the 1980's, 442 Squadron continues to operate the CC-115 De Havilland Buffalo, a slow but extremely agile SAR platform, that can move quietly along the air currents barely over its stall speed of 77 mph.[42] When these magnesium flares are dropped near a populated area they are often reported as UFOs to the local authorities.[43]

"John. It's Blaine. Those are search flares being dropped from a search plane. I used to load the flares when I worked with 442 Squadron in Comox."

"Really? How come I can't hear the plane?"

"It's a turbo prop flying out over the Strait of Georgia so the chances of hearing it from this position are pretty slim."

"Thanks for the info, Blaine."

With the mystery solved, and Ron's fears of a possible alien invasion put to rest, I moved back up to the spur landing. It was time to reheat my coffee and have a quick bite to eat. When I walked down the road to John and Ron's position Cindy was using the Thermal Eye to see if anything had trailed me. Unfortunately, nothing had. Or at least Cindy hadn't seen anything trying to sneak a peek through the woods.

"Matt, we're going to do another call blast."

"Okay. Do the same call as the first one. Is everybody ready?

"No, I'm not. Give me five or ten minutes."

For whatever reason somebody required more time to get ready for the call blast. Cindy and I swapped equipment so I now had the Thermal Eye. She was using her bionic ear. Both units were connected to a recording device. We waited in the darkness for the ten-second warning notice to be given and it didn't take long before everyone was set for another attempt.

Cliff must have cranked up the volume because this second call blast was much louder than the first. Once again the primeval howl descended the mountainside before crawling its way towards the rural residents across the valley floor. I was sure that our tactics were waking up the neighbors. Disappointedly, no immediate replies were reportedly heard by any of the teams at which point Cindy whispered to gain my attention.

"Is it starting to rain? 'Cause I'm hearing rain on the bionic ear."

This was an odd question. Everyone had been briefed on the weather conditions we were to expect over the weekend. Warm during the day, clear and cool nights, light winds and no precipitation. And besides, all you had to do was look up and see the stars shining brightly above the treetops.

"I'm still hearing it. Take a look with the thermal."

I didn't think that I could actually see the rain with the thermal camera. But looking through the eyepiece, I did want to see if the rocks had started to cool because of any rainfall. Scanning the area I could not see any effects of rain directly in front of me and yet Cindy was insisting that there was water falling right in front of us. Looking to the right, I witnessed the cause of the raindrops.

Sand and gravel was falling from the embankment overhanging the left side of the spur landing and rolling down onto road below.

"Cindy, it's pebbles falling from the ridge. Hold on! It's not just pebbles! It's mice!"

"What?"

Quickly switching on the digital recorder, I watched all manner of mice, voles, shrews and wood rats poured over the lip of the embankment. It was like the march of the lemmings and when they hit the road they weren't sticking around. Dodging and weaving, they appeared to be looking for a safe place to hide. Something had scared them!

"Blaine, I am hearing footsteps!"

"Where?"

"On top of the embankment!"

I quickly panned the thermal unit towards the top of the embankment to see if anything was up there. However, if an inquisitive 'squatch was trying to sneak a peek at us it wouldn't have to come all the way up to the lip of the embankment to do so. When John and I had scouted the area looking for the whistler, we noted that we could observe the spur landing from quite a ways back. And since a 'squatch was significantly taller, it would be able to look over the landing from an even safer distance.

The forest fell silent as the 'rain' ended with the last of the rodents exiting the plateau. Listening intently with the bionic ear, Cindy couldn't detect anything. So whatever had been walking around through the ferns must have been standing stock-still. We had neglected to call in this incident to the rest of the group so, I quickly raised them on the radio and filled everyone in on what had transpired. Matt quickly informed the group that Cindy and I were to continue with our surveillance while the rest would proceed with acting like campers. The call blasting and wood knocking was no longer needed.

Matt may have wanted us to continue monitoring the woods for signs of big shaggies but it was now near midnight and time to get some rest. Tomorrow was going to be busy with the main body of the attendees arriving throughout the day. We put away our chairs and loose equipment before crawling into our respective tents. As far as we knew there was still a sasquatch somewhere above the spur landing simply because Cindy had not heard it walk away and with one last look using the thermal I hadn't seen anything moving through the forest. Maybe the bipedal steps she had heard were made as it went past us. It was a possibility. However, I'm sure that the frightened rodents who were driven to leap off the embankment, would beg to differ. On the off chance that there might be a hairy visitor walking through the camp while we slept, I switched on a digital voice recorder before closing up my tent for the night.

Thursday... a day of revelation

I awoke thinking that this would be the last morning before the responsibility of the success or the failure of the expedition fell squarely on my shoulders. I was feeling pretty confident that everything would go off without a hitch. The base camp was well sited with access for our group alone. Several prime locations had been explored and we had already had some interactions. Best of all, I would head into Duncan later in the afternoon on a very important mission. Fred was coming over from the Sunshine Coast and I had to pick him up at a generic and yet easily identifiable location... the Tim Horton's coffee shop on the highway. Knowing that Fred was attending this expedition meant I would have someone who would watch my back in case the shit ever hit the fan. Trust me when I say that it is important to know someone who will not hesitate in an emergency, to drag your ass out of the woods, just as you would carry out his (or hers). Or be enough of a friend to be able to tell you to "Shut the fuck up!" without you getting pissy about it.

Until I had to go collect Fred, I would spend my time greeting the attendees as they came in and settling them into the base camp. Some of them would have needs or wants and most would certainly have questions of some sort for which I may have a solution. And if I didn't, I would have to seek out an answer from Matt. All in all, it would be a fairly relaxing day with time for some very spirited discussions about sasquatches and their suspected habits.

Shortly after noon Cindy, Derek, Dave and I went for a hike along the river. It was just supposed to be a leisurely stroll but I found myself pressed to keep pace with the three of them. We were on our way back to our vehicles when there was a distress call over the radio from Ron Crandall.

"BFRO! BFRO! Is anyone at base camp?"

"Who's calling?"

"It's Ron! I'm on my way down the mountain and I'm a couple of klicks from base camp. I need to talk to someone 'cause I think I saw something!"

"Ron! It's Blaine. Meet us at the trailhead by the bridge."

None of us believed that Ron had seen a sasquatch but, on the off chance that he had, we needed to talk to him as soon as we could. We picked up our pace towards our vehicles and as we neared the parking lot, we could hear Ron screaming down the road towards us in his off-white POS. When he spotted us at the trailhead, he ground to a halt and vaulted out of his car.

"C'mon quick! I saw one! C'mon. Let's go! 'Cause it may still be nearby!"

"Okay Ron. We'll go take a look. But first tell us where you saw it."

"I had driven a couple hundred metres past the spur road and went around a corner to the right. And there was this sasquatch, standing on the side of the road! C'mon! It may still be nearby!"

Derek, who had been quietly listening to everybody, came up with a plan. We would all follow Ron back to where he said that he had seen it. He was to stop about 100 yards short of that spot. Derek cautioned us that once we arrived at the location we could get out of our vehicles but no one, including Ron, was to walk ahead of him. Derek's request was self-evident. Derek was a tracker.

A quick drive placed us just past the gravel pit and the turn off to the spur road where we pulled over to the side in order not to block the road. We gathered at my truck and Derek went over his instructions again.

"I want everyone to stay here. I'm going to walk up the road and look for any tracks. The road is hard-packed. But there may be some kind of indication where it was and where it went.

Ron, I want you to come with me but stay twenty or thirty feet behind me so if there are any tracks in the dust they won't be accidentally rubbed out. Once I have covered the area, I will bring everyone up to look at anything I find."

Everybody agreed to Derek's requests. Even though I was the expedition organizer and therefore supposedly the defacto leader, I had none of the skill set that Derek was utilizing, so I stood back to watch a master tracker at work. Later, I would learn that Derek had been researching and tracking sasquatches for years. In 2000, he had been a member of the expedition to Skookum Meadows in Washington State, which culminated in casting the body imprint of a sasquatch.[44] So, with Cindy, Dave and myself watching from beside my truck, Derek coursed the road ahead looking for any telltale signs of a passing 'squatch. Starting on the right-hand side, he cautiously approached the spot where Ron had emphatically stated, it had been standing holding onto the branch of a tree.

"Where did it go from here? In which direction?"

Ron started to walk closer towards Derek but he was quickly told to stay put.

"It went across the road."

"Straight across or on an angle? How did it cross the road, Ron?"

"It walked along the road and then crossed towards those big trees on the left."

Once again Derek began to slowly follow the path Ron had indicated. Looking at every scuffmark, every displaced rock and every broken twig for some sort of confirmation of Ron's claim. We watched as he crossed and re-crossed the road and finally with a wave of his hand Derek beckoned us forward towards him. Quickly we advanced to his position.

"So? What's the verdict Derek?"

"I don't know yet. First, I have to take a closer look down in the brush on the left hand side of the road. C'mon Ron. Show me where you saw it walk off the road."

While Derek and Ron investigated further into the bush, Dave walked farther down the road happily taking nature photos. At least he was prepared to gather evidence if some big hairy thing walked out in front of us because I had mistakenly left my camera back at base camp. I don't know why but being prepared for such an event was becoming quite a problem for me.

About twenty minutes later Ron and Derek came back out onto the road. Derek wasn't saying awfully much, except that he had found a fresh pile of cougar scat and that he wanted to talk to Matt about his findings. Something was wrong. Either there had been a sasquatch on the side of the road or there wasn't. Neither Cindy nor I had seen any evidence of such an event but then again neither one of us had Derek's tracking skills.

"So? Was there anything here?"

"Fuckin' right there was! I saw it walk across the road with my own two eyes!"

"Well, before anyone starts jumping to conclusions, I want to talk to Matt first. I think we should head back to base camp."

Derek was right. A quick check of my watch showed that I would have to break the Cowichan Valley land speed record if I was going to be on time to meet Fred. On the way back to base camp a disturbing thought began to worm its way through the back of my mind. Why was Derek being so cautious in the face of Ron's adamant assertions that he had seen a sasquatch? In light of the interactions that Cindy and I had experienced less than a half-mile away, there certainly was a possibility that he had seen something but now I was not so sure.

I met Fred at the appointed place, loading him and his gear into the truck. It was good to see him again and I was buoyed by the fact that I now had someone who would be covering my six. While enroute back to base camp I brought him up to speed on what had been happening thus far. Armed with the knowledge of the goings-on at the spur road over the past couple of nights, Fred was enthusiastic about the prospect of seeing a sasquatch during the expedition, which is something that we all hoped for.

Base camp was a beehive of activity. The last of the newbies had arrived in my short absence and were sorting out their gear for later tonight. Over by the river bank Cliff and Bobo were having a discussion with several other investigators and then I saw Derek talking to Matt. Odds were that Derek was passing on his analysis of Ron's claim of seeing a sasquatch. I quickly parked the truck and as soon as I headed over towards them I was assaulted by a cacophony of voices…

"Hey, Blaine. Where were you? "

"Did you hear the news…? Ron said he saw a…"

"Squatch!"

Clearly, it would appear that Ron had not heeded Derek's advice to maintain a low profile as everyone was yammering about 'his sighting'. If he had seen one, the result would galvanize the attendees with the expectation that they too may see a sasquatch. Whereas the promotion of a false sighting would demoralize the attendees and would certainly put the BFRO in a bad light.

"Hi, Matt. Derek."

"Hi Blaine. Derek was just telling me about Ron's sighting."

"So Derek, was it a sighting or not?"

"Well, the first thing I noticed when I walked down the road was the fact that there were no tire marks where Ron said that he had suddenly stopped when he spotted it and then spun around to race back to base camp. The branch that Ron said the sasquatch was grasping above its head and was broken as it walked away is easily within Ron's reach. I saw no sign of anything weighing 300 to 500 pounds having walked across that road or into the bush where he said it had. To put it bluntly, if Ron saw a sasquatch it must have been levitating because there was no trail sign at all."

"I figured as much. The question is what are we going to do about it?"

"We could punt him off the expedition?"

"Nothing. We're going to do absolutely nothing!"

As per usual, Matt's experience, gleaned from dealing with hundreds of people during a multitude of expeditions, would prove to be invaluable to all of us. He explained that guys like Ron were bullshit artists whose woven web of lies and tall tales was created to elevate themselves above their own pathetic existence thus allowing them to curry status and property whenever possible. By sending Ron home early there was no guarantee that he would actually depart the area and in all likelihood he would simply dog our movements at every opportunity. Therefore, having him stay would allow the organizers to control his movements. To quote the Chinese general Sun-Tzu (400 BC) - "Keep your friends close and your enemies closer".[45]

And it wouldn't be long before Ron's bullshit began to pile up high enough to bury him. One of my personal faves was Ron's tale of being a big game hunter in Africa. A story that was accompanied by the serving of braised lion meat that tasted suspiciously like charbroiled beef.

Fast forward several hours.

The body of the expedition was split into three components. One group, with Matt and a number of investigators, was to head to the high ground. Utilizing Cliff's call blaster, they would broadcast down across the valley where two more groups, one lead by Rob and the other by yours truly, would listen for any responses. By all accounts, it was a great plan but I was concerned as to how we were going to fit everyone around the spur road because ten people could easily work that location and we had nearly four times that number. It was doable. It would just take a little bit of finesse is all.

Not to worry.

We weren't going to the spur road, a location where we had had considerable interactions. We were headed for a place that wasn't even on my bloody radar! A place I had not checked out for its usability or its safety for the attendees. A place, whose location was a total freaking mystery to me! This was the point when the 2007 Vancouver Island expedition had been hijacked out from under me. To this day I don't know why Matt had abandoned the spur road in favor of this new location. But his decision made me feel as if all of the hard work carried out had been a colossal waste of effort. All I could do now was go along for the ride.

It was dark when we caravanned out to the Chemainus River Valley. Cindy knew where we were going so she took the lead while I positioned myself as the Tail-end Charlie. We were going to set up an observation post about a mile or so downstream from Tony and his group of newbies. Both groups would be listening for any responses to the call blasts coming off the mountain above us.

Time to set up camp. It was now dark out and I didn't feel like packing all of my gear by hand so I put the truck into four-wheel low and drove down to the river while our newbies opted to park up on the main road. Over the next few hours we all sat by the river. With the aid of Cindy's bionic ear we listened for any responses to Cliff's call blasting. However, the sound of the rushing water drowned out pretty much everything else. From what I could gather, the newbies enjoyed the techno toys, listening with the bionic ear, looking up at a brilliant star field with the Gen2 night vision, and playing around with the thermal. So it came as a complete shock to me when all of the newbies in our group suddenly decided to call it quits for the night. With the aid of Jason, who ferried them in his car, they headed back to the comfort of their tents at base camp. That left me and several other BFRO member plus Ron, to hold down the fort. That was when it happened.

Fred, Cindy and I each crawled into our respective tents. We had positioned ourselves in a loose triangular formation. Cindy was to my left and Fred was across the path from me. Ron, who had crashed out an hour earlier, was fifty or sixty feet behind our position. After the requisite round of goodnights we all hunkered down to get some sleep. It had been another long day with several more to follow.

"Blaine!"

"Yeah, Cindy?"

"Did you feel that?"

"Feel what?"

"Something just thumped the ground near my tent!"

"No, I didn't feel anything."

As I lay in my sleeping bag contemplating what could have made the thump near Cindy's tent I began to feel a prickly sensation on my arms and legs. It was not unlike the feeling one gets when you have a limb fall asleep. The tingling intensified until my arms, legs, torso and neck felt heavy to the point whereby I was paralyzed. The only things that I could move were my eyes, and since I was on my back in the dark I couldn't see anything anyways. I felt a heavy weight sitting on my chest and try as I might, I could not call out. Whatever was happening to me was scaring the shit out of me. And then, I heard something brush against the wall of my tent. It wasn't up high. It was down low and right behind my head. Dragged slowly, from left to right, it took several seconds to complete and then it was gone. A minute later and I was back to normal; the weight on my chest, the tingling, and the paralysis everything was gone and I slipped into the Land of Nod.

I don't know what it was but whatever had palmed the wall of my tent would have had to reach around the trunk of the large fir tree that my tent was butted against. Was it a 'squatch? I don't know. But I do know that it wasn't a wolf or a deer or even a bear. None of these could have passed between the wall of my tent and the tree because the gap had been six inches or less. Additionally, I still don't know what had shaken the ground by Cindy's tent. The next morning, Cindy told me it was one single thump, as if something had fallen (or possibly jumped) out of the tree above her tent. Taken alone, these two events don't add up to much. But, when coupled together, it is possible that a sasquatch may have been observing us only to approach our campsite once the majority of the group had left for base camp.

Friday ... and they bailed on me again!

Fred and I were having breakfast when Mike Greene joined us. Today's morning meal consisted of scrambled eggs with sautéed wild chanterelle mushrooms, which Cindy had picked within fifty feet of the camp. Mike had spent the night camped up on the road. As we ate, the topic of discussion was why the newbies had abandoned us last night. It was as if, at the stroke of midnight, some magic spell had ended and they all had to run home before they turned back into pumpkins.

It's been a slice! Thanks for coming out!

Previous expedition experience dictated that following a night out in the woods the attendees would gather sometime around noon, in order to discuss any interactions that may have occurred and to formulate plans for the next night. When I had first organized this expedition I had made it clear to everyone that I felt that it would be important to hold a mid-day meeting for all of the attendees, both investigators and newbies alike, in order to have an open discussion and pass on any important information. Unfortunately, this didn't happen for several reasons, but primarily, since I was no longer seen as the defacto leader, everyone wanted to hear the plans from Matt.

And where was our fearless leader? After staying awake all night on the mountain, he had gone back to the hotel to coordinate the persistent administrative duties for the BFRO and to get his beauty sleep. In order to stay on top of the day-to-day operation of the BFRO Matt has to wear a lot of different hats.[46] I do not begrudge him the need to separate himself from the rest of the rabble. But, there are times when Matt's administrative duties run contrary to the needs of the expedition, leaving the participants to wallow until he reappears and this was just what was taking place during the 2007 Vancouver Island expedition. So, until Matt returned to base camp the expeditionaries were left to their own devices. Some took the initiative to explore the local area, some went into town for supplies, and some entered into discussions with seasoned investigators. And Ron continued to expound his tales of being on safari while offering everyone some grilled ostrich meat that tasted surprisingly like chicken. In the late afternoon everyone reassembled at base camp. It was time to rally the troops because we had a guest lecturer!

When I began to organize the expedition, I thought it would be interesting for the attendees, especially the newbies, if there were a guest to lead an open discussion on the subject of the sasquatch. For a number of reasons the most logical choice was to invite Dr. John Bindernagel. John lived close to the target area so it wouldn't be difficult for him to attend. He had been investigating the sasquatch for such a long time that many of the attendees would have heard of him and had probably read his book. Most importantly I wanted him to attend the expedition simply because he never had. From what I could gather, John's experience in the pursuit of the sasquatch was limited to investigating sighting locations after the fact, and searching the woods essentially by himself. When I first asked Dr. Bindernagel to attend, he balked at the idea, citing that he felt the BFRO did not approach the subject of the sasquatch in a scientific manner and therefore the evidence that we discovered was not being documented correctly. To which I reminded him that scientific or not, the BFRO had developed techniques that regularly incites the sasquatch to interact with us. In the end, John agreed to join us in the Cowichan Valley.

Having told only a few members of his impending arrival, the participants were completely surprised when Dr. Bindernagel showed up. Everyone greeted him warmly, welcoming him into their midst. To say the least, his round table discussion was engaging and informative with questions coming from both newbie and investigator alike. Although John did his best to answer them all, some of the more seasoned investigators gladly stepped up to the plate to help him out.

Dr. Bindernagel had brought along a portion of his collection of footprint casts for us to look at. He had brought along a number of reproductions of the track he had found at Paradise Meadows on Mount Washington as well as extra copies of his book to sell. It was a good thing that he had them because many of the newbies took the opportunity to pick one up. Unfortunately, I wasn't able to intervene before John had accepted a promissory note from Ron for a replica cast and a book. I knew that it was money that he would never see.

Okay, children! Show and tell is over. It's time to saddle up!

Tonight's operation would find the expedition participants once again split into three distinct groups. Cindy managed to get permission from a local logging company for Matt's group to access a private road on the opposite side of the river with the caveat that they would be locked in until a security guard released them in the morning. I felt that our attention should have been focused near the spur road since all the activity prior to the start of the expedition had occurred there. But despite my objections, both my group and Tony's would take up the sites we had occupied the previous night. I don't know what we were trying to accomplish at these locations. All that we could hope was that our techniques would be effective enough to attract a sasquatch, especially since Dr. Bindernagel was tagging along with Tony's group.

There was one other problem with going back to the Chemainus River. There was a fly in the ointment and its name was Ron. Because of all of his bullshit stories and his ever-present persistent, twitchy nature, no one wanted him in their group. He couldn't go with Tony since Dr. Bindernagel was with him and Matt certainly didn't want to be locked in on a logging road with him, so the final choice was yours truly. Well, there was more than one way to skin a cat and to do so I came up with a beauty of a plan.

Once we were out at the site, I gathered everyone around me.

"In order to make the best use of out tools we're going to divide our merry little band into three groups. Fred and I will set up our tents down the hill by the river. If any of you want to stay the night, you are welcome to join us. We will have one group down by the river using my night vision viewer to see if anything tries crossing the water towards us. I need another group to conduct a patrol along the road and with the Thermal Eye watch for anything trying to sneak up on us through the woods. Is everyone okay with this?"

There was a chorus of yeses.

"Okay then. Go ahead. Sort yourselves out and Fred will get you checked out with the equipment. And now, for the last position. Ron?"

"Yeah?"

Like a puppy anticipating the opportunity to play with his master, Ron was all ears.

"I need you to run a special operation for me. Can you do that?"

"What do you need?"

"I want you to take my bionic ear and set up a listening post. There is a pull-out about four hundred yards farther down the road. From there, the sound of the river will not drown out the sound of anything walking through the forest. It is important that you continue to listen in with the headphones. If you hear anything large coming towards us, give us a call on the radio. Are you comfortable doing this job?"

"Yeah, I can do that and I won't let you down."

I handed him the bionic ear and showed him how to use it after which he idled his P.O.S towards his special operation location. In one fell swoop, I had effectively promoted Ron to a position of importance, removed him from being such a pain in the ass to everyone and made a whole bunch of people very happy.

The remainder of the evening was spent assisting the newbies with the equipment and conducting roving patrols along the main road. At one point, Fred wanted to demonstrate a wood knock, to which I gave him the go ahead. Except, that I forgot to follow the protocol of radioing our intentions. As a result, Ron began screaming into the radio that he had heard a 'squatch. We tried to explain that it was our wood knock because we had forgotten to give the warning order. But, he wouldn't listen.

It was my fault. I had uncorked the genie and there was no way to get him back into his bottle. I spent the rest of the evening wandering down to his location over and over again to check out some noise or other. From previous experience, I knew that when using a bionic ear mice and squirrels can sound like a herd of elephants coming through the bush. Even without such a listening device the sound of a mouse probing around a camp at night can spook some people.

This was my fourth night out. The forest was at peace. It wasn't raining or windy and the stars were shining so brightly that we didn't even have to use our red lamps to move about. Other than having to deal with Ron's twitchy insecurity, everything was just a walk in the woods, so to speak. Our tents were placed far enough apart to invite an approach and yet near enough that communication was possible with a soft whisper.

It was near midnight and just like clockwork it was time for all the newbies to seek shelter from the bogyman. I wondered who was going to tuck them in. Over the course of the weekend, the new attendees had been told many times that sasquatches are benign and that there had been no known attacks on a person. Oh, they'll scream at you and throw rocks or sticks, push over trees and thump your vehicle but for the most part they don't mean any harm. Think about it. If a sasquatch actually did want to harm a human, there would be nothing he or she could do about it. With their size and strength, do you think that you would be safe even inside your vehicle? No! But none of this factual information, provided by people who had been in very close proximity to a 'squatch on numerous occasions, would dissuade them from climbing back into their vehicles and heading back to base camp.

Sleep tight and I'll see you in the morning.

Saturday... and I'm losing it!

Six a.m.

When I awoke, the first thing that came to mind was that I really wanted to sleep some more. I rolled over, buried my head deep inside my sleeping bag and closed my eyes. Fine. I couldn't see anything but how do I shut my ears? The river was only twenty-five yards away and the sound of the water rushing over the rocks was definitely not helping. Like some legendary Chinese water torture test the pain I felt increased with every drop. But, it wasn't on my forehead. It was my bladder that was crying out for relief. Well, so much for sleeping in.

Today would be our last-ditch effort for the group to find any real evidence of sasquatch in the area. We knew that they were here because of all the X's and arches that Cindy had already plotted and also because of the incidents that had taken place at the spur road location prior to the start of the expedition. So far there had been nothing new that we could demonstrate to the newbies and, more importantly, to Dr. Bindernagel that our techniques worked. His assertion, that since the BFRO does not consistently follow any evidence gathering or documentation protocols, any proof that the organization discovered would not hold up to scrutiny by the scientific community. However, properly documented or not, a sixteen-inch long footprint was still a sixteen-inch long track, an X was still an X and an arch was still an arch. To this end, it was my intention that before he departed from the expedition, I would take John to Area 1 in order to show him X's and arches of such dimensions that humans could not readily construct them. Then, he would have to believe me.

I discussed the idea with Fred as we broke camp. Fred said that he was keen on seeing Area 1 even if Dr. Bindernagel didn't want to. For now, it was time to head back to base camp to find out if anybody had any success last night or if their locations were just as quiet as ours. There was no rush since it would be some time before Matt and his crew were let loose from behind their secured position.

"Hey, guys! How's it going?"

It was the newbies. Those who were awake were greeting us as we drove in. The rest were still sacked out in their tents, getting their much-deserved beauty sleep. They might as well stay in bed since nothing would be happening until Matt showed up and who knew when the hell that would be. Fred and I took the time to kick back, brew up a pot of coffee and make breakfast. We sat away from the communal shelter because we really didn't want to be bothered by a slew of questions that wouldn't have required an answer if they had stayed out in the woods with us.

"Did you hear any wood knocks or whoops?"

"See anything on the thermal? If you did, you'd tell us. Right?"

"How'd ya sleep? You look tired."

I almost would have preferred talking to Ron. Almost. He was still at his listening post camp when we had left. On my last walk down to investigate something creeping around his camp, I had retrieved my bionic ear from him. After witnessing how he had scammed Dr. Bindernagel, I wasn't taking any chances with my equipment or that any belonging to the BFRO. And now I could hear the sound of his white POS rattling its way into base camp.

"Please Lord, let him park someplace else!"

Nope, he's headed right for us.

"Just great!"

"Hey guys. That was some night last night. With that bionic ear, I'm pretty sure I heard a sasquatch walking around through the forest. Hey Blaine, can I borrow it later on today? I want to go back to the spot during the day and see if I can hear it again."

"Sorry Ron but the battery is dead and I don't have a spare."

I didn't want to lie to him but Ron was acting flakier by the hour and I couldn't afford to have him damage my equipment or have it disappear with him after the expedition. It's one thing to loan a piece of equipment to a friend but no one knew Ron and with his actions thus far, he certainly wasn't winning any friends during this expedition.

Fred motioned that there were more vehicles coming into base camp. It turned out to be Matt and his crew. Since I didn't see Cindy's vehicle in the caravan I believed that she probably headed home to eat and take a shower. I did notice that Dave was riding shotgun with Derek. Dave was a pretty good guy. He handled himself with confidence out in the field and he looked at evidence with a discerning eye. I had already planned on sponsoring Cindy to become an investigator with the BFRO and was thinking that Dave would be a good addition to the organization as well.

Matt's crew looked pretty tired when they climbed out of their vehicles. Hopefully their lack of sleep was the result of being harried by 'squatches all night long and not from the long drive out. As I wandered over to see how things went for them Matt spotted me crossing the parking lot and also saw Ron tinkering with something on his car.

"Hey Blaine! How'd it go last night? Everyone make it back safely?"

"Oh yeah, everyone made it home safely because they all bugged out again!"

"What do you mean by bugged out?"

"At the stroke of midnight all the newbies said goodnight and goodbye. They climbed into their vehicles and headed for base camp. They did the same thing the night before. We even explained to them that all of the effort put into knocking and calling is usually rewarded after you crash out."

"That's right. A 'squatch is more likely to creep in after everyone is asleep in their tent."

"Because, that's when they feel safe from prying eyes."

"You're absolutely right. It's a shame they left. So, what about Ron?"

"Well, I knew that I was going to have a real problem with him unless I gave him something to focus his attention on. So, I set him up with my bionic ear and told him that he was to listen for anything coming from our right flank.

After that, it was just a situation of case management but he's still pretty flaky and I wouldn't trust him nor would I want to depend on him out in the bush."

"Thanks for the update."

"One more thing, Matt. I want to have Cindy and Dave signed up as investigators. They have the ability and the knowledge to be a great asset to the organization. What do you think?"

"Sounds good. After the expedition is over, send an email to the office and the admin people will walk you through the process.

The conversation was over so Matt headed back to his hotel. What I didn't do was broach the subject of abandoning the spur road. There was no need. The direction of the expedition had long since escaped my control and there was no going back. All I wanted to do now was show Area 1 to Dr. Bindernagel and endure the last night of the expedition. The long days and nights were really starting to wear me down. How Matt was able to go from one expedition to another, often with only ten days in between, and still have enough energy to carry on was truly a mystery.

It was around noon when we got out to Area 1. From my previous conversations with John, I was fairly positive that he was only humoring me by coming out to take a look. John's wife, who had no desire to see X's or arches, would hunt for wild chanterelle mushrooms that grew in great abundance. At least Fred had wanted to see all of the tree signs so he had come along for the ride too.

We walked towards the tree line. The salal was thick and clinging, almost to the point of tripping us. I wanted everyone to see the bowl shaped area at the bottom of the slope, which Cindy had named 'The Playground'. It held the greatest concentration of tree structures that I knew of and in the past there had been adult and infant tracks in the mud. I sincerely hoped that some imprints might still be evident despite the fact that there had been no rain in the past several weeks. If there were tracks in the area of the structures, then maybe Dr. Bindernagel would see that there was a correlation between the two. It's not that he did not believe that sasquatches built tree structures. It's just that he doesn't think that all structures are built by them. And, of course they're not. The vast majority of bent and tangled leaning trees are certainly natural in their occurrence. Wind, rain, animal interaction and natural decay can certainly twist and bend branches into a myriad of shapes.[47]

Once we reached 'The Playground', I pointed to the place from where Cindy had taken her photos. From that spot, the structures were very easy to see. I have to admit that at first, they did look like a simple tangle of twisted branches. But upon closer inspection, it was evident to me, that the branches had been woven together and was not caused by one limb accidentally falling from a height on top of a pile of other branches. There was an additional structure built out upon two large trees that had fallen (pushed perhaps?) into the center of the bowl. Again, the smaller branches were intertwined and did not look as if they had dropped out of a nearby tree. Some of these were from a species of tree that grew nowhere near the bowl. Surely, Dr. Bindernagel would have to agree that these were probably built by a sasquatch.

"Well, it is possible. But because it is so close to human habitation, there is a possibility that people could have done it."

This train of thought was really starting to piss me off. Why in the hell would anyone go through all the trouble to create a bunch of woven branches out in the woods? I don't know of any human who would do something like this without having a specific end purpose in mind such as building a temporary shelter.

"Okay then. Let's go back up to the ridge. There is a huge X and an arch that I want to show you as well."

On the walk up the hill, Fred inadvertently stepped on a yellow jacket nest prompting him to issue forth a string of expletives. Unfortunately, being the closest target, Fred took the brunt of the defensive attack while John, his wife and I emerged unscathed. Thank goodness he wasn't allergic to their venom!

"John. This is where we were when we saw, what we believe to be a sasquatch standing on the edge of the wood line. It was about three hundred yards down to the right, between the second growth and these younger trees."

"Did you see it move at all?"

"No. It was just standing there between the two stands of trees, rocking slightly back and forth. Cindy and I tried to swing around behind it but we had no luck."

"So, where's the X you wanted to show me?"

The Argument Sketch

"Ah. Is this the right room for an argument?"

"I told you once."

"No you haven't."

"Yes, I have."

"When?"

"Just now."

"No you didn't."

"Yes I did."

"You didn't."

"I did."

"You didn't."

"Did!"

"Oh look, this isn't an argument."

"Yes it is."

"No it isn't. It's just contradiction."

"No it isn't."

"It is!"

"It is not."

"Look, you just contradicted me."

"I did not."

"An argument isn't just contradiction."

"It can be."

"No it can't. An argument is a connected series of statements intended to establish a proposition."

"No it isn't."

Monty Python's Flying Circus, 1972

"Look up."

Set in amongst the trees directly above us was a huge X. Each individual pole was easily thirty feet long with the upper ends firmly anchored in the crotch of another tree. The positioning of these two poles had placed the center of the X nearly a dozen feet over our heads. All of the branches and limbs had been cleaned off leaving a bare pole. A close inspection of the bottom of each trunk showed that these two trees had not fallen as a result of natural causes because if they had there would have been a stump with roots still in the ground. There was no stump! The bottom of each pole was planted firmly in the ground.

Where were the tree stumps? Spiraling out from the X, Fred and I began to search for them. It took fifteen minutes to find one of them some seventy feet farther back from the edge of the wood line. We felt that this had to be a starting point since there was no corresponding tree trunk lying on the forest floor.

John was not convinced. In the absence of an eyewitness who observed a 'squatch fashioning the X in the forest and with the ease of access to the location, there remained the possibility that this structure could have been built by human hands. This was also his position concerning the nearby arch which was constructed from a thirty-five foot tall tree, stripped of its branches and bent to the ground with its top pinned down under several logs and a large rock.

This was going to drive me crazy. I knew that what I had just shown to Dr. Bindernagel may not have been empirical evidence but it was, in my opinion, evidence none the less of physical sasquatch activity. John was having none of it. What else could it be? Yes, there is a faint possibility that people could have created the X and/or the arch but I don't know of a single example of a person building such a structure or for a single reason as to why a person would build such a structure. Could John not understand this and concede to me this one little victory? No.

My back was up. I was ready to argue my point of view because a well-constructed argument can establish a person's claim even when he is factually wrong. Monty Python demonstrated this with their infamous Argument Sketch.[48]

Thankfully, Fred came to my rescue before I dug myself into a hole. Glancing at his watch, Fred noted that we should be getting back to base camp in order to prepare for tonight's adventure. Neither of us knew where Matt wanted us to be or what he wanted us to be doing. I was sure that regardless of the plan, come midnight, there would only be us; investigators hiding out in the weeds.

Our return to base camp did not go unnoticed. People were lounging about looking hungry and bored. I headed off to the washroom leaving Fred to dodge questions from the newbie interrogation squad.

"So, where were you guys?"

"Yeah! What were you boys up to?"

"Blaine was showing Dr. Bindernagel some tree structures. What have you been doing?"

"Nothing. We've been waiting for somebody to tell us what to do. Are there any plans for later this afternoon? Do you know what's happening tonight?"

Why were they sitting around base camp all day? Couldn't they have gone exploring all by themselves? There were numerous hiking trails and access roads throughout the area that could have been walked or were they waiting for me to hold their hand and lead them down the primrose path? Probably, because this was the group that went home early every night.

I quickly came up with an idea to get these people off their asses and out into the woods where they belonged. After all, this was a BFRO expedition and if they wanted to laze around a campsite they could have done that at home.

"A show of hands. Who here has seen an X and if you haven't, who wants to?"

My question elicited about a dozen or so arms in the air and my plan was to take them all back up to the area around the spur road. Across the road from the gravel pit was an X that I had spotted during the initial examination of the Cowichan Valley. It was easily accessible and there was plenty of parking for everyone.

"Okay kiddies! I am leaving in about ten minutes, so grab what you need. We're only going to be gone about an hour or so. Then we'll come back here before heading out for our final night of the expedition. Any questions? No? Good. We are out of here in nine minutes."

With a caravan of intrepid wide-eyed expeditionaries following closely behind, Fred and I drove out to the gravel pit and stopped at the start of the spur road. There was no room on the spur for everyone to park, so I had them position their vehicles at the edge of the main road and walk up to meet us. And why not? They needed the exercise after loafing around base camp all morning.

As the attendees trudged slowly along the spur road, moving above the gravel pit, I explained to Fred all that had taken place at this location before the start of the expedition. I told him about the whistles one morning and of the stealthy nighttime approach on the embankment above us that caused a rain of tumbling, terrified rodents.

"With all of the activity here, why in the hell are we spending our efforts on the other side of the valley?"

"Your guess is as good as mine Fred, but I'm not the one calling the shots! Hey, let's see if I can get some attention from the newbies."

"Do it!"

Cupping my hands up to my mouth I let go with a very powerful whoop. The sound rolled down the hill towards the valley far below. It also so it went right over the heads of the attendees walking up the road. I had not given the prescribed warning notice and as a result I was quickly inundated with radio calls asking if I had heard the vocalization. Once everyone had made it up to the spur landing, I told the group that it was me who had sent them into a minor state of panic. Some were upset that I hadn't given the warning but others accepted my explanation that I wanted them to experience the surprise of having an incident occur suddenly and without a prescribed warning.

You know what? They bought it!

"So, have any of you heard a wood knock while on the expedition?"

"What's a wood knock?"

Holy Crap! Didn't any of these people do their homework before coming out here? I know that the group I had down by the river was not exposed to any wood knocks simply because the sound of the water would have drowned out the knocking. However, wood knocks are often a topic of conversational amongst 'squatchers, you'd figure that they would have at least heard about it?

I was frustrated with these people so Fred stepped up to the plate and led a quick introductory lesson on the suspected whys and wherefores, including the concept of the wood knock station. Most of the attendees understood what Fred was telling them and the rest had that deer in the headlight look about them. Clearly it was time for a demonstration.

"So when we're out in the woods, the person coordinating the activities in a particular area will sometimes ask for a knock to be given. It could be a single, a double or even a triple. It could be a Barry Bonds home run smash or it could be as soft as Rush's drummer Neil Peart tapping on the high hats. The object is to elicit a response and possibly draw the 'squatches in for a closer look. If we have two groups operating on opposite ridgelines above a valley, we can carry out our own series of ask and answer wood knocks, which may lead a sasquatch to think that there may be some kind of party happening."

"Blaine, can you show us what it sounds like?"

"Not a problem."

Standing on the rim of the landing, where the ground sloped steeply into the canyon below, there was a large western red cedar tree. Its smooth brown bark was already marred from my previous knocks and it was about to be whacked again. I figured that I would do a double knock, Barry Bonds style. From this location, the echo would roll across the valley floor.

"Say we are out at night and Fred here is calling the shots. So he calls me on the radio and says that he wants a double knock. I then reply to Fred, telling him that I will let him know when I am ready. This also gives everyone else who is listening time to prepare themselves by sitting down or pausing long enough to hear the knocks and to listen for any replies. When I'm ready I will broadcast on the radio that I will carry out a double knock in ten."

"That means ten seconds, right?"

"Precisely. Give the man a cigar."

"Now, after the knock", Fred interjected, "it is very important that everyone stands still and listens. Sometimes a reply will be really faint and if you are busy yakking to your buddy, you'll miss it. Okay, Blaine. Do it."

Whack …pause …two, three …whack!

The echoes could be heard for several moments before the rabble started commenting on how loud it was or how much they liked the sound. The exact opposite of what Fred had told them to do. Stay still and listen. Since the protocols were not followed, I missed it but Fred didn't.

One of the newbies asked, "So Blaine, where's this X you were going to show us?"

"Didn't you see it? It's down at the bottom of the hill across the road from the gravel pit and just inside the tree line. You probably parked your truck right in front of it."

"Are you coming down to show it to us?"

"Sure. You guys start walking down the hill and Fred and I will take the truck down. We'll see you there in about ten minutes."

And off they went. As I watched them saunter down the hill, Fred turned to me and said, "Did you hear the reply?"

"What reply?"

"There was a knock reply to your wood knock, but you probably didn't hear it because they were all talking."

"Which direction did it come from?"

"From the bottom of the hill; probably down near where that X is, I would believe."

"Let's mount up and get down there before they do."

And with a bump and a jolt we were off, idling past the attendees as they walked down the spur road. A couple of them tried to snag a ride on the running boards as we went by but I warned them off. I really didn't want to be responsible for someone slipping off and going under my wheels. The first aid would be messy; not to mention the paperwork, which would be a bloody nightmare.

At the bottom of the hill Fred and I stepped inside the tree line at the edge of the road. The X, anchored firmly in the crotch of another tree, was ten or fifteen feet further on. As the two of us stood admiring the explicit simplicity, we could hear the rabble nearing the bottom of the hill.

"Hey, where are you guys?" Marco!

"We're standing at the X." Polo!

"Where is it?" Marco!

"Look into the woods on the passenger side of my truck." Polo!

I thought that I was imagining things and I didn't want to alarm anyone but I was pretty sure that when I had walked off the road, I distinctly caught the scent of a musty gagging putrescence clinging in the air. The attendees hesitantly picked their way through the roadside bushes and into the trees beyond. I soon heard the requisite "Oohs" and "Aahs" as they spotted the X, followed by the clicking of cameras and by a few of them saying, "What's that smell?"

"Fred? Can you smell it?"

"Yeah. I think we must have just missed it. I bet it was right here when you did the wood knock and when we pulled up it, simply walked off. We could take a look around for it but with all of these people here, it'll probably be long gone."

"I think you're right. Let's give them a few minutes more to take their pictures and then we'll herd them back to base camp. We can debrief them on our findings once we get there."

"Sounds like a plan".

Fifteen minutes later and the participants of my little outing were gathered in the parking lot at base camp. A quick round table discussion reinforced the key points of wood knock and vocalization protocols that should have been explained to them on their first night out and not their last. As for the pungent odor…Fred and I let them know that we felt strongly that there had been a sasquatch in the area of the X. Our opinion was based on the proximity of the wood knock reply. It had probably been there when they had walked up the spur road. The cloying scent hanging in the air near the X was also an indication that we had been very close to sighting a sasquatch. The attendees were shocked when presented with these pieces of evidence. Once again this points to Dr. Krantz's statement "believing is seeing". Whereby, if you can recognize the evidence for what it is, you will realize that the sasquatch is a denizen of the forest as much as a deer, or a bear, or even a raccoon.

There was time at hand for everyone to kick back and catch up on some rest. Not that the majority of the attendees had been expending a lot of energy up to this point. On the other hand, what with spending nearly twenty hours each day organizing the activities, carrying out road patrols or holding all-night vigils in the hope that there might be some sort of interaction; I needed some serious sack time. It was about three in the afternoon and I had gotten word that Matt would be here in a couple of hours to go over the game plan for the night. Well, I had already worked out a game plan with my "Six", and was going to put it into motion no later than six pm.

Tick tock.

I was seated at a picnic table in the shade with my head resting comfortably on my arms when I was roused by the sound of someone calling my name. What the hell did they want from me now? Can't I just have forty more winks? No, of course you can't! You have to be at the ready for everyone's beck and call.

"Blaine? I have a message from Matt.", Fred said from across the table. "He wants us to go back down to where we were last night. But we have the option of being in the same spot or taking over the place where Tony had been. Tony said that he was going someplace else tonight."

"Well, that's good news. At least we won't have the sound of the river to contend with."

"Oh, yeah and Matt wants to talk to everyone before we head out."

"Just fucking great! Do we know when he'll be here?"

"No idea. Probably in a couple of hours."

"Well it'll be dark in a couple of hours and I don't want to be setting my tent up in the fucking dark again. Let's round up all those who want to go out to our location and we'll head out in, say, a half hour."

"Do you want me to make the announcement to the group or do you want to do it?"

"I'll do it, Fred. But we are leaving in thirty minutes whether they are ready or not."

"Right."

Standing on top of the picnic table, I spoke with the clearest parade square voice that I could muster, informing all within earshot that in thirty minutes I would be heading out to tonight's location and all those who wished to come out with me should be lined up in their vehicles with their personal equipment. Those who decided to stay behind could tag along with either Matt or Tony to wherever they were planning on going. The fact that Dr. Bindernagel had agreed to accompany my group this evening was cause for a number of attendees to rally forth. All together there would be a little more than a dozen people in my group. How many of that number would remain throughout the night, would be another question.

Ten, then twenty minutes went by. A line of vehicles of those who were ready started to form in the parking lot. I was sitting in the cab of the truck, half awake and not paying attention to the passing of time, as another twenty minutes slipped by. Attendees started to ask aloud if we were still going, as I continued to slump in a dazed state, feeling the breeze on my face blowing through the open windows and seeing nothing beyond my dashboard.

Finally, Fred had had enough of my inactive bullshit. He radioed the group to let them know that we were pulling out with me in the lead and Roger, once again acting as the Tail End Charlie. Getting into the truck, he commanded me, "Start the fucking engine!" and like a mindless automaton I obeyed by turning the key in the ignition. Then, putting the truck in gear, I rolled forward at the head of the convoy until all the participants were lined up to go, at which point I stopped and turning in my seat, I looked at Fred to say, "Thanks. I needed that."

Thanks for forcing me to focus on the task at hand and

Thanks again, for being my Six!

It wasn't long, maybe twenty minutes or so, until we arrived at the place where Tony had spent the two previous nights. Although the road did lead down to the river it was far enough away that the sound of the water would not interfere with any audio amplification or recording devices. While there was still daylight available, I had Fred quickly set up a campsite while I briefed the group as to what our plan would be for the evening. It wasn't anything special. Just the standard camping on the road / roving patrol technique with some wood knocks thrown in for good measure. It had worked in the past and if the participants would only give it half a chance, it should work again. I was about to pair everyone off and assign patrol areas when Matt showed up.

"So how's it going? Is everyone ready for tonight? Has Blaine described what's going to happen and how things are supposed to work?"

"Uh, no he hasn't yet."

"Matt, I was just about to do that when you drove up. But, I was still waiting for Dr. Bindernagel to join us first. I think he would probably like to hear what the game plan is for the evening. He'll be here just as soon as he finishes setting up his camp."

"Okay. So what's going to happen is this…"

And with that Matt began his explanation of how we conduct our roadside patrols, the use of wood knocks and how we can entice an inquisitive sasquatch into coming closer by acting different from what they are used to seeing. I don't know why he was giving this lecture now, on the last night of the expedition. In order to give the newbies some sense of the expedition's direction, these methods should have been explained on the first night at base camp with everyone in attendance and not at the end. There is a possibility that Matt had hoped that by putting in an appearance at my location it would bolster the newbies' hope of having an interaction. After Matt left, for parts unknown I might add, their attitude had certainly changed with the majority of the group actually participating in the roadside operation.

"We've got movement on the right! We've got movement on the right!"

One of the groups patrolling the road was calling excitedly on the radio net. They were equipped with a bionic ear and reportedly were hearing something uphill from their position.

"Is it walking or moving?" I inquired.

"There's something up there and it's moving! Wait! It stopped. But we know that something is up there! Here, Donnie! You have a listen!"

This was the middle of three groups. Positioned about a hundred yards down the road from our spot, the four-person group was tasked with walking along the road from one end to the other and visiting with those who were standing at their post at either end. It was our hope that this patrol technique, which in the past had elicited a response from an inquisitive sasquatch, would work once again. If only the participants would hang around long enough to actually experience the results of their hard work and not fuck off once again when the clock strikes twelve. No such luck. When midnight came, they all chickened out and went back to base camp leaving me, along with Fred, John, Jason, Roger and Dr. Bindernagel holding the line. However, before being abandoned, our time was occupied with chasing after every twig snap and rustling leaf followed by additional cries of, "There's movement on the right!"

Once the newbies had left, Fred, Jason and I retired to our camp. I was beyond tired. The only adjective that could describe my condition would be fully baked. Cognitively impaired from the lack of sleep, I was stumbling around in a mental fog. A whole troop of squatches could have passed right through my tent and I wouldn't have noticed nor cared one iota about them. You wouldn't believe it, but besides the irritability, dizziness, body ache and memory loss, a little-known symptom of sleep deprivation is uncontrolled humor. The three of us must have made quite the sight, laughing loudly at one another's stupid quips, jokes or innuendos. So much for following the BFRO's lying low at night protocol. At which point Matt materialized out of thin air.

"Hey, guys. What's shakin'?"

"Absolutely fuck all!"

Matt had come to retrieve any of the technical equipment that may still be out in the field. The last thing he needed was for someone to 'forget' to return an $8,000 USD Thermal Eye. I handed over the Gen3 night vision I had been using earlier in an attempt to spot "the movement on the right". Leaning against his rented SUV, Matt listened to our rambling jokes and rolling punch lines. Nothing was taboo. There wasn't a subject or a person that was spared from our venomous derision. No malice was intended because this was simply method of venting all of the displeasures that had cropped up during the course of the expedition.

"You have a good time on the expedition?"

What was I going to say? Should I tell Matt that I was pissed at the way he hijacked the expedition out from under me? Or ask why he had ignored the obvious 'squatch signs recently found near the spur road in favor of a location identified by a single BFRO report? One thing was for sure. The expedition was pretty much over so there was no sense voicing any concerns. I fell back on the words of a former squadron member.

"Sure Matt. All expeditions are good. It's just that some are better than others."

"Ain't that the truth. I've got to get going. Tony's up at the gravel pit and I think he has one of the thermals. If I don't see you tomorrow, have a safe trip home."

"Yeah, see you later Matt and thanks for everything."

It was two in the morning and Matt had more than a dozen miles to drive from one side of the valley to the other. He appeared to be just as tired as we were and I knew that none of us would attempt to go to the gravel pit at this time of the morning. Falling asleep at the wheel and ditching your vehicle would be extremely bad form. There would have had to be an entire sasquatch family tied up in the back of Tony's truck for me to risk life and limb to drive there.

Sunday...and that's all folks!

Damn, I'm sore.

Lying in my tent, awake after a mere four or five hours of sleep, I quickly realized that I would need at least a dozen more hours of rest in order to eliminate the massive sleep debt my body had accumulated over the past five nights. Every joint in my body ached from five consecutive nights of rocks and roots hiding under my sleeping pad. Clearly, like many of us who sleep on the ground, I was another victim of masochistic acupressure. And laying there, I began to create an itemized mental list of all that had to be done before I drove north.

1. Get up, eat something, pack up this camp and head to base camp.
2. Coordinate and assist with any departure plans the newbies might have.
3. Drive Fred back to the RV point.
4. Tear down my gear at base camp.
5. Do a garbage sweep of base camp to ensure we leave BC Parks on a good note.
6. Head for home.

Maybe it was the notion that since "the best laid schemes of mice and men go often awry"[49] but I felt that the odds of completing the list were not entirely in my favor. For example, the first item on the list: Get up, eat something and head back to base camp. After a quick breakfast, I had packed up my gear, tossed it in the truck, turned the key in the ignition and... nothing. The electric cooler had drained my battery. Thankfully, Roger was there to give me a boost.

But I flatly refused to let this minor setback get the best of me. After all, this was now Sunday and I would soon be sloughing off all that had occurred once I got into my bathtub. In fact, there would be a direct correlation between disappearance of expedition annoyances and the depth to which I sank into my bathtub and an exponential correlation when compared to the amount of time I spent in my bathtub.

With my truck now operable, Fred and I drove back to base camp. Upon our arrival we found most of the newbies were simply lounging around the pavilion looking like a flock of lost sheep. Lacking the shepherd to point them in any particular direction, they simply began to graze until they spotted the two of us.

"Baaaaa?" they chorused. What's happening?

"Not much. Fred has to pack and I have to run him back into town."

"Baaa?" they queried. Did anything happen last night?

"Yeah man!" Fred replied. "A whole herd of 'squatches walked right through our camp. Too bad you missed it. We took tons of photos but, of course, they're all blurry."

"Baa! Baaa?" What! Really?

If it hadn't been for the fact that we had a job to do the discussion between the Newbies and us, could have turned ugly in a hurry. After being bailed on three nights in a row, I had no patience left for these people. It's as if we all went to a theatre to watch a movie and then, right after the previews, they all went home only to ask you about the movie the next day. Well, if you really wanted to know the details, then you should have stayed for the show. Secretly, I wished a big hairy sasquatch had walked into the middle of our camp last night providing us with some eighteen-inch tracks that we could stick right under their noses.

After Fred rv'd with his wife in Duncan, I returned to base camp only to bump into Ron. He had spent the night entertaining Matt's group with a raucous ad-lib comedy routine, which, from all indications, was an extremely funny presentation. Given the amount of everyone's sleep deprivation and Ron's reputation for spewing bullshit, something tells me that his audience was laughing at him and not with him. Earlier during the expedition Ron had asked me where the bus station in Duncan was located because he was having his sniper's ghillie suit shipped to him.

More bullshit.

I was packing my gear for a departure later in the day when I noticed some of the newbies were starting to leave. They had ferry schedules to meet and planes to catch so I said my goodbyes and bid them a safe journey home. I had hoped that they had enjoyed themselves on the expedition but the fact that many of them chose to return to base camp at the time when most approaches usually occurred, greatly reduced their chance of having an interaction. Maybe the fact that they were able to meet with Dr. Bindernagel as well as Cliff and Bobo had compensated them in some manner.

It was just after lunch when it was decided that the requisite "family" photo be taken before more of our group parted company. So we all gathered near the pavilion in a huddled mass. Tony's family had come over from the Sunshine Coast the day before bringing their dog as well. I know that the BFRO expedition protocols explicitly state that you cannot bring a dog on an expedition and that there are no exceptions to this rule. It's quite understandable that an expedition organizer does not want twenty or more people each bringing along a dog because the associated problems would be immense; the whining, the barking and fighting, not to mention the faeces. And then you would have to worry about the dogs.

As the organizer, I didn't even know that they were coming on Saturday until I saw them on Sunday. As for the dog, it's a well-behaved animal that I had previously met so I had no problem with it being there, except for the fact that it smelled like it had been gleefully rolling in a mixture of fish entrails and steer manure on a daily basis.

You know what it's like when you're in a crowded elevator headed for the 30th floor of an office building and a third of the way up someone, who must have eaten three bowls of chili the night before, lets loose a one-cheek-sneak that threatens the life of everyone in the elevator. The point is, you can't even move away from the stinky bastard. First, because you don't know who it is and second, there is no place to go. So, no one had really noticed that the composting fumes were emanating from the dog. However, once the dog was held steady for the group photo, the source of the rotting stench was positively identified. After the photo, Tony came over to have a chat.

"Hey Blaine. You have any action last night?"

"No. The only thing that happened was that Matt came and picked up the electronics. Then he left to go find you guys."

"Yeah. He showed up to get his stuff and left five minutes later."

"Tony, were you camped at the gravel pit?"

"Yeah."

"Did you have anything happen?"

"I'm pretty sure that we had something check us out after we had all gone to sleep. Darcy was in his truck. Adam had borrowed Darcy's tent because he didn't bring his along. The wife and I were in our tent and the kids were sleeping in the van. Sometime around two this morning she wakes me up and tells me to go put the dog in the van because she can hear it walking slowly around the tents in the gravel pit."

"Was it the dog?"

"Hell no! I told her that the dog was sleeping in the van with the kids. But whatever was out there was walking around very slowly on two feet as if it knew the sound of the gravel moving could wake us up. In the morning we found that something had pulled the rain fly off Darcy's tent."

"Holy shit! He heard the fly being torn off of his tent?"

"No, it wasn't torn because it hadn't been attached to the tent. You're thinking that it could have been the wind, right? But there wasn't supposed to be any wind last night so Adam didn't attach the fly to the tent."

"So Tony, how do you know that something pulled the fly off the tent?"

"Before going to sleep Darcy had set an audio recorder on the dash of his truck. He left the window open so the microphone could record anything outside the truck. When we woke up and saw that the rain fly was on the ground in front of the tent we started to compare notes. Darcy replayed his audio recorder and we could hear the sound of the fly being pulled off but nothing else."

"Did you guys look for any tracks?"

"We didn't notice anything else but I told all of this to Cindy. She said that she was going to head up to the pit to take a look around."

"Thanks for the info, Tony. I'll talk to you later."

I didn't know if anyone else was going to take a look at the gravel pit with Cindy but I knew that it would be safer if there were two of us present. And besides, if there was any secondary evidence at the scene, I wanted to share in its discovery, too. It wasn't surprising to hear that, of all the places where expedition participants had slept, the one place where an approach had occurred, was the very location where Cindy and I had had two separate incidents prior to the start of the expedition. To this day, I cannot fathom why we did not maintain an outpost camp presence on the spur road or in the gravel pit below.

However, the door had not yet closed on this expedition.

I met Cindy up at the gravel pit and once there, we scoured about, looking for any possible prints. We looked at the approaching slopes and the floor of the pit itself. We saw nothing discernible. Nothing that would stand up to any sort of scrutiny and certainly nothing that would compare to the wide selection of castings Dr. Bindernagel had shown us on Friday. With nothing to show for our efforts, we quickly left for base camp to bid farewell to the remaining participants.

Cindy was driving ahead of me, the swirling road dust obscuring her vehicle from my sight. Just to be safe, I stayed back by several hundred yards, but rounding a corner, I suddenly had to stand on the brakes and veer over to the far right-hand side of the road. Cindy's van was parked in the middle of the road and she was charging off into the woods.

"Cindy! Where the hell are you going?"

"There's an X! A brand new one!"

She was right. All weekend long, expedition participants had driven up and down this road and not one of them had spotted this tree structure, because up until yesterday, it was not there. Bashing my way through the trees, I stood next to Cindy, admiring a near perfectly aligned X. A pair of twenty-five foot trees had been stripped of their limbs and securely locked between living upright supports. The butt end of one tree was some twelve feet off the ground with a root ball still attached. The fact that the earth on the roots was still damp, told me that this X had most assuredly been constructed within the last twelve to twenty-four hours and next to actually watching a structure being built, this would be as fresh as it would get.

For a few moments we pondered the ramifications of where this X had been placed and why it had be placed at this point in time. On the opposite side of the road there was a clearing. It was more like a field, really, stretching a hundred yards or more back from the road. The entrance to the field was a fifteen yard-wide gap in the bushes that would easily be missed when you were hurtling down the road. From the road, the X structure was visible only to the trained eye. However, when viewed from the middle of the field, it stood out against the vertical trees like a sore thumb. It was clearly a marker of some sort but once again its specific purpose remained a mystery.

There were still a few people left at the campground when we pulled in, so Cindy went to say goodbye to some of the newbies while I returned to my task at hand. By now, it was well into the afternoon and in order for me to make my own departure; I had to finish loading my truck with all of my gear. This is where my military training as an Aviation Life Support Equipment specialist really came in handy. Having the technical ability to pack parachutes and survival kits has been best described as knowing how to cram forty pounds of shit into a five-pound bag. So with a little bit of effort, I was able to tetris[50] two tents, a couple water jugs, a Coleman stove, a five gallon fuel can, a camp box, my backpack, two sleeping cots, a cooler, a pair of sleeping bags and a myriad of other gear that had all been necessary for the expedition, into and onto my truck. An hour later I was finished. After a quick last-chance check, I said farewell to the few who remained and headed for home. I may have been dirty, hungry and over-tired but most of all I was happy that this expedition was finally over.

Postscript

Several days after the expedition, I finally had a chance to read through the comments posted on the expedition forum. It provides a medium for everyone to share their expedition experiences. There were a number of postings thanking the organizers for the all of their hard work and a similar number expressing their delight in meeting Matt, Bobo, Cliff and Dr. Bindernagel. Some attendees also used the forum to report incidents that had occurred away from the main expedition body and after the expedition had been concluded. One such incident took place on Sunday night after the conclusion of the expedition.

Officially, the expedition ended on Sunday. But a number of people decided to remain in the area for an extra day or two because of their personal travel arrangements and it was these intrepid individuals who decided to roll the dice one last time in the hope of having an interaction with a sasquatch. One attendee went on to post an incident that had taken place on Sunday night after the expedition had been concluded. What follows is the actual message that was posted to the expedition message board. It is copied here with the permission of the author and has been edited only to correct the spelling.

WOW! You should have been there last night!!!!

(Sunday night)

My husband Mike and I decided to stay another night at camp and hopefully find some other people who wanted to go back out again. (We hadn't been up to the gravel pit at night yet) Tony and his family, Alex and Ron were the only people left there that day.

Tony invited us to go with him out there that night (Thanks Tony!!!!!!) It was pouring rain and very dark already by the time we ventured out. We took two cars, Tony's van and our Rodeo and headed up the road towards the gravel pit. I'd say about half a mile or so before we had planned on stopping we shut off all our lights and opened the windows to listen for knocks (didn't hear any) and drove slowly up the road in the dark.

We stopped and parked (shut off our dome lights too) and quietly got out our cars. We sent Alex and Ron up the road about 200 yards on foot to try some of Ron's "moans". (We had heard he got a knocking response that morning at ****). Tony, Mike and I stayed by his van and communicated in whispers by radio to the guys. We all sensed that they were very close and heard steps in the woods close by. I had a "feeling" they were near the side of the van but couldn't see anything. Then a car came from up the road and blew our cover!

So...we repeated the same thing down the road... lights out and very quietly. Sent the guys up the road again and told them to stand shoulder to shoulder next to each other facing opposite sides of the woods. Ron did a series of three moans. He radioed back and said that a rock had just hit him in the chest and asked what he should do? Tony told him to moan again. He did and next time they threw a little bigger rock, which landed next to Alex..., then they hurried back a bit shaken up!

Well I was really excited because I had never experienced that before and I wanted to go out with them! SO we repeated the procedure the exact same way except this time I walked down the road with them.

Ron moaned...we waited...he moaned again...we waited...then again and waited, listening very quietly. Nothing happened. Alex tried to radio back to Tony but his batteries went dead and we lost contact....sooo we stood there for a while and then Alex turned to us and said "it didn't feel Squatchy", and Ron and I agreed. Alex was in the middle of his next suggestion to head back towards the van when a big rock about the size of baseball landed right behind him!! Well... he screamed really loud (sorry Alex) and started running down the road! Mike and Tony heard the scream and didn't know what in the world was going on so they rushed down the road towards us to see what happened!!

As for me I was just thrilled to death to actually have had an experience like that! I know there is no other explanation for what happened because I saw it and heard it myself! Everyone had a bit of a fright but I thought it was awesome and I was thankful we decided to stay that one more night! I wouldn't have wanted to miss that!!!

We got a hold of Matt and his crew and they came out with all their equipment to check it out. They stayed out there for quite a while after us because we had to leave early in the morning. I will be looking forward to hearing if they got anything that night on film?

Thanks again to everyone! It was so nice to meet you all and can't wait to do it again!

Jeanne [51]

At first I was very skeptical of this incident simply because of Ron's involvement. Over the course of the expedition his BS had piled so high that from the top of the heap a person could have seen Vancouver on the other side of the Salish Sea. However, after reading Jeanne's post, and after cross-examining the other people in attendance, it is my opinion that these individuals did have an interaction with a sasquatch. An interaction that occurred close to midnight on a lonely logging road with no lights on and where the response to their vocalizations was to have several rocks accurately tossed at them. It is interesting to note that according to the witness's information the site where this interaction took place was in close proximity of the new X, which Cindy had spotted less than twelve hours earlier.

Welcome to **W**onderful **W**orld of 'Squatching.'

*Matt Moneymaker and Mike Greene at base camp
(BFRO Sunshine Coast Expedition 2005)*

First X (BFRO Sunshine Coast Expedition 2005)

Setting up a remote camp (BFRO Sunshine Coast Expedition 2005)

Fred on over watch duty during the Beaver Pond Operation
(BFRO Sunshine Coast Expedition 2006)

Wood Knocks & Tossed Rocks

Expedition members (BFRO Sunshine Coast Expedition 2006)

*Suspected woodknock station
(BFRO Sunshine Coast Expedition 2006)*

*Woven tree limbs at Area 1 Vancouver Island,
photo by BFRO Investigator Cindy Dosen*

Suspected woodknock station at Area 1 Vancouver Island

*Similar tree structures from Texas (left) and Vancouver Island (right),
photo supplied by BFRO Investigator Cindy Dosen*

Teepee structure found at Baird Lake, August 2007

Chapter Four
Tips and Tricks While on an Expedition

So, you have decided to face your fear of what goes bump in the night and you're heading out on an expedition. It might be a BFRO expedition or it might just be a camping trip with your pals. Well, here are some tips and tricks that I have either learned the hard way or I have picked up from someone else. In any case you may want to try them as they may be of some benefit to you.

Your Vehicle

Despite what some people may think you do not need to drive a huge four wheel drive SUV in order to participate on an expedition. While most of the expeditions that I have attended could be completed with a simple four door sedan those who drove a pickup truck had the added benefits of more cargo space and a greater ground clearance. But, you might want to check with the expedition organizer beforehand as some expedition sites are only accessible by four wheel drive vehicles.

Your choice of vehicle is totally up to you and your budget however you should ensure that it is in good running order before heading out into the woods. Fill up all your fluids and ensure that you have a usable spare tire and the necessary equipment to change it. This would include a vehicle jack, a lug nut wrench and a method of inflating a tire. I would also recommend carrying an aerosol can of flat tire repair. The same goes for a can of radiator stop leak and a spare wiper blade.

Take the time to look after your ride and it will certainly look after you.

Clothing

The clothing that you choose to wear on an expedition is important and in order to have the correct clothing you have to consider where you are going, when you are going and what you are going to be doing. For example, if you are coming to the Pacific Northwest, you must realize that the area is classified as a temperate rainforest so bring a rain suit. If you were heading to Arizona in the summer months, clothes made of loose fabrics will allow for natural cooling. Another good point is to layer your clothing. If you are too warm, you can always take a layer of clothes off but if you are cold, it is kind of difficult to add on additional layers when you don't have them.

When I retired from the Canadian military, I was lucky enough to be allowed to keep several sets of combats (BDU's). For my purposes, they are lightweight, layer well for extra warmth and have a multitude of pockets for carrying stuff. The benefits of these clothes are endless but the one thing that stands out above all the rest, is the material from which they are made. You can be soaking wet one moment and after standing in front of a fire for only ten minutes, on either side, you will be comfortably dry. This type of clothing may not be readily available in your area but there are a number of similar styles available at Wal-Mart, Cabela's or from any other outdoor equipment outfitter that will be just as acceptable. I don't think that they need to have a camouflage pattern on them but if you like wearing camouflage, the decision is yours.

Your footwear is an integral part of your gear. A proper set of boots will ensure that your feet will last during the expedition. Boots come in all shapes, sizes and colors. You can select whatever kind you fancy; in fact I recently saw a pair of hunter pack boots in a lovely shade of hot pink camouflage on sale at a local sport shop. The footwear you select should provide good traction, great ankle support, and some degree of waterproofing. They should be snug enough that your foot doesn't slide around causing blisters and loose enough to accommodate a thicker pair of socks. For goodness sake **do not** buy your boots right before the expedition. New boots need to be broken in so they will be comfortable on your feet. This has to be done over a length of time so if you are looking at getting new boots be sure to purchase them well enough in advance to provide time to break them in.

Hygiene and Bathing

Keeping your body clean is important no matter where you are and obviously this will not be a problem if you have the luxury of staying at a motel while on your expedition. If you are not quartered at a local inn, one option is to take a quick dip in the nearest body of water. However, if you want to keep your body clean and you cannot have that daily bath because the lake is too cold or if your portable hot tub is on the fritz, then use this simple tip passed on by another BFRO investigator: Bring along a re-sealable package of disposable moist baby wipes so you can give your grimy nether regions a daily cleansing swab before putting on fresh skivvies and bedding down for the night. If they are good enough for a baby's butt, they're good enough for yours. I know that Coleman has a similar product marketed as Bio-wipes. Inside a re-sealable pouch you will find thirty 8 x 10 inch cloths. The cloths are moist enough to wash all of your important parts and the package can easily fit any pocket of your backpack. All you would need now is a small towel for drying.

Something that goes along with your personal hygiene is the basic bodily functions. I am not about to tell you how to do it but where to do it. Naturally, if there are public washrooms at a campground or at a nearby restaurant, then it would be best to make use of them. However, there will be times when you do not have access to such a facility, so simply go for a walk down the road, hang a left or right into the woods and find yourself a comfortable spot. You want to be twenty feet or more away from the road not only for your own privacy during the act but also because there is nothing worse than seeing a pile of excrement topped with a Charmin turban on the edge of the road or beside a well-traveled hiking path. This is another reason why I carry a shovel in the truck. Out of sight, out of mind. And don't worry about it being unhealthy or un-natural because if a bear can shit in the woods, so can you.

What do you do if you are in your tent and you desperately need to relieve the pressure on your bladder in the middle of the night? People who are younger than me don't have to worry about this because I am sure that you can last the night. If you can't wait until daylight, then you could easily get dressed, grab your flashlight and go for a short walk. The only problem is that waving a flashlight around at night does tend to scare off the quarry. The alternative is to use the tip I learned from another BFRO member, which is to have a bucket. I know it sounds disgusting but if you are the only one in your tent, you can easily make use of a one gallon ice cream bucket or, for the men, a large recycled mayonnaise jar. As long as it doesn't spill inside your tent while you're sleeping, you would be in the clear. But the smart thing would be to gingerly set it outside your tent so you can easily dispose of it properly when you wake up.

Personal Equipment

People attending an expedition do not need the best equipment that money can buy but everyone must be expected to bring along all of the equipment that will be required for the duration of the trip. However, instead of bringing along four tents, four camp stoves and four sets of cooking pots, the total amount of gear can be substantially reduced if a group of attendees were to pool their resources in order to have a single set of common items. Not only would this reduce the volume of a personal kit being dragged from one end of the country to another but it would also reduce the overall cost as well.

Besides bringing your clothes, boots, shelter, bedding, rain gear and food, the one thing that I think that you will need is a good knife. It does not have to be a huge jungle-clearing machete nor do you need a great big Jim Bowie Special because, despite it being a testosterone-fuelled cultural icon, you won't have to defend yourself from any grizzly bears. All you really need is a folding clasp knife with a three or four-inch long locking blade. Another option is a small fixed blade sheath knife. There are many knife manufacturers in the marketplace today but some of my favorites include Buck, Gerber, Columbia River Knife and Tool (CRKT) and Kershaw. All you need is something that cut some rope, whittle a stick, peel a carrot or cut open a bag of Cheetos.

Take the time to test all of your equipment before coming out into the big woods. Set up your tent and take a really good look at it. If it has more than three supporting poles, it might be too complicated to bring with you. If you think that it's going to be a piece of cake to set up, then try doing it in the dark while you're holding a flashlight in your mouth which is something that can easily happen on an expedition. I would also suggest that you spend a night or two sleeping in your new tent, just to make sure that you are going to be comfortable hiding inside it.

The same thing goes for your radios. Like any other piece of equipment, they all come with an instructional manual. *Please take the time to read it.* Become familiar with the features on your radio. While on an expedition there are certain radio protocols to which attendees must adhere. For example, knowing what the "Roger Beep" is and knowing how to shut the damn thing off would make life easier for everyone involved. Most of these radios come with a rechargeable battery pack. I suggest that you figure out what size of standard batteries will fit your radios because unless you have a method of recharging your radios in the field, they may become as useful as two tin cans and a string. Another thing that comes to mind is the fact that not all handheld radios are compatible. Recently I purchased a second set of GMRS radios with a much greater range than my first set. However, this second set cannot communicate with the first set because they are digital and the first set are analog. As a result, the second set was useless to me and, as you can well imagine, I was lucky to have discovered this flaw before going out on an expedition.

Caring for your equipment after an expedition is just as important as it is before you head out into the field. I feel the two most significant items to check would be the presence of excess moisture and the condition of the batteries. Every item that you used out in the field should be hung up to dry and then packed away to avoid the growth of mold and mildew. When it comes to batteries you must remember to remove them from all of those tech toys, especially if you are not going to be heading out into the field in the next little while. Just as you would not want to open up your tent to find it all smelly with mold, I doubt if you would want to find your more expensive equipment corroded by battery acid. I made this very mistake and as a result I am still trying to replace the battery pack for my night vision unit.

Most expedition attendees are a fairly responsible group of individuals but the one thing that really irks me is how some people can be so careless about their gear. There are some who will blindly abuse their equipment. Like the guy who hammered in his tent pegs with an aluminum coffee pot to the point where the pot will no longer hold water. Or the lady who totally forgot to dry out her wet hiking boots only to find them reduced to a mound of moldy leather mush the following year. Then there are my favorite people: the individuals who just cannot keep track of their own equipment. You've met these individuals, haven't you? You can recognize them by their haunting call: "Has anyone seen my...?"

or "I've lost my...can I borrow one of yours?" Sometimes these individuals will feebly attempt to disguise the fact that they have already started to lose things on Day One of a four-day expedition by vocalizing: "Does anyone have a spare...?"

Personally, I think that last one could be classified as the mating call of the migratory *North American Lost Equipment Reporter* (LosER). And if you're smart, you'll keep quiet because this guy is looking for someone to be his never-ending supplier of bungee cords, coffee cups, tent pegs, matches, flashlight batteries and plastic spoons. Hey, if you have a spare spoon and you don't mind parting with it, that's great because when you're out in the woods your fellow expeditionaries are all you have and you never know when you might just need to borrow something, too.

In regards to these LosERs, maybe their mommies always cleaned their rooms so they never had to look after their stuff or maybe they now have more money than God, which allows them to purchase new equipment before every expedition and leave the used stuff in the woods. I don't know the reasoning behind it but I have seen pieces of clothing, tent parts, dishes, cutlery, cameras and even personal identification documents forgotten or simply left behind at a base camp or even worse out at a remote site. I can recall on one particular expedition a certain member who was forever misplacing his wife's new digital camera. He'd walk over to visit someone's campsite, set the camera down and then simply walk away. Once he realized it wasn't in his hot little hands he would frantically begin scouring the entire base camp looking for the camera. This process of losing, searching for and then finding the camera was repeated time and again throughout the expedition to the point where he became the running joke with everyone wondering what he would lose next. The final straw took place immediately after he had talked to a couple of members who were driving into town to get something to eat instead of going with the rest of the group. The expedition organizers were in the process of getting everyone rounded up for a group photo, which was going to be taken at a very scenic location overlooking a nearby fjord. Suddenly, for the umpteenth time, this clown can't find his camera. Only this time his wife was nearby so he's really in a stage three panic attack trying to find it. Running from campsite to campsite he yelled for anyone and everyone within earshot to help look for this camera. It was nowhere to be found and since we would soon be losing the available daylight everyone wanted to get out to the site for the photo shoot.

So now this guy really starts to snap. In his mind it became quite evident that if the camera wasn't lost and could not be found then it must be stolen. As a result he began to curse everyone and launch false accusations of theft, threatening to bring in the RCMP to conduct a property search and that no one was going to leave base camp until he had his fucking camera!

Well, enough was enough and we all had had enough of his craziness so we got in our vehicles and headed to the photo site. The drive was great and the scenery was fantastic. Despite having driven the general area many times already I had not been on this side of the mountain range so the panoramic view of the inlet far below was quite the treat. After the photos were taken we drove back to base camp where, lo and behold, the missing camera was discovered. It would appear that after talking to the guys in the car, he once again just walked away while leaving his wife's digital camera behind. This time it was left on the right hand side of the vehicle's hood. Luckily, the passenger spotted the camera before the vehicle had gone very far. He then secured the camera with the intention that he would return the camera to its rightful owner the next time they met. When that meeting took place I was, along with the majority of expedition members, really impressed at the amount of apologizing, groveling and general sucking up that took place once his grievous error came to light.

The point of this little tale is that when it comes to your personal equipment, there are two simple axioms:

1. Never bring a piece of equipment on an expedition that you cannot afford to have damaged or lost. And more importantly...
2. One Man – One Kit. You and you alone are responsible for your gear; not the campsite operator, not the other attendees and certainly not the expedition organizer. So you had better look after your own stuff!

GPS, Maps and Compass

In today's world, just about everyone has heard about the global positioning system (GPS). This system can identify or locate a spot on the earth with pinpoint accuracy with the use of simple triangulation between three or more of the twenty-four geo-synchronous satellites and the receiver (that's you) on the ground. Sounds great! Who in their right mind would not want to have a system that can not only tell you where you are but show you how to get to where you want to go and how to get back again. Well, there are several drawbacks to using a GPS. First, like any handheld electronic device, the batteries can and do die out, usually at the most inopportune moment. If you don't have any spare AA's, or whatever size your particular GPS unit uses, you may find yourself lost in the deep dark woods. Unless of course, you have been dropping breadcrumbs along the way.

Another fundamental problem with GPS units is the loss of satellite reception. It's not because a satellite has suddenly blown a widget, although that could happen. The loss of signal can be due to dense clouds or heavy overhead cover such as trees, branches and leaves. When this occurs, the screen of the handheld GPS receiver may display a message stating something to the effect of 'Unable to Receive Signal. Need Clear View of Sky'. This error can be rectified once the cloud cover clears off or by moving out from under the trees, but until that happens your GPS is just a very expensive paperweight.

Finally, the prime GPS difficulty is simply finger trouble. In other words, the operator has no clue which button controls which function and the continual random selection will simply exacerbate the confusion. Clearly, an individual should practice identifying and locating positions with a GPS unit well before attending an expedition. It is just not practical to review the instructional manual on a particular piece of equipment while walking down a trail at night.

If you really want to be able to navigate your way around in the woods spend some time using just a map and compass. And

How Many Norths?

I realize that you know that the "N" on the compass indicates north. But did you know that there are three different Norths?

1. **Grid North** - The top of your map is always to be considered to be Grid North.

2. **True North** - The geographic North Pole is the northern point where the lines of longitude converge.

3. **Magnetic North** – The place where the compass needle points. The angular difference between True North and Magnetic North is called the Magnetic Declination.

make sure that it is a topographical map, one that shows the contour lines, and not some mimeographed road map, available at the local mortuary and tackle shop aka Ike's Bloat n Bait. Learn how to orientate your map by identifying the physical features that you can see in front of you on the ground and then verify those features on your map. Some objects that are easy to verify would be a lake, an island, a saddled mountain, or a radio tower.

To align your compass to your map, follow these three steps:

1. Turn the dial on your compass until you have the "N" at the top of the dial.
2. On a flat surface, place your open compass on the map with the edge of the compass aligned, with a grid line running from top to bottom.
3. Now, with the compass still aligned with a grid line, turn the map until the compass points north. Congratulations, you have now successfully aligned your map to Magnetic North.

To find out precisely where you are on a map you might have to learn how to do a resection. By shooting compass bearings at prominent objects and translating that information onto your map you can plot your position to within a hundred square metres or less.

Accommodations

Everyone, including yours truly, enjoys having some level of personal comfort while on a BFRO expedition. In order to achieve one's own preferred comfort level, each individual will have a different set of accommodation requirements. There are those who must have a hot running shower on a daily basis, sleep between fresh sheets and be able to order room service to obtain their food. At the other end of the scale, there are individuals who want nothing more than to plunk their butt on the tailgate of the truck with the coffee percolating on the camp stove while they contemplate having either the instant oatmeal, a freeze dried omelet or a couple of tins of sardines in tomato sauce for breakfast. Instead of a queen-sized mattress, this person's simple bedroll has only to be crammed back into a protective stuff sack.

The point is this: When you are out on an expedition, you will spend long hours being on the go and sometimes the weather can be down-right miserable so you will have to make yourself comfortable whenever and where ever you can, and in the end it will be your accommodations, be it a hotel, a tent or the back of a pickup, that will recharge your batteries for the next day. So, snuggle up and get some rest. You will need it.

Food

The food that you want to eat on an expedition is very much your own dietary decision. Some people prefer to bring freeze-dried military-type rations, while others fancy the real flavor of fresh meats and veggies. I've even seen some people live on nothing but sodas and Cheetos for four days. Regardless of your preferred diet, you will want to take food that is nutritious and lightweight because you will have to carry it in and, more importantly, pack out the trash. If you are traveling any distance to the site of the expedition, it may be difficult to bring your foodstuffs with you, so ask your expedition organizer for the nearest places where you can purchase your groceries.

There is something new that has been taking place on some of the BFRO expeditions. A number of the organizers have started their expedition by hosting a potluck dinner. This is a great idea as it give the attendees an opportunity to sit back and relax under the atmosphere of a sociable "Meet & Greet". It's kind of fun too, since some of the regular BFRO members have gone so far as to present their favorite recipes for a critique by their peers; a pretty daring act, especially when, in the spirit of a friendly competition, no quarter is offered and none is given.

Ah, but it's all in good taste.

Extra Items

If you are traveling to an expedition by vehicle, you should give some thought to what else may be of use on your expedition. Along with your tent, sleeping bag, food and any technical toys that you normally have with you, it might be a good idea to bring along some other useful items. With an extra plate, bowl and cup, I am able to share my meal with a fellow participant if they're hungry and at the very least, enjoy a cup of coffee. I always carry a shovel, an axe, maybe a camp saw and a couple of ropes that are greater than thirty feet in length. Another handy item is a roll of string, or better yet, a spool of 550 parachute cord.

What about batteries? Just about everything runs on them, so make sure that you have enough spare batteries in all of the popular sizes, as well as any specialty type cells you may need. You don't have to supply everyone in the group. Just bring what you need plus a few spares. Again, if someone else runs short and you can provide, that would be great.

If you have some medical aptitude or if you have taken a first-aid course, please let your expedition organizer know about it. Also, you might want to bring a first-aid kit of some kind. There is no sense being qualified to do something and not having any tools to use. As far as I know there have never been any severe accidents on a BFRO expedition but if the need arises knowing who has some sort of medical training is good to know.

Since you are participating in an investigative venture, you should be bringing items that will allow you to document your findings. You should have a notepad, pens or pencils, a measuring tape and a camera of some kind. Having photos of any tracks or stick structures that you can show to your friends back home, is great and you never know if you might just be the one to snap the picture that definitively proves sasquatch's existence to the world. It is clearly understood that any photos that you take while on an expedition are legally yours; however, there are a couple of requests about taking pictures on an expedition that you need to know. First, I would suggest that you ask the other attendees if it's okay to take their picture, simply because it is a matter of personal privacy. Believe it or not, there are some individuals who don't want their friends to know that they have been bitten by the Bigfoot Bug. Go figure! The second request is that before you post any pictures online, please let the BFRO look at them first. It is not because the organization would deny you your right to post them, but imagine if you will, the repercussions of posting a picture that you believe shows a sasquatch, only to have the BFRO later refute your assertions that the fuzzy blob in the upper left corner of an otherwise pristine panoramic photo of a lake, is clearly a sasquatch. Obviously, this would place both you and the BFRO at odds with each other. It would be better for everyone involved if you simply forward them to the expedition organizer so your photos can be analyzed, and verified, by the BFRO's extensive resources, so neither party ends up with egg on their face.

The extra equipment that an individual brings to an expedition may vary with the location and with the season. I like to bring a couple of 12 x 12 foot tarps in order to provide some extra protection from the elements. Let me assure you that your fellow expeditionaries will be very thankful when someone can jury-rig a temporary shelter to keep them out of the pouring rain or the sweltering sun. There is something else that I have been meaning to bring along. I need to bring a pair of 6 x 6 inch pressure treated beams, about five feet in length. If any of you have been out on a BFRO expedition on Vancouver Island or any place where the logging roads have been deactivated, you may benefit from this idea as well. When a logging company deactivates a road, they often dig a short deep ditch across the road in order to keep people like you and me from enjoying a casual drive in the woods. It would appear the more desperate a company wants to keep you off the road, the deeper and more numerous the ditches. Sometimes there will be two or three of these traps in a row. By placing these beams in the ditches and then retrieving them after the last vehicle traverses them, an expedition convoy can proceed beyond the No-Go Point imposed by the logging company. Could this action be considered to be trespassing? No, because the group is already operating in a publicly accessible area or has secured the owner's permission. In my opinion, temporarily bridging these ditches is not an illegal act.

Keeping things dry is extremely important, especially here in the Pacific Northwest. Most of the technical equipment that you would want to take on an expedition will probably have some built-in level of moisture protection. Cameras have protective cases, video/audio cables can be neatly coiled, and when personal gear is not in use it should be stowed away. Realistically speaking, looking after your gear is pretty much common dog:

Keep it clean, keep it dry, and keep it together.

Subject Matter Knowledge

Take some time to learn as much as you can about the subject matter. There are a vast number of informative books on the bigfoot/sasquatch phenomena. Some of them are great and some of them are not so great. I'm not about to tell you which are which because that should be up to each individual to decide for themselves. But I will suggest that a quick glance at my reference material will reveal the titles and authors that will offer you a starting point for your own sasquatch library. A good friend of mine has such an interest in the subject that his burgeoning collection has hundreds of books, magazines and newspaper clippings.

Another subject to read up on is the location of the expedition. Not so much about the specific location but more about the general area. For example, I have never been to Kentucky or to Tennessee. I would surely love to participate in any expedition in the Lower 48 and if given half the chance I would. But before departing on such a trip I would take some time to learn what I could about the history, the geography and the people within the target area. Doing so would only broaden my knowledge and enhance my overall experience.

Night Moves

As much as every attendee of a BFRO expedition would love nothing better than to have a daylight sighting of a 'squatch, the odds of that happening are very slim. From my experience, most of the interactions between humans and sasquatches during an expedition take place at night when the range of human vision, without artificial assistance, is reduced to nearly nil. With its exceptional night vision, a sasquatch can see easily what people are doing; like sitting around the fire in their camp chairs and rooting around looking for stuff in their coolers or in their tents. It can also see where we are looking and in which direction we are going by simply watching our flashlights stab into the inky darkness. These human behaviors would appear to be fairly routine to an observant sasquatch, but what really piques a sasquatch's interest are the night-time activities that occur during an expedition because they are anything but routine. At night when regular campers stay close to their campsite with their lanterns shining brightly to ward off the bogeyman, you will often find expedition participants sitting in the dark or wandering along some cart-track with no lights whatsoever. Of course there are a few tricks to be learned in order to move around at night.

First and foremost, while there is still usable daylight, you must try to visit wherever it is you are planning to camp or pre-walk the trail you will be taking during a night hike. This will give you the opportunity to see the lay of the land and to get your bearings. Once it does get dark, the knowledge gained in the daylight may reduce your chance of getting seriously injured. This scenario was played out several times on my first two expeditions and it was only once the sun rose that I quickly realized how close I had come to walking off a cliff when I went to go for a leak in the middle of the night. Additionally, pre-scouting the trail may give you the chance to spot some secondary signs like X's and arches. At the start of the Sunshine Coast expedition, in 2006, I had followed Tony deep into the woods and in the fading light I had set up my camp. Later that night, after Fred had joined us, we sighted a sasquatch with the use of a starlight scope. However, it wasn't until the morning, when the sunlight was filtering through the treetops that we realized that there were more than a half dozen arches within a forty-foot radius of our camp. Some large and some small but all of them were perfectly bent with their tops firmly secured with rocks or logs.

Second, humans have very poor night vision. In order to protect what little ability we do have, there are protocols in place that pertain to the use of light during an expedition. Obviously, wandering around base camp waving a flashlight is out of the question, as this may have a negative effect on the 'squatches. Most BFRO members have a headlamp that utilizes a red lamp feature. Some of these even have two different intensity settings which allow them to look at things up close in the dark, without damaging their night vision all that much.

As previously mentioned, it is best, whenever possible, to have your campsite or your observation post set up before it gets really dark. Try to have the items that you will require for the evening readily at hand. So, take the cooler with your munchies out of the vehicle. Grab your backpack, holding your extra clothes, and anything else you might need, out of the car. Set up the portable table, the Coleman stove, prep the coffee pot and your tent, if you're planning on staying the night. Now, why should you go through the trouble of setting all of your equipment outside? Wouldn't your belongings be more secure if they were left inside and retrieved only when required? Well, if you are planning on leaving in a hurry, don't bother unpacking anything. But the main reason for pre-positioning your gear is due to the light protocols. Let me give you an example of why this is important.

In 2008, I organized the Vancouver Island expedition. It was a small expedition with only a dozen and a half people camped at a location that was about an hour's drive north of Campbell River. There had been some questions raised as to why I had selected this particular location when there had been no reported sightings or incidents in the vicinity. The answer was quite simple: the scientific process. I could have easily held the expedition elsewhere but I wanted to test out the following hypothesis: Given what we knew, up to that point, of the sasquatch's basic requirements of food, water and security, could evidence be found of the existence of the sasquatch at a location where there had not been any previous reported sightings or incidents? The experiment worked. Although we did not have any Class A sightings, we did find a number of older tracks. A couple of minor tree structures were spotted and two individuals were trailed and had rocks thrown at them. Not bad for a location with no previous history of activity.

During the expedition a problem arose when two attendees decided that they didn't have to follow the BFRO expedition protocols. During the daylight hours on Friday the group had traveled in caravan-fashion, exploring more of the surrounding mountains and searching for locations to set up a couple of observation posts during the night. Ideally, these posts would be located outside of visual range but within radio range of one another. For example, one group might take up a position high on a ridgeline, while a second group may be on the opposite side of the valley and a third may be sitting at a chokepoint created by topographical features. Unfortunately, on this particular night several high ridges separated the two groups and as a result radio communication between them was completely impossible. I was directing one half of the expedition at a site closer to base camp, while Cindy took the rest of the group over to the location sited along-side a lake that had demonstrated some excellent echo returns earlier in the day. My group, containing both members and newbies alike, conducted themselves with the quasi-scientific deportment as directed by the expedition protocols. They coordinated the use of wood knocks and vocalizations using either no lights or, if necessary, red lights. And they had ensured that the damned "Roger Beep" feature on their radios was turned off. Cindy, on the other hand, may have had a couple of newbies in her group but for the most part they were all seasoned expedition members or at least she thought they were.

On their return to base camp, Cindy informed me that her group had arranged themselves in a loose formation along the lake and then, shortly after it got dark, prepared to conduct some vocalizations and wood knocks. All was going well except for these two "experienced bigfooters". It would appear that these guys had not read the BFRO expedition handbook and they chose not to abide by Cindy's requests to abide by the approved protocols. They were constantly entering and exiting their vehicle, which initiated the interior vehicle lights and sounded the horn when the doors were re-locked. When one of the pair volunteered to do a wood knock, he attacked the tree with a series of rapid blows as if he were attempting to subdue the tree trunk into submission.

The use of light at night and how you move around is very important if you are going to attract a response from an inquisitive sasquatch. During the 2007 Vancouver Island expedition, a seasoned BFRO member demonstrated his method of walking down a pitch-dark logging road without the use of any lights at all. First, he centered himself on the road. Next, he looked down the road while glancing towards the point where he could see the sky through the tops of the trees. Now, keeping a wary eye on this point, the ambient light provided by the moon and stars was enough for him to navigate the road in the dark. By scouting the area in the daylight, he was able to discover any obstacles or dangers that would have to be avoided on a night hike. An important point to remember is that if you feel that you are in danger, and then by all means stop where you are and turn on your flashlight.

Think Safety First.

Packing Up

You have just spent four days out in the woods and now the expedition is over. Sure, you're tired from being awake nearly twenty hours a day and sore from sleeping on the ground but, all things considered, you have probably had a pretty good time. If you attended the expedition with the attitude that you were going to have fun, that you were going to meet some new friends and that you may even learn something then I am sure that you will have achieved your goal. To top it off you may have experienced the thrill of having an interaction with a sasquatch or you may have even been lucky enough to have a rare visual sighting. I've said it before and I'll say it again: In my opinion there is no such thing as a bad expedition. They are all good and some are better than others.

However, the party is not over yet. You still have to pack your gear and get home safely. Please take some time to ensure that you have all of the equipment that you came with. Often attendees will purchase equipment when they arrive that they cannot possibly bring home. This is especially true for those who fly in to an expedition with only the clothes on their back. If you have to leave behind a tent, a sleeping bag or some other cumbersome items please ask the organizer if left over equipment can be donated to a local Scout troop or some other needy youth group. I am sure they will appreciate it.

After all of your belongings are all secured for the trip home you should conduct a Last Chance Check. Take a look around your campsite. Is there anything left behind? Is all of your garbage picked up? Have you returned any items that you have borrowed over the weekend? Last, but not least, after you get home please send a quick email to the organizer to say that you have arrived home safely.

Chapter Five
Investigators, Investigations and Questions

Why would a person want to investigate the sasquatch phenomena?

There's certainly no money in it and everyone you meet thinks that you're crazy!

So, why do some people feel the need to go deep into the forests of North America only to bang sticks on trees and howl at the moon? Then there's the whole lack of sleep thing. It sounds like a ludicrous way to spend a weekend by anyone's standards. It has been suggested that the time spent investigating the sasquatch may stem from simple curiosity or a desire to rationalize a personal incident or it might be an individual's scientific pursuit.

After returning home from the 2005 expedition on the Sunshine Coast I tried my very best to let my interest in the pursuit of the sasquatch fall by the way side. But, as any of you who know me can attest, if there is something that I am truly interested in then I don't do it half way. It's all or nothing. If I'm in for a penny, I'm in for a pound and it's full steam ahead.

One of the first items on my agenda was to file a BFRO report of my own based on my experiences on the expedition. The report was summarily reviewed and posted on the BFRO website under the heading of "Notes from Previous Expeditions".[52] Looking back, I am glad that I wrote it and I am still grateful to Matt for giving me the opportunity to attend that first expedition.

Time marched on. It was back to the real world of employment, schooling and family life. Sure, I still checked the BFRO website on a fairly regular basis looking for any newly posted reports. I was sincerely hoping that I would be able to go back to the expedition site sometime in the future. My wife had even suggested that since I had met some people in Sechelt that there was no reason why I couldn't camp out with them again.

There was only one problem with that plan. If I had gone back to the target area after the expedition I would have been in breach of the Expedition Non-Disclosure Clause, a document that everyone must sign before proceeding on a BFRO expedition. The purpose of this clause is to prevent expedition members from disclosing the precise location and restricts them from returning to the location, outside of another BFRO expedition for a specified length of time.

Squatchaholism

Squatchaholism is a broad term generally used to mean compulsive and uncontrolled consumption of Bigfoot themed material via: The Internet, books, national conferences, expeditions, etc. It is usually to the detriment of the person's health, personal relationships, and social standing. There is no know cure.

–Sybilla Irwin

Why would it be necessary for the BFRO to have such a document in place?

I would think that the answer would be pretty clear. Imagine, if you will, what might happen if a troop of sasquatch were to be discovered at a location that was easily accessible by the public. Let's say, inside a National Park or off some logging access road on public land. Obviously a research organization like the BFRO would not want this location publicized, since the opportunity to set up any future operations would suddenly end with the mass influx of Looky-Lou's and media hounds.

It didn't take long before everything squatchy once again crept to the forefront in my life. I began scanning the BFRO website again, methodically going through all of the published reports from each state and province. Reading not only the newly posted reports but also the older ones listed from years past. One of the Twelve Steps of Addiction is the admission that a problem actually exists and I freely admit that I had become a Bigfoot Junkie. I already owned several books on the subject. I dusted them off and began to secretly re-read them for the umpteenth time. When I was online I voraciously ate up the BFRO and the Bigfoot Encounters websites. I looked through the Sasquatch Research Initiative (SRI) and the West Coast Bigfoot sites as well. For a brief moment, I even scanned Autumn Williams' Oregon Bigfoot website. However, if you want to read anything new or listen to any reported sasquatch sounds on her site you had better be prepared to cough up some dough, re, mi. It seems that these things are only available to those who sign up and pay her a monthly subscription fee.

It soon became quite obvious that of all of the bigfoot groups I found on the web, the Bigfoot Field Researchers Organization was the only group that routinely and consistently placed individuals, both investigators and laymen, in a close proximity with sasquatches on a fairly regular basis. Am I being biased just because I am now a member of the BFRO? No, I don't think so. But don't take my word for it because you can check it out for yourself. Just do a little digging and make up your own mind. Compare the number of outings that each bigfoot seeking organization actually conducts. Ask if its members really go out into the field or are they just a bunch of armchair 'squatch investigators who, from the safety of their own homes, contemplate what constitutes real evidence without ever getting their feet wet or their hands dirty? Look at the number of reports submitted and the number of reports posted as well as how often the publicly viewed website is actually updated. Once you have done all of this you will soon realize, just as I did, that the BFRO is truly a leader in the field of sasquatch investigation.

And I desperately wanted to be a member of that group.

Several months had passed since the 2005 Sunshine Coast expedition and I had heard nothing from Matt. I thought that he would have called me after the expedition but it was obvious that he missed on my indicated interest at becoming a full-fledged BFRO investigator in British Columbia. I continued to talk off and on with Tony. He was still having lots of activity in Sechelt, which was good to hear. But to answer my question, he didn't know how an individual could become an investigator other than by going through Matt, who at the time was a veritable willo'wisp. You knew that he was around but you just couldn't catch him.

A couple more weeks went by before I finally made contact with Matt and when I did it was a case of... Blaine? Blaine who? What with the traveling to various expeditions and the administration of the BFRO it's a wonder that Matt can remember any of the multitude of people that he meets out in the field. After refreshing his memory of who I was, we discussed the possibility of me becoming an investigator. Up until this point it had been an American investigator who had sifted through the witness reports submitted from British Columbia. I felt that I had a lot to offer the organization with my military experience and my current schooling in the field of criminology. I don't know what convinced him, but Matt must have agreed with this train of thought because I was soon accessing the raw reports submitted to the BFRO. Once I was able to see behind the public web page, a whole new world was opened up to me. What amazed me the most was the number of reports in B.C. that had gone unchecked for years. Looking at the long list before me I felt that the best way to proceed would be to start with the older reports at the bottom of the list and work my way up to the newer ones at the top.

Over the next few months I plowed my way through the inventory. I began phoning witnesses, emailing them and tracking them down through their various changes of address. In my heart I felt that if just one of them had seen something special that could be brought forward in a finished report, it might even be enough to revolutionize how the naysayers viewed the subject.

To complete each report, several conditions must be met. Most important is the oral interview with the witness. This must be done either in person or via the telephone. If a witness cannot be spoken to directly, then his or her report will go nowhere, which is to say it cannot be completed to a point where it may be published on the website. I know that some investigators will dump a report into an unusable file if they can't contact the submitter. I try to complete as much of each report that I take on because, even without the interview, it may contain anecdotal information that may shed some light on other incidents in the same area. I also try to keep track of these unfinished reports in the hope that someday in the future I will have the opportunity to speak to the primary witness and then finish off the report. Believe it or not, this does happen on a fairly regular basis. Just because a person submits a report doesn't mean that he will be sitting around pensively waiting for the phone to ring or for his computer to announce "You've got mail". Daily life goes on. Good luck trying to reach the long haul trucker or the waitress on night shift. Additionally, the reporter may only contact with the investigator when he or she is alone to avoid being embarrassed in front of his coworkers, family or friends.

These conditions have become evident time and again in a number of the reports that I have completed. On Vancouver Island, there was a case of a possible stalking where a sasquatch had shadowed a pair of biologists as they conducted a survey around a lake.[53] That case had sat partially completed for months. I finally ended up contacting the witness's parents who informed me that their son would be home for a holiday sometime in the near future. It was only then that I could finally verify his submission and complete the report. Another file contained information from a hunter in Alberta who had watched a sasquatch walk a hundred yards along a mountain ridge and go into the safety of a tree line.[54] That particular individual worked at a remote northern location where there was little or no digital access with the outside world and as a result he was finally interviewed five or six months after I started working on his report. To cope with a situation like this I usually leave a simple voicemail and / or email requesting the submitter set a time or date when we could discuss the report.

Do a lot of reports go uncompleted? Yes they do. As previously mentioned, any report that I cannot verbally verify will only go so far. People move, phone numbers and emails change or get disconnected, couples divorce and witnesses move on or die. The list of reasons why a report is never finished is virtually endless. It must also be understood that the number of negating factors will rise exponentially as the time between the date of submission and when an investigator first makes contact with the witness increases. As a new investigator the lure of jumping on a submission as soon as it hit the New Reports Page was very strong. A fresh report means that the evidence and the witness' ability to remember specific details of the incident will be much clearer. At least you would think so but this is not always the case.

Experience has shown that a person, any person, who has actually seen a sasquatch will be able to remember the details of the sighting even thirty years later as vividly as the day that it had happened. If you don't believe me then go attend a presentation on the sasquatch where Bob Gimlin is a guest speaker. Listen to him as he relives the incident when he and his late partner, Roger Patterson, surprised a female sasquatch walking along Bluff Creek in California. I would dare to say that after more than forty years he has not forgotten a single lick of what had happened on that eventful day.

One of my very first investigations was a report from Courtenay, BC[55] where a lady, as a young girl, had spotted something large and human-like standing in a ditch across the street from her home. Her report, submitted many years after the fact, said that it was very late at night and her family had just returned home from visiting some relatives in a nearby town. She remembered that the moon was shining brightly and her father had been trying to get them into the house as they had to get up for school later that same morning, when something caught her eye.

"Dad, what's that?"

"Dad?"

"Dad! What's that over there?"

After a quick glance in the direction she was pointing, her father, concerned for their safety, ordered them all to get quickly into the house. The witness told me that the process of pulling in the driveway, getting out of the car and into the house took several minutes. During that time the creature had stood stock-still while trying to hide behind a hydro pole.

You can tell by the low report number that hers was one of the first reports submitted to the BFRO. Before I got a hold of it three other investigators had tried their luck at completing it without any success. Needless to say my own investigation took several months of dogged snooping to find her. It had been nearly 40 years since the sighting and during the course of the interview I found her memory to be as sharp as a tack. After answering my questions she began to recall several other disturbing details that she had previously believed to be unrelated to her sighting when in fact they actually strengthened her case.

One winter morning the witness looked out from her upstairs bedroom window and saw that during the night her neighborhood had received a fresh dump of snow. Everywhere she looked it was like a pristine blanket of cotton except for a line of large widely spaced footprints that marched their way across her yard. Initially, she thought that one of her brothers had been playing out in the snow but she soon came to realize that it would have been impossible for them to straddle the four-foot stride length without disturbing the snow in between the individual steps.

As shocking as this may have been, she went on to tell me how her neighbors would occasionally have a sheep go missing from their flock and how they always laid the blame on her dogs. The witness was adamant that her dogs never left the confines of the yard unless someone was with them and they were never out of the house at night.

Could a sasquatch have stolen her neighbor's sheep? It was possible. But before jumping to any conclusions, I thought it more important to look towards the more logical culprits. Today, just as it was back in 1968, the known large predators on Vancouver Island consist of wolves and cougars and bears. Bears, despite being omnivorous, don't usually prey on livestock unless they are really, really hungry. Wolves will prey on a flock of sheep and so will a cougar. However, an attack by any one of these three predators would most certainly have caused the flock to raise an alarm loud enough to wake the shepherd. By looking at this situation logically a few points have lead me to believe that a resident 'squatch may have been picking off the occasional sheep.

First, there was never any blood nor a carcass found. Wolves almost always feed where they kill their prey. To my knowledge they do not waste precious energy removing their victim to a secluded spot for consumption. However, a cougar will stash its victim in a place that is inaccessible to its competitors and allow it to feed in peace. But, even with a cougar kill there would still be some blood evidence present.

The second piece of evidence was the secure fence line. The witness could not recall a time when the neighbor's fence was found to be broken after a sheep was discovered missing. If a bear had gone in to dine on some tender lamb chops not only would the fence have been broken but also there would have been nothing to prevent the rest of the flock from escaping afterwards.

Another reason for a sheep going missing may have been the actions of some teenage miscreants. For the sole purpose of being a butthead some local kid could have easily opened the gate and shooed a sheep out of the pen. But why would he stop at just one little lamb? Any juvenile delinquent worth his salt would have let every one of them out by opening the gate and letting them wander out on their own accord. I don't think this was the case either.

And a final point is that despite her assertions to the contrary, could the witness' dogs have killed the neighbor's sheep? They most certainly could have. Domesticated dogs, especially those living in more rural

areas, such as on farms or acreages, have been known to form a pack and run down neighboring livestock or a deer. However, once they accomplish this biologically driven primal goal, they rarely complete the task by feeding on their kill. They simply gambol about the carcass before heading home to once again become the family pet. Like a canine Dr. Jekyll and Mr. Hyde, their killer instinct now masked by puppy smiles and wagging tails. So, if the witness' dogs had harassed the neighbor's flock, I am sure that the associated noise, an uneaten carcass and any dried sheep blood on the muzzles of the accused would have been enough to convict them. However, none of this was in evidence.

Now that all of the known possibilities have been eliminated, it only stood to reason that it may have been a sasquatch that was preying on the sheep, especially since the witness had seen one across the street from her house. Personally, I believe the sheep wouldn't have raised much of an alarm either. Their natural predators are four footed not bipedal. To a domesticated sheep an approaching sasquatch would probably have appeared to be just another farmer, only taller, until it was too late. A quick snap of the neck, a twist of the leg and that's all. No noise, no blood and no broken fence either since the big fella can simply step over it.

To fully appreciate the fantastic opportunity that Matt Moneymaker has given me, I have had to adopt three axioms to be an investigator within the BFRO. The first comes from the late Dr. Grover Krantz who coined the phrase "believing is seeing". Thom Powell recorded in his book, *The Locals,* that by this statement Dr. Krantz implied "that the evidence supporting the Bigfoot hypothesis is seen by many people who visit the woods or live in its margins (but) they don't grasp the evidence they are seeing, though, because they never took seriously the possibility that Bigfoots might exist"[56]. The second is from Sir Arthur Conan Doyle's detective sleuth Sherlock Holmes who stated "that when you exclude the impossible whatever remains, however improbable, must be the truth"[57]. Both of these two ideas are pretty straightforward. However, the third axiom is much more thought-provoking and has been adopted by many scientists as a means to logically approach a subject. Called Occam's Razor, after the 14th Century logician and friar William of Occam, it states that "entities should not be multiplied unnecessarily" or "if you have two theories which both explain the observed facts then you should use the simplest (theory) until more evidence comes along."[58] In the military this is often referred to as the KISS principle, which stands for Keep It Simple, Stupid.

When these three ideas are placed together in some semblance of a working order I, as a BFRO investigator, am able to identify or recognize sasquatch evidence when I see it after which I am able to eliminate the impossible before paring down my observations to its simplest truth. Viewed in this manner, these concepts support and strengthen each other while still leaving room for the acceptance of additional facts. It is very important to remember that the accumulated worldly knowledge on the subject of the sasquatch is, in all probability, only the tip of the proverbial iceberg. In other words, what we don't know is far greater than what we think we know. I honestly believe that public acceptance and, more importantly, recognition by the scientific community will only be through the continued investigation of the reported sasquatch sightings by inquisitive individuals, the dedicated members of the BFRO and by any scientist who is willing to risk going out on a very shaky limb. These people are not out for glory or riches and those who are in it for the money, simply do not last very long in the field as their greed eventually gets the better of them by tainting their investigations with stench of ill-gotten gains. Think about this for a minute. Say that you had a sighting or an unusual experience while out in the woods. Whom would you rather talk to? An individual who wants to be paid to come and check out your story only to twist it around to better corner his market share. Or, someone who wants nothing but the facts and who protects your right to privacy by protecting your anonymity.

Looking after those who submit reports to the website is a cornerstone of the BFRO and I can assure you that any member who cannot adhere to this simple principle would soon find himself or herself on the outside looking in. The reasoning behind this is very simple. Humans are, by nature, a pretty chatty species. For some unknown reason, we always feel compelled to tell someone something, to confess that we have been a witness to something special or out of the ordinary despite the fact that we know that individuals who have come forward with their reports of sightings, vocalizations and tracks are quite often ridiculed by their peers.

'Hey, Bob. Guess what I saw?'

'What?'

'A bigfoot.'

'Suuuure you did.'

'I really did see one, Bob. Last Friday after work, I was heading out to the cottage and as I got to that hairpin corner, this tall dark thing stepped out of the ditch right in front of me. I almost ditched the car myself.'

'Yeah right! Get any pictures?'

'No, really! I saw one!'

'Hey guys! Guess what? Bob said he saw a bigfoot.'

'Are you sure that it wasn't that big black bear that's been hanging around the park? Bob, was this before or after you had some of your homemade beer?'

What to call them?

If a group of cows is a herd and a group of baboons is a parliament there should be a name for a group of sasquatch. In keeping with the primate theme I have decided to refer to a group of sasquatch as a troop.

The decision to garner a witness's privacy is an ethical one that must be considered by every investigator and doing so only increases the likelihood that if another incident does occur, the individual will feel confident in calling you because there is a level of trust that exists between you.

I can assure you that by revealing their identity any subsequent sightings will go unreported and therefore will not be investigated. The need for this level of trust is most important if cases of habituation between humans and sasquatch are to be discovered. I say discovered because I have no doubt that cases of habituation have been taking place and it is unimaginable that they have not been taking place. I am sure that somewhere on the North American continent, in some little backwater out of the way place, a human family has been having almost daily peaceful interactions with a sasquatch or maybe even a number of them. Some of these incidents have been reported but I think the vast majority of them are unknown simply because the people want to be left alone. And they want the sasquatches to be left alone. Think what the media circus would be like at your house if suddenly there were photographic evidence showing that your kids played kick ball with a bigfoot. It would be absolute pandelerium.

In dealing with the people who are connected to this sub-culture, these Bigfoot Investigators, especially those in the BFRO, it has become very apparent to me that it will be us who will eventually find the solution to this hairy conundrum and not the trained scientists! Why do I say this? The answer is really quite simple. It's because we are not resting on our proverbial laurels like a lot of the academics do. That's why. As investigators, we are the ones who are out in the weeds looking for the evidence, talking to witnesses and asking the thought-provoking questions.

Gee whiz, Blaine, what kind of thought-provoking questions?

Well, since you asked…other than some of the more obvious questions such as, what does a sasquatch eat or how does it communicate, some investigators that I know, have started to ask about seasonal migration routes, the sociology of a sasquatch troop and the length of a sasquatch gestation period. This last question came from a friend of mine.

Sasquatch Math

Cindy became a BFRO investigator after the Vancouver Island expedition in 2007. She has a diploma in Animal Sciences with strengths in biology and chemistry. Cindy is an outdoors person who probably knows more about animal traits than most big game hunters do. On a recent visit to see her, Cindy said that she had been checking on the number of reports from across the Pacific Northwest and she was wondering why there seemed to be more vocalizations reported during the late summer and early fall as opposed to the rest of the year. Personally, I hadn't thought about this characteristic but now that she mentioned it, I became very intrigued. Cindy went on to explain that she believes that a seasonal increase in sasquatch vocalizations being reported may be a possible result of a sasquatch gestation period. Call me crazy but I really think that she is onto something and unlike a lot of other bigfoot theories, it was really quite easy to follow along as she filled me in on her hypothesis.

We already know that many large animals living in a temperate environment tend to breed at only one specific time of the year. Through some Darwinian evolutionary process this trait has been genetically wired in order for the offspring to take full advantage of the abundance of food and the fair climate. Deer, elk, and moose all mate in the late fall to early winter and give birth to their young in the late spring to early summer. Once weaned from their mother's milk, baby fawns and calves will have an abundance of new plants to browse on. Bears, on the other hand, are slightly different. Black bears breed in the early summer, late June or early July, and with a gestation period of about 210 days the cubs will be born the following January or February. "This may seem like a very long gestation period, but in fact the embryos stop growing a few days after fertilization and do not implant in the uterus until the beginning of the denning period in early November. This pause in the embryo's development, called "delayed implantation," is common to all bear species" [59] and these new cubs will only weigh about eight ounces (half a pound) at birth, which is 310 times less than the sow. By comparison, a human infant at birth is about 12 times the mass of a bear cub.[60]

Cindy and I also discussed the following hypothesis: Given that the sasquatch is believed to be a large unknown primate, would its gestation period be similar to that of the large known primates, including humans? It would seem reasonable but how would a person go about proving or defending this opinion? After a couple of weeks spent mulling things over, Cindy's question really started to bother me and I decided to do a little more digging to find a possible explanation. By simply Googling the phrase 'animal gestation periods' I arrived at a website belonging to Thayer Watkins, a gentleman who just happens to teach economics at San Jose State University.[61] I know what you are thinking. What the hell does economics have to do with the gestation of animals that are not usually intended for the market place? Being an economics professor, Mr. Watkin's forte is in dealing with numbers and there appears to be a mathematical formula that actually demonstrates the relationship between the size of the animal and the length of its gestation period. I don't know if he discovered this formula or if he posted it on his site just for interest's sake because it uses a logistical algorithm. For those of us who barely squeaked through high school algebra, it might be a bit difficult to comprehend but all you have to do is simply push the 'log' button on your calculator to figure this out. Mr. Watkins' formula looks like this:

Log (Gestation) = 2.075 + 0.189(log (Weight)

This equation is actually pretty simple. You can either solve it for the length of gestation or reverse the equation and solve it for the weight of the mother. Either way, in order to complete the equation you have to know the value of at least one of these variables. The most readily available value would be the mother's weight and, according to Watkins, the female body weight would be the body weight without fat represented in kilograms.[62] The reason kilograms are used in the equation is because metric measurements are easily divisible by base ten.

Sounds simple. So, let's go ahead and plug in some numbers, shall we? If the average pregnant human female, without any body fat, weighed about 50 kilos, the gestation equation would be thus:

Log (Gestation) = 2.075 + 0.189(log (Weight)

Log (gestation) = 2.075 + 0.189(log (50)

Log (gestation) = 2.075 + 0.189(1.698)

Log (gestation) = 2.075 + 0.320

Log (gestation) = 2.395

Gestation = 248 days

There is an inherent problem in that we already know from experience that human gestation is, on average, about 266 days. That's an eighteen-day difference between our solution and the statistical average. This difference could be explained if several incalculable factors such as diet, exercise or personal habits such as smoking are taken into consideration. But, the prime factor is the value or amount of the female body weight used in the formula. Because we know the average gestation period for a human fetus, the formula can be resolved for the value of body weight instead.

If - log (Gestation) = 2.075 + 0.189(log (Weight)

Then - log (weight) = (log (gestation) - 2.075) / 0.189

Log (weight) = (2.425 – 2.075) / 0.189

Log (weight) = 0.35 / 0.189

Log (weight) = 1.852

Weight = 71.09 kg or 156 lb.

I believe that this recalculated weight would appear to be more in line with that of the average pregnant human female, without body fat, before giving birth. This would reflect her body mass plus that of the fetus and any extra muscle that she might have gained during the pregnancy.

The point of this mathematical exercise is to demonstrate the ability of calculating the potential gestation period for a sasquatch. To do so accurately we would need a specimen, which we just don't have. However, on October 20, 1967 Roger Patterson and Bob Gimlin did not encounter just any sasquatch at Bluff Creek. What they saw was a *female* sasquatch, a fact easily proven by observing her swinging breasts on the film, and "from the impressions left on the sandbar they guessed her weight at about 350 pounds."[63]

This weight estimate may not be all that far off because William Roe stated that the creature he had observed in 1957 was "probably weighing somewhere near three hundred pounds"[64] and in a follow-up letter he added that "if this animal should have been seven feet tall, it would have weighed close to five hundred pounds."[65] The only other historical mention on the weight of an identified female sasquatch that I could find, comes from Albert Ostman. As you know, Albert claimed to have been kidnapped and held hostage by a family of 'squatches. According to his description this troop was comprised of an adult male and an adult female, apparently a father and mother, and two juveniles, a male and a female. In his affidavit, Ostman gave no indication as to how old he believed the younger one to be but he stated that the chest on the younger one was "flat like a boy – no development like young ladies."[66] I believe that his observations would indicate that she was probably pre-pubescent and may not have been capable of producing offspring. In regards to the older female, Ostman described her as somewhere between 40 and 70 years old in age, standing over seven feet tall and weighing between 500 and 600 pounds.[67] If Ostman's physical description was accurate then this individual may no longer have been capable of breeding successfully.

Based on Ostman's observations, let us consider that if the weight of a female sasquatch who is capable of breeding is in the neighborhood of three hundred pounds or maybe even four hundred pounds, in the formula this would be one hundred fifty to one hundred eighty-two kilograms. Once these numbers are plugged into Watkins's formula, it is possible to arrive at a probable gestation range of three hundred and six to three hundred eighteen days for a typical sasquatch pregnancy.

Log (Gestation) = 2.075 + 0.189(log (Weight)
Log (Gestation) = 2.075 + 0.189(log (182)
Log (Gestation) = 2.075 + 0.189(2.260)
Log (Gestation) = 2.075 + 0.4271
Log (Gestation) = 2.5021
Gestation = 317.75 days

Are these numbers too far out into left field? I think that as preliminary numbers, they are within the ballpark but are certainly not definitive by any means. You must remember that all of this is just speculation on my part. Until an actual sasquatch specimen can be scientifically studied, there is no way of really knowing even the most basic of biological facts such as size, diet or longevity. However, this does not mean that we have to sit on our collective academic asses and wait for the body to drop into our lap. By taking a closer look at the world's largest three primates there are other statistics that can be viewed that may support this conclusion.

According to the wonderful people at Sea World, an adult female orangutan will weigh between 30 and 50 kilograms (66 to 110 pounds)[68] and it can live for more than forty years. This does not mean an orangutan mom will be pushing out a dozen babies in her lifetime. Far from it. Female orangutans will give birth to their first infant at about fifteen years of age and "with the maternal investment in raising young, there is usually an eight to ten year span between births."[69] The gestation period for a pregnant orangutan is about two hundred fifty-five to two hundred sixty days or about eight and a half months, after which the mother will give birth to an infant weighing only one and a half kilograms or three and a third pounds. In the wild, a healthy mother orangutan will probably only give birth to three or four offspring during her lifetime.

The weight of an adult female chimpanzee ranges between 26 and 50 kilograms (57 to 110 pounds) and its life span can reach upwards of sixty years in the wild.[70] Females enter into puberty near the age of seven and on average will give birth to their first infant at age fifteen.[71] The gestation period is about two hundred and thirty days but this can fluctuate up to thirty days plus or minus. Like orangutans, chimpanzees usually give birth to a single infant who will weigh in at about two kilograms, and there is span of three to six years between the birth of one offspring and the next.[72] The difference in the rate of birth between these two species may be due to the fact that chimpanzees have more of a social structure to their lives than the orangutan. Living in a social group allows the offspring to progress at a much greater pace than a single mother scenario and once it can provide for itself in a limited fashion, the mother is then able to concentrate on reproducing once again.

A female gorilla enters into sexual maturity at around seven to eight years of age but it does not normally reproduce until it is ten years old. The gestation period is about eight and one half months which, like the other great apes, usually results in the birth of a single infant.[73]

If all of this holds true for the advanced primates that we already know about, why could it not hold true for the ones that we know very little about? When family groups of sasquatch have been observed there is usually a fair bit of difference in the size between the adults, the juveniles and any toddlers or infants that may be in the troop. From the earliest reports, Ostman's affidavit indicates that there was clearly an age and size difference between the male and the female juvenile sasquatch. As I had mentioned earlier, his description leads me to believe that the younger male may have been closer to adulthood, while the female may not have reached adolescence. But this is not the only report where both adult and juvenile sasquatch had been seen. Dr. John Bindernagel and John Green have both chronicled the troop of sasquatch that was seen by Glen Thomas in Oregon's Mount Hood National Forest.[74]

In the mid 1960's, Mr. Thomas was a professional logger. One day he decided to go for a short hike. Following a trail, he discovered some rocks that had been recently turned over. He knew this because all the other rocks were still wet from the prevailing fog and yet the newly exposed undersides of these were still dry. Continuing along the trail, he suddenly came upon three human- like creatures. Taking cover behind a small tree, Mr. Thomas watched as a male, a female and a baby, which was no taller than her hips, hunting in amongst the rocks for rodents with great agility. At some point, Mr. Thomas realized that he had been detected since all three sasquatch suddenly became alert to their surroundings and then moved quietly to a safer location behind some nearby trees. He noted that when they left, they moved in an upright fashion with the mother holding the infant to her body as she ran.[75]

These are some of the ideas, concepts and puzzles that investigators are faced with. But just as each new discovery answers one question, it inevitably raises a dozen more. And so it should. You must remember that while many sasquatch investigators are professionals in some kind of field, the vast majority of them are not scientists and evidence observed or collected is often not done using scientific protocols. This is a point that Dr. Bindernagel is all too quick to point out. Due to our lack of scientific training the conclusions or answers to the questions raised are taken with a grain of salt. For example, from being in the field we have observed that a sasquatch has a great amount of flexibility in its toes, which answers the question of why individual tracks may differ within the same track way. On the other hand, a trained scientist would look at this same question and, if he gives you an answer at all, it will probably involve some highbrow lingo on how the variation in tarsal positioning is due to the greater amount flexation in the dorsal and anterior tendons while the fibrous bands of muscle are laterally supporting the tarsals.

Do we really need the scientists?

Even though we, the laymen, are the ones spending a lot of effort, not to mention the money for fuel, equipment and personal time tramping about in the weeds to learn more about this mysterious primate, we still need those individuals with letters behind their names because that's what provides validity for the general public. We especially need those individuals who have decided to stretch their necks before the Axe of Ridicule that is so often wielded by their peers. Believe it or not, there are some scientists who just don't care what their peers think. In his book Thom Powell wrote, "Dr. Grover Krantz was well aware of the professional penalty for taking Bigfoots seriously. His willingness to weigh the evidence brought him personal ridicule and loss of promotion at Washington State University."[76] Ostracized by his peers, Dr. Krantz felt that the reconciliation of the sasquatch issue was more important than kowtowing before the establishment.

Bravo Dr. Krantz!

Dr. Jeff Meldrum has also faced criticism from the scientific community for his pursuit of bigfoot. He went out on a limb and wrote "Sasquatch: Legend meets Science" which, by the way, is a fantastic book that should be on the required reading list for anyone interested in this subject. In regards to Dr. Meldrum, Dr. George Schaller wrote the following:

> "Dr. Meldrum is a scientist, an expert in human locomotor adaptations. In *Sasquatch: Legend Meets Science* he examines all evidence critically, not to force a conclusion, but to establish a baseline of facts upon which further research can depend. His science is not submerged by opinion and dogmatic assumption. With objectivity and insight, he analyzes evidence from tracks, skin ridges on the soles of the feet, film footage and DNA, and he compares it to that of primates and various other species. He disentangles fact from anecdote, supposition, and wishful thinking, and concludes that the search for yeti and Sasquatch is a valid scientific endeavor."[77]

While on an excursion in northern California, Dr. Meldrum had his own encounter with something that had "left sixteen-inch footprints, apparently walked on two legs, dexterously opened backpacks, rifled its contents without mark of tooth or claw, and accurately lobbed a rock"[78] in the direction of his party. As a result, Dr. Meldrum concluded that he "would have to pursue the question of the sasquatch to its resolution, one way or another."[79]

Thanks for joining the party Dr. Meldrum.

Dr. John Bindernagel is another scientist who has spent a great deal of his lifetime doggedly pursuing the sasquatch. Moreover, he has been trying to make the public more aware of its existence. According to John, the biologist not the Apostle, he was in the midst of his wildlife biology courses at the University of Guelph when he happened across an article detailing a sighting from northern British Columbia. When John asked his professor whether there was any additional information about this strange ape-like animal, he was told that it was just make-believe and that he should forget the matter.[80] This exchange took place in 1963, and although his career has taken him all around the globe, Dr. Bindernagel maintains that there must be something to the sasquatch phenomena. Maybe it's because he knows there must be something that is making all of the tracks or maybe it's because he finally saw one himself.

While being interviewed by Matthew Kruchak for the Times Colonist, Dr. Bindernagel was asked "What would it be like to live your entire life without seeing (a) Sasquatch?"[81] To which John replied, "I've seen one."[82]

And that was all he said.

Well thanks for telling us about your good fortune, John!

I find that this is a problem with a lot of scientists. For all of the times that we (laymen) have shared witness information and the details from being out in the field, you would assume that when a scientist like John has his own personal sighting he would at least pass along some amplifying details to the rest of us.

No.

Thanks for sharing, John.

In an effort to find additional answers to questions pertaining to the sasquatch, I decided to enroll in an anthropology course offered through the University of Manitoba. I wanted to learn about the primate evolutionary tree and where the sasquatch may hang from it. All in all it was an informative course but I did have some difficulty with my instructor. One of the course assignments was to find an anthropology paper that had been published online, read it and then write a review of the paper for the rest of the class to examine. Before I had a chance to post anything, some students were posting their assignments and it soon became clear that many of my fellow classmates were a lazy lot. I believe that their choice of articles was done thoughtlessly and without considering that this was an opportunity to inform the other students of something they may not have seen before. Instead, with the same articles being assessed over and over, it was clear that many of them had simply Googled the phrase "anthropology papers" and then picked one of the first three listed. Not wanting to be a part of the herd, I decided to throw my class a curve ball by reviewing Dr. Meldrum's paper entitled "*New Perspectives on the Evolution of Bipedalism*"(2004)[83].

In his article, Dr. Meldrum explains the characteristics of the primate foot and how bipedal propulsion works with a foot that is flexible. Dr. Meldrum states that this flexible footstep takes place at the position known as the mid-tarsal break, which allows the foot to "bend around the axis of the transverse tarsal joint".[84] A prime example of this would be the foot of a chimpanzee. If you have ever seen a chimp either in photos or on film you would have seen that this adaptation aided the animal in climbing trees and it can carry objects with its feet. Humans no longer have this flexible foot because "after the transition to habitual bipedalism, these grasp-climbing adaptations were compromised by the evolution of the longitudinal arch, which permits increased mechanical advantage of the flexors of the ankle and improved endurance for long-distance walking and running."[85] Dr. Meldrum goes on to point out how "early (3.5 million years ago) hominoid footprints from the Laetoli excavation, confirm midfoot flexibility, including repeated suggestion of an associated pressure ridge"[86]. Evidence of what created this mid-tarsal break was demonstrated when a "reconstruction of the *Australopithecus afarensis* foot skeleton was superimposed over the Laetoli footprint".[87] Dr. Meldrum then presents findings from the Patterson – Gimlin film where the subject, a large upright hominoid, was filmed walking along a creek bed with a bent-kneed flat-footed step, while leaving behind a series of deep impressions that exhibit a distinct pressure ridge that has been interpreted as a mid-tarsal break.[88]

Even if you don't believe the sasquatch to be real, Dr. Meldrum's insightful and well-written paper introduces his interpretation of how prehistoric evidence, found at a well-known archaeological site, relates to physical evidence found in the Pacific Northwest. My review of his online paper wasn't just for the benefit of the instructor but to convey something new in the field of anthropology to my fellow students. I had expected a minimal response from my peers but I wasn't prepared for the drumming handed out by my instructor. She wrote that I had discussed the article well, that it was a bit too long and it would have been better if I had "omitted the last paragraph where you seem to have been led astray by the lunatic fringe and sasquatches again."[89] This comment from my instructor left me stunned. Clearly, she wasn't calling me a lunatic but rather those who had lead me astray with their belief in the sasquatch were. And who would that be? Maybe she was thinking that it was all of the witnesses who had seen a 'squatch? Could it be the First Nations members for whom this is part of their culture? How about Dr. Meldrum? Possibly, since he wrote the article in the first place.

With nothing but fear and common sense to prevent me from defending myself, I sat down and wrote a rebuttal letter informing my instructor that I felt insulted by her comments and how I believed others should be informed of her close-mindedness. For a split second I thought she might respond. You would think that an instructor, any instructor, would or should respond to a student's rebuttal. Maybe, in her mind, she believed that she didn't have to respond because her lofty position as a Distance Education Instructor at the University of Manitoba. After waiting a reasonable amount of time, a week or so, there was still no response from my instructor, I forwarded her comments and my rebuttal letter to the head of the U of M Anthropology Department. As I recall the email went out on a Friday and by the following Monday I had a reply from the professor.

"Thank you for forwarding me your letter. It seems to me that your point is a relevant and very important one. Has (the instructor) contacted you yet to have a chance to respond? I will speak with her directly, as the Department values highly the promotion of critical thinking and open engagement with/ from a diversity of ideas and perspectives."

Surprisingly, the Department Head also invited me to have a sit-down meeting with my instructor. If I had been living in Winnipeg, Manitoba I would have immeasurably enjoyed presenting my instructor with a mountain of the most current evidence available, including the track casts that I have collected, and challenge her to prove to me why the sasquatch could not possibly exist. Unfortunately, I had neither the time nor the funds to fly half-way across Canada to confront her.

But, I wish I had.

X's and Arches

As an investigator, I have often been asked about tree structures that have been attributed to the sasquatch. These structures are commonly referred to as X's and arches. Are the forces of nature forming these structures? In some cases the answer is yes. I am sure that if you were to take a look through the forests and woodlands, you would assuredly find similar structures that are the effects of wind, snow and wood-rot. These forces can cause trees to bend or twist and fall against one another. If the wind can be strong enough to blow apart a house, then it is certainly strong enough to bring down a tree and lean it against another.

This is commonly referred to as a wind-blow. Additionally, where a tree has succumbed to the ravages of disease or insect activity, it may fall against another tree that is already leaning over. The main difference between this and a structure believed to be built by a sasquatch is the fact that wind-blown trees all tend to fall in the same direction with the larger ones pulling down the smaller ones, whereas tree signs such as X's or arches have been purposely built. Of course, the specific purpose for such a structure would be anyone's guess.

August 2007 I was camping with my parents at Hidden Lake, BC. I had not been there since 1978 and it was exciting to be back at this lake. Not just for the personal nostalgia but because I had also completed the investigation of several BFRO reports from this area. It was intriguing that nearly fifty years had passed since Mrs. Bellvue's sighting and there was still ongoing sasquatch activity. If we had been camping alone, I would have done some wood knocks and vocalizations just to see if I could elicit any responses but since there were quite a number of other people camping at the lake, I felt that it was prudent not to scare the hell out of them. However, a good place to look for some secondary evidence would be around the smaller lake that sat at the top of the mountain due to the lack of human traffic.

A wheeled skidder is commonly used in logging operations. It is an articulated vehicle with plenty of clearance to go over rocks and tree stumps. Mounted with various accessories it has the ability to create its own roads in the forest.

Located three or four miles farther down the road from Hidden Lake is Baird Lake. It sits at 2650 feet above sea level, which is about 700 feet higher than Hidden Lake. One afternoon, when the fish weren't biting and while my Dad was having a nap, I tossed my two sons into the truck and headed off up the mountain. During the drive, the first thing that I had noticed was that the road to the upper lake had been greatly improved since the last time I had traveled it. Years ago the road up to Baird Lake was not much more than a skidder trail and only a serious 4 x 4 truck or a motorbike would have been capable of making the trek up the mountain. But now the road was smooth enough that a Honda Civic would have little difficulty traveling on it. My concern was that the ease of access may have allowed the public to encroach on the available sasquatch habitat and I may not find any secondary evidence in the form of X's, arches, structures or tree breaks.

It had not rained in the area in over a week so there was little chance of spotting any distinctive tracks on the road, but then again I was looking into the woods for arches and X's. On the slow drive to the lake I had seen nothing inside the tree line on the left-hand side of the road that would indicate that a sasquatch might have been nearby. Once I had reached the shore of the lake, I turned around. This would allow me to view the opposite side of the road on my return trip down the mountain. I had not gone more than 200 yards down the road at the most when I saw what appeared to be an X. It was uphill on the left-hand of the road. Although the bush was surprisingly thick, I had a clear view of the structure but only from a specific position on the road. If I moved as much as ten feet, either forward or backward, it simply disappeared from my sight, melding into the background clutter of branches and leaves.

After I parked the truck off to one side of the road my sons and I bailed out to take a closer look at the structure. I slowly approached the X looking for any tell-tale tracks or signs of recent activity but with the sustained high temperatures the moss, which normally would be resiliently water-logged, was so desiccated that my footsteps crushed the delicate plants to a powder.

Looking back towards the road from the X there was a clear path or a route, rather like a laneway, that continued on the opposite side of the road and lead down to the lake. I went down this path but I could not find any other tree signs that had been constructed. Once I had reached the lake I turned around and looked back up the hill. The X was plainly visible against the background of vertical standing trees. Was this structure visible from above its position as well as below? It most certainly was. However, when the X was viewed from a position of 90 degrees to either side it was not distinguishable from the regular forest trash.

As investigators in the field, many of us have seen X's set into the woods. The reason for their creation has never really been clear but indications would demonstrate that the sasquatch might be building these X's as a means to identify locations that are important to them. I believe that this may be the case simply because they stand out so clearly against the background of vertical trees.

The clearest evidence that I can offer to support my claim that the X's may be used as some kind of a direction indicator is from BFRO report # 13390. In the photo provided by the witness you can see a clear line of suspected sasquatch tracks heading across a muddy field. Looking at the tree line in the background there is an X-like structure that is clearly visible to the left of the direction of travel. In a discussion with the witness he indicated that he must have surprised the sasquatch since the tracks did not reach the tree line at the opposite side of the field and instead turned 90 degrees to the left. The track stride length increased from 4 feet to close to 7 feet after it had turned to the left. This would indicate that whatever had made the tracks wanted to get out of that muddy field in a hurry. When I asked the witness why he felt that it had turned to the left as opposed to continuing straight ahead, he stated that from the point where it had turned there was some protective cover (trees and bushes) to the left side of the open field that were closer than the tree line in the back ground.

In conducting her own sasquatch research, British Columbia's BFRO investigator Cindy Dosen has photographed, documented and plotted many of the X's or structures that she has found. While pouring over the evidence Cindy realized that a number of these markers were lined up in such a way that they charted a path from one side of the valley to the other. Again, were they built to mark a path or were they created for some other purpose?

Cindy has the ability to get out into the field far more often than I and she has also been able to attend more expeditions than I have including those in Washington State. With this in mind, I asked her if she had seen as many structures in Washington as there were at home. I also asked her if there was a sizable human population within the expedition site. The answer to both of these questions was no. This information brings up the notion that in those areas with a higher density of human habitation the X's are being created to mark a pathway that would enable a sasquatch to best avoid human activity. It is plausible, isn't it? If you were a huge bipedal primate who wanted to remember the best way to go around farmyards and houses armed with guns, dogs and, God forbid, motion sensitive yard lights, it might be to your benefit to put up some kind of signage to assist you in your navigation, especially in the dark.

Another prevailing idea is that an X may indicate where not to go. I know of some reports where hikers have gone down a trail only to find an X of logs placed clearly across the path on their return journey. Was the X placed to tell people to stay out? Or, as suggested by another BFRO investigator, could it have been constructed to warn an infant or juvenile sasquatch that they could risk contact with humans if they were to go past the X? In his book, *Impossible Visits*, author Chris Noël documented how trees had been broken and placed across the primary path he had been travelling in order to access his research area. Instead of being fashioned into an X, Chris discovered that these two trees, "six or seven inches in diameter (had) been snapped cleanly in twin right angles and laid, a clear No Trespassing sign".[90]

Given a choice of all the possible shapes that could be easily built with a couple of logs, I would have to say that an X would be the most perfect because at night all trees look alike with smaller horizontal bars (branches) sticking out from thicker vertical bars (tree trunks). You can conduct your own X-test by placing two poles of similar diameter and of similar length at a 45-degree angle to the perpendicular trees at the edge of a tree line while positioning them at right angles to each other. Now stand back twenty, forty, or even sixty yards and you will see how easily your X can be spotted. Now try looking from inside the tree line, out towards the edge and I bet that your X will still be visible as a marker. When viewed by an eight-foot tall primate this marker would stand out like a proverbial sore thumb. Maybe, once someone actually witnesses a sasquatch building such a structure, then we will begin to understand what the real purpose is behind its construction.

The other type of structure that has, on occasion, been attributed to the sasquatch is the arched tree. Whenever I see one of these structures I have to ask myself two questions: why was it built in this location and what was the purpose behind its construction? I suppose the first question should be – Could some other natural force have created this structure? Arches are a very good example of a structure that can be the result of natural creation. Simply take a tall willowy tree of whatever species you like. It should be anywhere from ten to forty feet tall and with branches only at the very top of the tree to catch the snow. Allow the snow to pile up on those upper branches until enough weight accumulates as to bend the top of the tree down toward the ground until the trunk of the tree forms an arch. Depending on the thickness of the tree trunk, this naturally created arch may not occur after a single winter season but may require several successive snow loads before the tree is permanently bent. In the spring when the snow melts, the tree now, released from its burden, will try to return to its original vertical position.

The difference between a natural arch and one that may have been constructed by a sasquatch is the fact that the top of the tree has been pinned to the ground and is held in place by a number of logs or rocks or both. The truly significant point is that the articles used to secure the treetop are almost always not native to the location. It wasn't a wind blow that fell on top of a snow laden tree. No, in my opinion, these logs and rocks had been brought for the sole purpose of holding down the top of the tree to form the arch. Although it is possible for a person to construct structures similar to those attributed to an unrecognized primate, the one remaining question is why? Why would a person do such a thing? Generally speaking, people don't do things without a reason. They may do things without thinking them through, like when they've been drinking, but they will still have a reason as to why they did them. So, what would be the purpose or the benefit for a human to drag a pair of thirty-foot logs a mile or more from the nearest road and anchor them, without the mechanical aid of ropes or pulleys, up in the trees in such a manner that even the heaviest of windstorms could not dislodge them? The answer is…there isn't one!

On the BFRO website there is an interactive section, known as the Blue Forum[91], where ideas and questions can be raised between those who are interested in the sasquatch phenomena and BFRO members. This forum, like many others that can be found on the internet, is moderated to keep things on track and running smoothly. Recently a question cropped up that piqued my interest. The poster wondered how a sasquatch spent its waking hours.

In order to answer this question you would have to consider what a sasquatch would need to exist on a daily basis and how much time would be spent fulfilling those needs. As mentioned before, the requirements for the survival of any animal would include food, water and security. The BFRO and other sasquatch investigators have found many secluded spots providing the security and the resources that a 'squatch would need during the daylight hours. Yes, sasquatches are active during the daylight but assuredly they are more cautious around people than when it is nighttime because the darkness of night provides a sasquatch with a very large security blanket. Grazing animals spend more time on their feet obtaining their nutrition than those who hunt them. If you don't believe me, have a quick look at any National Geographic film featuring life on the African savannah. It will display thousands of four legged animals moving across the plain happily munching every green leafy substance in sight while the animals with the sharp teeth spend the majority of their time lounging about waiting for their table to be called. "Ah yes. Madame and Monsieur *Pantera Leo*. Here is your Gnu for Two. Served just as you requested. On the bone, with a side of carrion. Hold the salad"

It is commonly believed, at least by those of us in the field, that sasquatches are omnivores, meaning they harvest their food as both a grazer and a hunter and therefore the amount of time spent being active may vary with its diet for any given period of time. For a clear example of a seasonal dietary variation you only have to look at some of North America's largest known animals-the Alaskan brown bear (*Ursus arctos*) and the North American grizzly bear (*Ursus arctos horribilis*). Both of these fearsome creatures with their massive canines, bone crushing jaws and razor sharp claws, can kill a human with one swipe of a paw. But for all their ferocity, these bears are both omnivores that "derive up to 90% of their dietary food energy from vegetable matter".[92] It's hard to believe, but it's true. If it weren't for the time spent gorging on the spawning salmon or indulging themselves on any winter killed ungulates that they might find, bears would probably be classified as herbivores.

During a field study one scientist had observed grizzly bears spending a vast amount of time turning over rocks high up on a mountainside far above the tree line. It was long believed that these bears were hunting rodents like marmots or picas. However, the bear's activity never involved a chase of any sort, so whatever they were eating wasn't trying to run away. A closer investigation revealed the bears were munching on army cutworm moths. These moths can be found resting on the underside of rocks high on mountain slopes. At first it doesn't sound like much but an analysis of the moths' nutritional value shows that 40 to 72 percent of their body weight is comprised of fat.[93] These moths are so nutritious that "they become the richest food in the ecosystem, with more calories per gram than elk or deer meat"[94] and "observers have calculated that a silvertip grizzly bear can eat 2,500 moths an hour and 40,000 a day. A month of such steady feasting could fulfill nearly half the bear's energy requirements for the year."[95]

It is unclear as to precisely which foods make up a sasquatch's diet but if a varied food intake can support the growth of a bear to over 1000 pounds, it should be accepted that a similar omnivorous diet could sustain a population of large bipedal primates roaming the boreal forests of North America. The BFRO database keeps track of any food stuffs a sasquatch is observed to be eating or stealing from people. The First Nations people of the West Coast have consistently reported seeing sasquatches digging shellfish on beaches at low tide and stealing salmon from drying racks or smoke houses. In their statements, both Ostman and Roe said the sasquatches they saw ate leaves, green shoots, and ground nuts and at no time was meat of any kind seen consumed.[96] However, the most compelling indication concerning the make-up of a sasquatches diet often involves the theft of wild game that has been harvested by big game hunters. Every year the BFRO receives new reports from armed sportsmen who have seen one or more sasquatches at an extremely close range. Sometimes the two parties are close enough for the hunter to see the facial expression of the 'squatch before it walks off with the deer or wild pig that the hunter had just shot. As unnerving as this could be, one of the most harrowing incidents of sasquatch predation took place in the early days of the BFRO. Thom Powell wrote extensively of the incident in his book - *The Locals*.

Entitled "*Easy Pickin's*", Chapter 4 of *The Locals*, documents a situation involving a group of landowners in LeFlore County, Oklahoma who would regularly pit lamp for deer in the field near the house. The deer were initially attracted to the field to feed on the Austrian peas, planted by the landowners to support the deer population, thus allowing them to harvest the deer from the comfort of their back porch. The increased size of the deer herd did not go unnoticed by the sasquatches living nearby and they quickly learned that not all the deer that the hunters shot at were killed. In fact, most of the deer would simply stampede back to the safety of the woods where the 'squatches would be lying in wait to pick them off. If this wasn't bad enough, the inquisitive sasquatches also learned that stealing the cleaned venison from the big outdoor freezer eliminated the need to gut the deer themselves. In desperation the landowners called in the BFRO in the hope that the organization had a method of removing or eliminating the irritating bigfoots once and for all. They were sadly disappointed when it was discovered that the mandate of the BFRO is to investigate and preserve the species not harm them.[97]

Going back to the original question from the BFRO Blue Forum of "How does a sasquatch spend the hours in its day?" I would ask anyone who is a math whiz to try to devise a logarithm that could be used to satisfy the following question:

Where the daily amount of calories required (CR) to sustain an eight foot 600 + pound bipedal primate (again that would be anyone's guess) would be the mathematical constant. Then, by comparing the caloric value (CV) in the types of food available to how much time spent in gathering (TG) those foods will result in a calorie / time spent harvesting ratio. This ratio would allow you to accurately compare the various foods available for consumption by an omnivorous primate.

The number of hours in the day can be easily divided up into times of activity and inactivity. Activity is the waking hours when gathering food, travel and social interaction takes place, whereas inactivity is the physical rest the body requires. Simply subtracting the amount of time required to physically rest results in the time available to be active. The type of food gathered multiplied by the amount of time required to obtain the necessary daily caloric intake subtracted from the available waking hours would provide a result demonstrating the amount of free time (FT) when neither metabolic rest nor physical needs must be met. Mathematically speaking, I think the necessary equations could look something like this:

24 (Hours in the Day) – RT = TA

CV x TG = CR

(CV x TG) – TA = FT

In the wild, animals tend to consume only the calories required to maintain their daily activity level. If the calories required to maintain this level are greater than what can be gathered, the subject would go hungry or even starve to death.

However, if the calories required are met and a metabolic rest is not required, the subject would have the time and the energy to accomplish other desired tasks. In the case of a large bipedal primate, this time could be spent travelling to find a new food source, socially interacting with other members of its troop, manufacturing intriguing structures or scaring the hell out of campers at night.

Looking at the examples that already exist in nature could help to solve this equation. But, examples must include the daily dietary habits of herbivores, predators and omnivores in order for a wide variety of foods and the harvesting methods to be fully examined. Most animals spend their entire day in the pursuit of the calories required to sustain them leaving just enough time in the day for self- preservation from predators, competing for position within the social group and procreation. Herbivores, such as deer, bison, sheep and the like spend their days grazing, then ruminating, all the while keeping a wary eye out for something that wants to take a bite out of them. Predators like lions, cougars or wolves spend less time acquiring food and more time lying around digesting it because, if they are successful hunters, the food they eat will provide a large amount of calories for the amount of energy expended to gather it. This in turn leaves them with more free time for social interaction. Omnivores seem to have the best of both worlds, allowing them the freedom to choose or adaptively consume a wide variety of foods as they present themselves. When bears emerge from hibernation, they are confronted with fresh green grasses, which they will contentedly eat like cows grazing on a farmer's field. However, the scent of a deceased moose would certainly garner their attention, as will the salmon spawning in the rivers.

If it is an omnivore, the sasquatch would be able to capitalize on a wide selection of foods. It would be able to consume vegetation (grasses, mushrooms, berries, seeds) as it comes into season and sasquatches, acting either alone or as a group, would actively pursue prey animals. I contend that sasquatches have a higher intelligence level than most forest denizens. This is suggested by their actions with regards to human foods such as the opportunistic theft of downed game animals, the liberation of poultry or livestock without releasing the remainder of the flock or herd, and the ability to skilfully enter outbuildings in order to feed on grains without damaging the structure; not to mention raiding smokehouses and drying racks for stored fish.

As an investigator with the BFRO, I see my role as one that allows me to process the information gleaned from the reports submitted to the organization in order to propose analytical questions that hopefully, once solved, will gain additional insights into the sasquatch phenomena. Therefore, I ask you to please continue to report your sightings, your interactions and incidents to the BFRO where the investigators, like myself, will dauntingly complete your report in a timely manner. Always remember that your anonymity is assured because your personal information is always held in the strictest of confidence.

Is there a lesson in all of this? Of course there is. For anyone who happens to read this book, and it does not matter if you are a member of the BFRO or any other organization or even if you are an independent researcher, the following four truths must be observed:

1.Be true to your witnesses.

2.Be true to your organization.

3.Be true to your spouse or partner.

4.Be true to yourself.

If you, as an investigator and moreover as a person, cannot abide by these simple guidelines then you might as well be pissing into the wind. If your witnesses want to remain anonymous then grant them that security. If members of your organization ask for your assistance, you should provide it knowing that it will be returned in your time of need.

What does the future hold for the realm of sasquatch investigations? That is the $64,000 question. If you watch the news you will routinely see people coming forward saying they have the body of a bigfoot in a freezer or they know where a family of 'squatches are living or some such story. The big key to recognizing these charlatans for what they are is the fact that there will be a media circus circling them like a pack of wolves and the primary witnesses won't reveal anything for free.

On the legitimate side of the fence are the members of the BFRO and a number of smaller localized groups as well as individuals, like Thom Powell and Chris Noël, who quietly go about doing their own sasquatch research. Quite often the aim of the expeditions is to coax our big hairy friends to come out to play just long enough for us to get those few minutes of irrefutable footage. However, with the advent of YouTube, every hoaxer with a digital camcorder is producing his own "sasquatch discovered" video and as a result, this form of evidence is rarely accepted as proof. In regards to the sasquatch phenomena, the scientific community routinely has its collective head in the sand, or somewhere else where the sun doesn't shine, and it will not accept the data gathered by laymen as evidence. It is my belief that evidence in the form of vocalizations, footprints, hair strands, fingerprints and secondary signs like X's and arches is proof of an unknown North American primate and therefore, it is imperative that it is identified, documented and verified as scientifically as possible.

As I had previously stated, it is often quite difficult to have witnesses come forward to report their sightings due to their inherent fear of being ridiculed. This has all begun to change with the advent of the "*Finding Bigfoot*" television program.

But, wait a minute! Hasn't this type of televised investigative bigfoot chasing been done already? Well, yes and no. Over the years many such programs were produced by people who, in my opinion, knew nothing about the sasquatch and where clearly the producer's aim was to create a highly sensationalized program that would garner a greater market share of the viewing public. As a result, almost all of these television programs were highly inaccurate even in their depiction of the most celebrated incidents such as Albert Ostman's kidnapping and the assault on Fred Beck's cabin. And that's another point. It seems that every one of these programs has re-hashed the same old stories. It was always Ostman, Beck, Roe and the Bluff Creek film. Ad infinitum.

In 2007 two new television programs that investigated legendary phenomena hit the airwaves- *Monster Quest* and *Destination Truth*. *Monster Quest* aired for four seasons from fall of 2007 to the spring of 2010. "Produced by Whitewolf Entertainment, the program (*Monster Quest*) deals with the search for various crytozoological creatures (cryptids) and paranormal entities reportedly witnessed around the world."[98] Sixty-eight episodes were produced in total with seventeen of those being devoted to the sasquatch or bigfoot type creatures from across North America and around the world. I have watched quite a few of the episodes and I found them to be well researched and very informative with reported incidents recreated using digital graphics interspersed with interviews from real witnesses. In short, *Monster Quest* was appealing to a wide audience.

On the other hand, there is *Destination Truth*. Described as a "paranormal reality television series"[99] *Destination Truth* relies heavily on creative editing to build suspense and excitement, which is typical of any reality television program. Is the program entertaining? Sure it is but is it realistic? In my opinion, it is not and I'll tell you why. The concept of an investigative team launching itself to far-flung points on the globe in the search for proof of paranormal or crypto-zoological sightings is nothing new. This same production formula has been used for international crime fighting or rescue teams. But it is truly amazing how the *Destination Truth* team can routinely deploy to precisely the right place at the right time to discover tracks, vocalizations or ghostly images on their hand-held FLIR units after questioning a number of the local inhabitants and spending only one night in the field.

In my opinion, there can only be three possible explanations for being able to achieve these astounding results. First, the team from *Destination Truth* may have conducted far more research on the target subject and location than what is portrayed and in order to maintain the reality television format the entire behind the scenes work simply ended up on the cutting room floor. If that is the case it would be extremely easy to make mention of the work carried out before the team winged its way to Outer Slobobia in search of the Phantom Phoolie or some other mysterious creature. In my mind this small act, taking only seconds of airtime, would have lent greater credence to the *Destination Truth* team. Second, the ability of *Destination Truth* members to locate or find any evidence of their quarry points strongly to the notion that their vast amount of luck is derived from the load of horseshoes each of them is carrying rectally. The third option is that the show is pure bullshit and the team, along with the producers, have carefully edited the program in order to create an air of discovery and excitement that in the end bolsters the show's ratings.

I strongly believe that, given the amount of time the *Destination Truth* team appeared to be in the field, it would have been impossible for them to make any credible discoveries and as such the television program should be viewed purely for its entertainment value.

But, how does *Finding Bigfoot* differ from this program? Does it have hype? Sure it does. Is there suspense and excitement? Of course there is. After all, *Finding Bigfoot* is a reality television program where the viewing audience lives vicariously through the actions of the team members. *Finding Bigfoot* is the brainchild of Matt Moneymaker. It is something that Matt has worked very hard to develop and I am sure that he did not want it to be another Monster Quest or even less, another Destination Truth. As a member of the BFRO, I can confidently state that what you see on television is very much what happens on an expedition.

However, for the benefit of the viewing public, *Finding Bigfoot* does follow a consistent format. First, a team of investigators heads to a location that has had a high number of sighting reports. Unbeknownst to most of the public, many of the reports for this area have been completed independently by other BFRO members. Next, once they arrive, the team carries out a general examination of the geography in order to get a feel for the area. Again, what may not be common knowledge is the fact that because of the number of incidents, other BFRO members may have already conducted expeditions in the area. Then, during a town hall meeting, Matt and the team listen to additional local reports in order to better focus on a specific site. Deployed in pairs, the team utilizes vocalizations and wood knocks, which are the very same techniques employed on any other expedition and unlike Destination Truth, the actions of the *Finding Bigfoot* team does result in similar types of interactions, from wood knocks to vocalizations and approaches, that are experienced by the participants on many BFRO expeditions.

Why does the *Finding Bigfoot* team have successful interactions when other similar reality shows do not? Maybe it's

> "When they turn the pages of history
> When these days have passed long ago
> Will they read of us with sadness
> For the seeds that we let grow
> We turned our gaze
> From the castles in the distance
> Eyes cast down
> On the path of least resistance
>
> The hypocrites are slandering
> The sacred halls of Truth
> Ancient nobles showering
> Their bitterness on youth
> Can't we find
> The minds that made us strong
> Can't we learn
> To feel what's right and wrong"
>
> *Rush - A Farewell to Kings (1977)*

because the *Finding Bigfoot* team has forty or more years of active sasquatch investigations among them. Maybe it's because the methods they use have been honed over the dozens and dozens of expeditions. You may not believe in the results and you really don't have to, but I do know that the methods do work. For my efforts I have experienced approaches into my camp, piercing screams and tossed rocks.

So, if you have the desire to seek out what goes bump in the night or if you want to experience the primal fear that comes when something slaps the back of your truck, then I suggest that you come join us on an expedition. Information on how to join an expedition can be found on the BFRO website, www.bfro.net.

Glossary
Bigfoot Researcher's Quick Reference Guide
Prepared by Charles Lamica
BFRO Investigator, Northeast Washington
Updated: 8 September 2009

Abominable Snowman: Another name for the Yeti and other hairy, man-like, bipedal creatures. This term was popular in the 1950s and 1960s, but is seldom used now.

Almas: A Mongolian word meaning "wild man." Used in reference to bigfoot-like creatures reportedly inhabiting the Caucasus Mountains of central Asia.

Anthropoid: Resembling a man in shape and appearance. Often used to describe manlike apes.

Anthropology: The study of human beings, past or present. Scientists working in this area are called "anthropologists."

Ape: In layman terms, "ape" typically refers to a tail-less primate such as gibbons, chimpanzees, gorillas, orangutans, and humans. They are omnivorous and (except for adult gorillas and humans) agile climbers of trees. The term "great apes" refers to humans, chimpanzees, gorillas and orangutans. Members of the gibbon family, the largest of which is the Siamang, are considered "lesser apes."

Ape Canyon: Located near Mt. St. Helens in Washington, Ape Canyon was the scene of a 1924 incident in which several miners were "attacked" by bigfoots throwing rocks at their cabin. The "attack" was reportedly the result of the miners having fired rifles at a bigfoot earlier that day. The incident was reported by a Portland newspaper, *The Oregonian*, on July 12, 1924. In 1967 one of the miners, Fred Beck, published a book about the encounter which he titled, *I Fought The Apeman of Mt. St. Helens*. Ape Canyon suffered severe destruction when Mt. St. Helens erupted in 1980.

Ape Cave: The longest continuous lava tube in the continental U.S., Ape Cave is located in Gifford Pinchot National Forest, south of Mt. St. Helens. The origin of the name is in dispute. Some believe the name refers to bigfoot-like creatures that inhabited the area. Others insist the cave got its name from a youth group called the "Mt. St. Helens Apes," who were among the first to explore it.

Bait Station: Sometimes called "baiting". A location where various foods (typically fruit, peanut butter, jams, syrups, etc.) and or pheromones are left for the purpose of luring a bigfoot to the area.

Base Camp: The main gathering place and campsite for members of a BFRO expedition. Under ideal situations, the base camp is in or adjoining the expedition research area. In other cases, the base camp is located some distance from the research area and researchers must "convoy" to and from the research area each night. Group meetings, planning sessions, and training events are usually held at the base camp.

BFRO: The Bigfoot Field Researcher's Organization, founded in 1995 by Matt Moneymaker.

Bigfoot: During the late 1950's construction crews working in remote forests of northern California found large human-like footprints. They, and subsequent newspaper writers, used the word "bigfoot" to describe the creatures that made the footprints.

Bipedal: The ability to walk on two legs. Animals who primarily use this type of locomotion are known as "bipeds."

Biscardi, Tom: Enough said.

Blobsquatch: Refers to a poor quality, blurry, vague, or otherwise questionable photograph of a supposed sasquatch. The "sasquatch" is just a dark blob on the photo.

Blue Forum: The publicly available internet forum within the BFRO website. This forum is stringently monitored to ensure the discussions remain bigfoot-related and do not degenerate into off-topic or inappropriate subjects.

Bluff Charge: These have been documented many times in encounters with bears and primates. It is a form of intimidation in which the animal charges at the intruder, stopping short of engaging in an actual attack. Some bigfoot witnesses have reported this behavior.

Bluff Creek: Located in northern California, Bluff Creek is legendary in the bigfoot researcher's world. The first widely reported modern newspaper stories of bigfoot occurred in 1958 when road construction crewman Jerry Crew made a plaster cast of a bigfoot track and showed it to reporters. In 1967 Roger Patterson and Bob Gimlin filmed a female bigfoot in the same area. In Loren Coleman's book, *Bigfoot! The True Story of Apes in America,* he lists the "Twenty best places to see bigfoot". Bluff Creek is #1 on that list.

Boq: The name for bigfoot used by First Nations people of the Bella Coola region.

Bossburg: A small rural community in northeastern Washington. Bossburg gained national media attention in 1969 when numerous bigfoot tracks were found there. The tracks were unusual because they indicated the creature's right foot was deformed. This has resulted in these tracks becoming known as the "Cripplefoot" tracks. The tracks resulted in a deluge of bigfoot hunters and investigators descending on Bossburg. Among them were Rene' Dahinden, Roger Patterson, and Bob Titmus. To this day, the Cripplefoot tracks are considered some of the most intriguing pieces of evidence in the bigfoot mystery.

Buk'wus: Kwakiutl word for a male sasquatch.

Byrne, Peter: Irish-born big game hunter and bigfoot researcher Peter Byrne saw his first Yeti footprint in 1948. He subsequently was a key player in Tom Slick's Himalayan Abominable Snowman and North American Bigfoot expeditions of the late 1950's and early 1960's. Byrne wrote *"The Search for Bigfoot: Monster, Myth, or Man?"* He directed the Bigfoot Research Project, based in The Dalles, Oregon, from 1992 to 1997. He has appeared in several documentary shows about bigfoot.

Call Blasting: Using a megaphone or portable stereo speakers to broadcast tape-recorded bigfoot vocalizations in the hopes of receiving a response from any bigfoots in the area.

Casting: Using a plaster-like substance to preserve impressions found in soil or snow. Footprints, handprints, and other body impressions have been found and cast.

Chiye-tanka: Lakota word for bigfoot. "Chiha-tanka" in the eastern Sioux (Dakota) dialect.

Class A Report: As used in the BFRO report database, these are reports involving clear sightings of a bigfoot in circumstances where misinterpretation or misidentification can be ruled out with greater confidence.

Class B Report: As used in the BFRO report database, these are cases of a possible bigfoot being observed at a great distance or in poor lighting conditions, or possible bigfoot activity occurring under circumstances that did not afford a clear view of the subject.

Class C Report: Most second-hand reports and any third-hand reports, or stories with untraceable sources, are considered Class C because of the high potential for inaccuracy. Those reports are kept in BFRO archives but are not listed publicly in the database.

Coleman, Loren: A well-known cryptozoologist who has authored many books on mysterious creatures such as bigfoot, the mothman, and thunderbirds. He earned degrees in anthropology and psychiatric social work. He has appeared on many television shows and documentaries to discuss cryptozoology subjects.

Cowman of Copalis Beach: In the mid-1960's a family living near Copalis Beach, Washington reportedly had several encounters with a bigfoot-like creature. The creature apparently visited their home on several occasions because one of the young children nicknamed it the "Cowman" due to the fact it was big and smelly, like a cow. The boy reported the Cowman sometimes came to his bedroom window at night and "talked" to him using grunting noises, and it could imitate bird calls. The creature supposedly caused damage to the family's house and behaved in a frightening manner. The family eventually sold the house and moved away.

Cryptozoology: The study of hidden animals. Cryptozoologists research legendary creatures such as bigfoot, yeti, the Loch Ness Monster, etc.

Dahinden, Rene': Born in Switzerland, Dahinden moved to Canada in 1953, where he became enthralled with the bigfoot mystery. He was involved in many famous investigations, including the Bossburg Cripple case. He owned the photographic image rights to the Patterson film. With Don Hunter, he wrote one book entitled *Sasquatch.* He died in 2001.

Dermal Ridges: Most commonly known as "fingerprints". Dermal ridges are found on the hands and feet of humans and primates. Some casts of bigfoot tracks have been found to show evidence of dermal ridges.

Dsonoqua: A Kwakiutl word for a female sasquatch.

Expedition: As it applies to the BFRO, an expedition is a sponsored event led by a BFRO Expedition Organizer for the purpose of searching for evidence of bigfoots, exploring techniques and methods for attracting them, and testing equipment for monitoring and documenting them. Expeditions have been conducted in many different states and provinces, including Alberta, Arizona, British Columbia, California, Colorado, Florida, Georgia, Maine, Michigan, Minnesota, Missouri, New Hampshire, New Mexico, New York, Ohio, Oklahoma, Ontario, Oregon, Pennsylvania, Texas, Tennessee, Utah, Washington, West Virginia, Wisconsin, and Wyoming. Most expeditions are about four days in duration although some have been longer. Most of the expeditions are open to the general public, with the approval of the Expedition Organizer. Persons who might prove to be disruptive, ill mannered, deranged, or otherwise unable to adhere to the standards and policies of the expedition are not allowed to attend.

Eye Glow: There are a number of sighting reports in which a bigfoot's eyes are said to "glow," actually producing light rather than merely reflecting light. If true, the source of such light is currently unknown. Many researchers doubt the existence of this phenomenon.

Eye Shine: When light is shone into the eye of an animal having a tapetum lucidum it is reflected back at the viewer. It can occur in a variety of colors. Because eyeshine is a form of iridescence, the color can vary with the angle at which it is seen and the color of the source light.

Family Group: It is believed by many researchers that a typical grouping of bigfoots consists of an adult male, an adult female, and one or two offspring.

FLATS: Follow-up Logging and Tracking System. The computerized clearinghouse and database used by BFRO investigators. Not available to the general public.

Footprint Measurements: When possible, sasquatch footprints should be measured in three areas: Total length from heel to toe, width across the ball of the foot, and width across the broadest part of the heel.

Frame 352: Probably the most well-known image of a bigfoot to date. Frame 352 of the Patterson-Gimlin film shows a female bigfoot turning to look at the camera as she walks away towards the woods.

Freeman Video: In 1994 Paul Freeman obtained a brief video of a supposed bigfoot near Deduct Springs in the Blue Mountains of southeast Washington.

Game-cam: See Trail-cam.

Georgia Body Hoax: In August 2008 two men from Georgia, Matt Whitton and Rick Dyer, announced they had a dead bigfoot. The story gained national media attention, partly because Whitton's position as a deputy sheriff enhanced his believability. Notorious huckster Tom Biscardi got involved and "confirmed" the existence of the body. He also started selling photos of the body on the internet. The "body" turned out to be a Halloween costume and animal entrails.

Gigantopithecus: Some scientists suspect sasquatches may be related to, or a remnant population of, *Gigantopithecus Blacki*, the largest known ape. Known only from fossilized jaws and teeth, Gigantopithecus is estimated to have been up to ten feet tall and may have migrated from Asia to North America along the Bering Land Bridge.

Grassman: Also called the "Ohio Grassman." A local name for bigfoot-like creatures in Ohio.

Green, John: John Green started collecting sasquatch stories as a newspaper publisher in British Columbia in the 1950's. In addition to doing field research, he wrote *Sasquatch: The Apes Among Us* in 1978. As of 2009, Green lives near Harrison Hotsprings, BC and still shares with others his passion for bigfoot.

Gugwes: Micmac word for a bigfoot-like creature, similar to the "Windigo."

Habituation Case: A situation in which one or more bigfoots have become accustomed to, and sometimes interact with, humans on a regular basis. Such cases often begin with humans leaving offerings of food and the relationships develop over long periods of time.

Hair Morphology: The structure and configuration of hair. A number of hair samples suspected to belong to bigfoot-type creatures have been studied by scientists such as Dr. W. Henner Fahrenbach, a BFRO curator, and Dr. P. Fuerst, of Ohio State University. As might be assumed, some hair samples have been proved to be from commonly known animals but there are some samples that have defied identification efforts. Some scientists have declared suspected bigfoot hairs to be clearly related to, but not identical to, those of the great apes. The greatest challenge to bigfoot hair identification is the lack of a known standard for comparison purposes. It's a Catch-22 situation: We can't positively identify a sasquatch hair until we have some sample hairs that are positively from a sasquatch.

Hallux: Often called the "big toe" on humans.

Harry and the Hendersons: A 1987 movie starring John Lithgow and Don Ameche. "Harry" is a bigfoot accidentally struck by a car and who comes to live with the Henderson family. The film won an Academy Award for Best Makeup.

Heuvelmans, Bernard: Belgian zoologist Dr. Bernard Heuvelmans was born in Le Havre in 1916. His interest in mysterious animals led him to invent the word "cryptozoology," and was known by many as the "Father of Cryptozoology." He authored at least a dozen books on cryptid animals. His 1955 book, *"On the Track of Unknown Animals"* is considered a classic in its field. In 1975 he founded the Center for Cryptozoology in France. From 1982 until 2001 he was president of the Washington D.C.-based International Society of Cryptozoology. Throughout his life he traveled around the world to investigate mysterious animals, receiving many awards and recognition along the way. He died at home on August 24, 2001.

Hoaxer: Anyone who falsely reports a sighting, plants false evidence, or otherwise acts in a manner calculated to deceive others in regards to bigfoot.

Hominid: Also known as the "great apes", hominids form the taxonomic family that includes chimpanzees, gorillas, humans, and orangutans.

Howl: A type of bigfoot vocalization characterized by long, powerful screams or moans. These sounds are longer in duration than those known as whoops.

Human: A member of the bipedal primate species known as *Homo Sapiens.*

Infrasound: Sounds so low in the sonic range that humans can not hear them, but they may feel them. Many animals use infrasound for communication, including elephants, alligators, hippos, lions, and tigers. Anecdotal evidence leads some researchers to suspect sasquatches may also use infrasound, especially to warn away intruders.

Investigator: A volunteer BFRO member who investigates and reports on bigfoot sightings and evidence. BFRO Investigators are selected by invitation only, and usually only after a prospective individual has attended one or more BFRO expeditions.

Jacko: On July 4, 1884 a British Columbia newspaper, the *Daily British Colonist,* reported a hairy creature, similar to a gorilla, was captured by railroad workers near the town of Yale. The animal was given the name of "Jacko" and was confined to the local jail. The animal later disappeared and was never seen again. Although this story has been repeated in several bigfoot books, it is thought by many researchers to have been a newspaper hoax.

Jacobs Creature: On September 16, 2007 a game-cam in northwest Pennsylvania captured two photographs of what many people believe to be a juvenile bigfoot. The camera was put in place by a man named R. Jacobs. Some have offered the suggestion the subject in the photos is nothing more than a skinny, mangy bear.

Knuckle-walking: A form of quadrupedalism in which the fingers are curled and the hands are used in a walking motion, resulting in the weight of the upper body being taken on the knuckles. Gorillas and chimpanzees regularly use this form of locomotion. It is suggested that juvenile bigfoots may do the same.

Krantz, Grover: Born in 1931, Dr. Grover S. Krantz was a physical anthropologist at Washington State University who believed bigfoot-type creatures may be related to *Gingantopithecus Blacki*. Krantz was very interested in the bigfoot mystery and wrote several books on the subject. He died of pancreatic cancer in 2002.

Kushtaka: A Tlingit (southeast Alaska) word for a shape-shifting creature that sometimes appears as a man and other times appears as a land otter. The word is also used to describe bigfoot-like creatures.

Legend of Boggy Creek: A 1972 low budget movie directed by Charles B. Pierce depicting events reportedly involving bigfoot-like creatures near the town of Fouke, Arkansas.

Meldrum, Jeff: Jeff Meldrum, Ph.D., is a professor of anatomy and anthropology at Idaho State University. His interest in bigfoot has resulted in his participation in bigfoot field research and led him to assemble a large collection of bigfoot casts and photographs. His book, *Sasquatch: Legend Meets Science*, was published in 2006.

Melted Out: Refers to tracks found in snow, that have been through one or more cycles of thawing and re-freezing. This process distorts the shape and size of the track, often making the track look bigger than it was. As a result, some people have mistakenly believed they found some bigfoot tracks when, in reality, they found the melted out track of some other animal.

Memorial Day Video: On May 27, 1996 Lori and Owen Pate obtained video footage of a sasquatch near Chopaka Lake in northern Washington. A third witness, Tom Lines, observed the creature through binoculars. The creature was filmed running across a clearing, and some researchers have suggested it is a female with an infant riding on its back.

Midtarsal Break: Apes do not have a fixed longitudinal arch, such as found on human feet, resulting in an ape's foot being more flexible than a human's. This area of flexibility is known as the midtarsal break and is the reason why sasquatch tracks in loose soil, snow, or mud often show a "pressure ridge" in the middle of the footprint.

Minnesota Iceman: In 1967 the corpse of a hairy manlike creature was exhibited at fairs in the American Midwest. The creature was contained in a block of ice and several conflicting stories about its origin were told by its owner. Cryptozoologists Ivan T. Sanderson and Bernard Heuvelmans were allowed to examine the body through the ice. Heuvelmans believed the body was that of a Neanderthal-like creature. Sometime after these examinations the owner had a life-sized model made of the body. The model was subsequently used for exhibits and the location of the original body is currently unknown.

Moneymaker, Matt: Matt holds a BA degree in English Literature from UCLA and a Juris Doctorate degree from the University of Akron School of Law. In 1995 he founded the Bigfoot Field Researcher's Organization. In 2001 he wrote and co-produced the Discovery Channel's *"Sasquatch: Legend Meets Science."* He is recognized as an expert on bigfoot and has appeared in many newspaper, magazine, internet, radio, and television reports on the subject. Based out of southern California, Matt personally attends many of the BFRO's expeditions.

Monster Quest: A television series appearing on the History Channel that deals with various cryptozoological and paranormal mysteries. Bigfoot is featured in several episodes.

Myakka Ape: On December 22, 2000 an elderly woman living in Sarasota County, Florida mailed two photographs to the Sarasota County Sheriff's Department. The photos were taken at night and show a large primate-type animal which, according to the anonymous woman's letter, was "six and a half to seven feet tall in a kneeling position."

No-Shoot Policy: Unlike some researchers who believe the best way to "prove" bigfoots exist is to shoot or capture one, the members of the BFRO adhere to a no-shoot policy. This means their research is done is such a way as to avoid causing physical harm to the creatures.

Oh-mah: Also known as "Oh-mah-ah." The Hoopa (northern California) word for bigfoot.

Orang Pendek: An Indonesian word meaning "short person." Used to describe a cryptid primate-like creature supposedly inhabiting the island of Sumatra. Unlike bigfoot, which is unusually large, Orang Pendek is reportedly less than five feet tall.

Ostman, Albert: In 1924 Ostman was camping alone near Toba Inlet, British Columbia. His story, told to John Green in 1957, is that he was asleep in his sleeping bag when a male sasquatch picked up the bag and carried it, with Ostman inside, off to a remote valley. Residing in the valley were a family of sasquatches consisting of the male, an adult female, and two juveniles. Ostman was held captive, but was not mistreated, for several days. He managed to escape by allowing the male sasquatch to eat a quantity of snuff. When the sasquatch became violently ill, Ostman ran for his life and was able to return to civilization.

Overlapping Bear Tracks: Sometimes called "registered" tracks. At a normal walking speed a bear's tracks are distinctly separated, clearly showing four feet. When a bear moves faster its front and rear footprints often overlap each other. In some cases the overlapped prints will appear to be one large, almost human-like footprint. Such prints are sometimes mistaken for bigfoot tracks.

Paralleling: Many researchers and witnesses have reported sasquatches following them as they hike through the woods. Often, the path taken by the sasquatch is not the same path as the human, but may be on a parallel trail or ridgeline. This seems to be a result of the sasquatch's curiosity about "intruders" in their territory.

Patterson-Gimlin Film: On October 20, 1967 Roger Patterson and Bob Gimlin filmed a female bigfoot on Bluff Creek in northern California. Frame #352 of the film is probably the most widely known bigfoot image in the world. Also known as the Patterson film.

Patty: An affectionate name given by researchers to the female bigfoot filmed in 1967 by Roger Paterson.

Piloerection: As part of an aggressive display or in response to fear, some primates can cause the hair on their bodies to bristle or stand on end. This same action has been reported in some bigfoot sightings.

Pongid: An anthropoid ape of the family Pongidae, which includes the chimpanzee, gorilla, and orangutan.

Primate: The taxonomic order of Primates includes animals such as lemurs, monkeys, apes, and humans.

Quadrupedal: The use of four legs for locomotion. Animals who do this are called "quadrupeds."

Redwoods Video: On August 28, 1995 a film crew in a recreational vehicle in Jedediah Smith Redwoods State Park in northern California saw and briefly filmed a nearly eight-foot tall, hairy, bipedal creature. The video was originally called the "Playmate Video" because the film crew was hired to make a video for Playboy Magazine.

Rock Clacking: Some witnesses have reported sounds seemingly made by striking two large rocks together. The exact purpose of such activity is unknown.

Rock Formations: Some researchers have found curious piles or stacks of stones and rocks in areas where bigfoots are suspected to inhabit. Like stick structures, the purpose of these formations is subject to conjecture.

Rock Throwing: There are a number of reports of rocks being thrown at or near hikers or campers, apparently by sasquatches hidden nearby. There are also reports of sasquatches throwing rocks towards tents prior to a "Type 1 Inspection". It is thought this particular kind of rock throwing is done to see if anyone reacts to the noise. If no one reacts, the campers must be asleep, and the sasquatch feels more confident in walking into the camp.

Rugaru: Ojibway word for bigfoot.

Sagittal Crest: A bony ridge found on the skull of some primates, especially male gorillas. The resulting "peaked head" is reportedly seen on some sasquatches.

Samurai Chatter: Vocalizations supposedly made by several bigfoots in the early 1970's in the Sierra Mountains of California. These deep muttering, grumbling voices were tape recorded by Ron Morehead and Al Berry and are featured on CDs entitled, "Bigfoot Recordings, Volume 1 and Volume 2". In 2008 the recordings were studied by linguist R. Scott Nelson, who believes the creatures are using a complex language.

Sanderson, Ivan T.: Born in Scotland in 1911, Sanderson became a naturalized US citizen after World War Two. He earned degrees in zoology, botany, and geology and traveled to many parts of the world to study wildlife. It was Sanderson who coined the word "cryptozoology." He wrote a number of books, including *Abominable Snowmen: Legend Come to Life.* He died of brain cancer in 1973.

Sasquatch: J.W. Burns, a journalist and teacher at the Chehalis Indian Reserve near Harrison Hot Springs, British Columbia, popularized the word "sasquatch" in newspaper and magazine articles of the 1920's and 1930's. The word is an anglicized version of an Indian word for large, hairy, man-like creatures.

Sassy: A name used by some to describe a female bigfoot. Derived from "sasquatch".

Satellite Camp: A remote camp, located some distance away from base camp. Satellite camps are often used when a small number of people wish to stay in a specific research area rather than travel back to base camp. Expeditions with large numbers of participants will sometimes establish one or more satellite camps so as to avoid over-crowding any one campsite.

Scat: Animal fecal matter. Scientific analysis of scat is important due to the fact most wild animal scat contains parasites. These parasites are often "host specific," meaning they only inhabit one particular host species. Some suspected bigfoot scat have been found to contain parasites not usually found in humans, bears, elk, moose, deer, or other large animals inhabiting the same area.

Sighting: An eyewitness report of a bigfoot.

Sign Cutting: The act of looking for clues in order to find a starting point to begin tracking.

Skookum Body Cast: A very large casting (over 200 pounds) made by BFRO investigators in 2000 during an expedition near Skookum Meadows in southern Washington. The cast shows impressions made in moist soil by a bigfoot while it was in a semi-reclining pose, reaching for some fruit left as bait.

Skunk Ape: Local name for large, hairy, bipedal creatures reportedly seen in Florida. Some researchers suggest Skunk Apes are more ape-like in appearance and behavior than bigfoots of the western United States.

Slick, Tom: A Texas millionaire, Tom Slick funded and participated in several large expeditions to hunt for yetis in the Himalayas and bigfoots in the Pacific

Northwest in the 1950's and early 1960's. He died in an airplane explosion in Montana in 1962.

Snow Mounds: In June, 2005, while participating in a BFRO expedition in the Sierra Nevada Mountains, Bart Cutino and Robert Leiterman found several waist-high mounds of snow covered with an insulating layer of wood debris and bark. Examination of the mounds indicated they were carefully created for the apparent purpose of preserving a quantity of clean snow. The location and circumstances surrounding the finding of the mounds made it unlikely they were man-made. The exact purpose of the mysterious mounds is not known.

Squatch: A contraction of the word "sasquatch".

Squatch-bait: In spite of the shy and elusive natures of sasquatches, researchers have determined the creatures are very curious about humans who enter their territory. This curiosity may result in behavior such as paralleling and type 1 inspections. Sasquatches seem to be especially curious about, and attracted to, women and children. As a result, some researchers intentionally use women and younger expedition members as "squatch-bait." Typical squatch-bait tactics might include having women or younger people gather around a campfire to sing, laugh, and behave in a light-hearted and conspicuous manner, or have a similar group hike along trails or roads at night.

Squatching: A word derived from "sasquatch", describing the act of searching for signs or evidence of bigfoot.

Squee'noos: A Coast Salish word for bigfoot.

Step Length: The measurement from one point on a footprint to the SAME POINT on the next footprint. Example: From the heel to the heel. This is not the same as a "stride length".

Stick Structures: Logs, branches, or sticks found arranged in a manner unlikely to have been a natural occurrence. These can be in the form of branches arranged in a "tipi" formation around a central tree trunk, or "X" formations found across trails, or limbs that are twisted or woven together. Some structures may mean "keep out", some may be a territorial sign, while others may be created simply as entertainment.

Stride Length: A measurement from one point on a footprint to the SAME point on the next print of the SAME foot. Example: From the heel of the left footprint to the heel of the next left footprint. This is different from a "step length".

Tall Boy Trails: Trails or paths suspected to regularly be used by bigfoots. The main characteristic of these trails is the absence of limbs or branches protruding into the pathway. This includes branches as high up as eight to ten feet above ground.

Tapetum Lucidum: A layer of tissue in the eye of some animals, immediately behind or sometimes within the retina. It reflects light back through the retina, increasing the animal's vision in low light conditions. Humans do not possess a tapetum lucidum, but some researchers believe bigfoots do, which is the cause for reported "eye shine".

Thermal Imager: A generic term used to describe heat detection devices that allow the viewer to "see" body heat emanating from animals or people. Particularly useful for spotting animals at night.

Titmus, Robert: Born in 1919, Titmus was a taxidermist in Redding, California when bigfoot tracks were found at Bluff Creek in 1958. He taught Jerry Crew how to make plaster casts, resulting in Crew's famous newspaper picture holding a cast of a bigfoot track. Titmus began searching for tracks and amassing a collection of bigfoot casts. His field efforts resulted in two separate sightings of a bigfoot. He was acquainted with Roger Patterson and casted several of the footprints left by "Patty" in the Bluff Creek footage. In 1997 Titmus died of a heart attack in British Columbia at age 78.

Tracking: The act of following a continuous chain of clues (sometimes called "sign") left by the passage of a person or animal.

Trail-cam: A type of camera used to take photographs or video of animals in the wild. They are often mounted on trees or in concealed locations along trails or places where bigfoots may be active. Motion sensors trigger the camera whenever something moves in front of it. The newer models use infrared flash for night photos and can store hundreds of photos in digital format.

Tree Twists: Small trees and saplings that have been broken and twisted in a forceful manner. The break is usually four to eight feet above ground and the twisting of the tree trunk is evidence of immense strength. It is speculated these tree twists are not a product of environmental forces, but are made by someone or something with hands.

Tsiatko: Nisqually (western Washington) word for bigfoot.

Type 1 Inspections: The purposeful visit of a bigfoot to a campsite or campground. These visits have been documented on a number of BFRO expeditions. They often occur in the early morning hours (between 3:00 and 4:00 AM seems to be a favorite time), and only after a bigfoot has decided all campers are asleep. During these visits the bigfoot will often examine and touch cooking gear, tents, or other equipment.

Vocalizations: As it pertains to sasquatches, this refers to any sounds made by the creatures. Such sounds can include long mournful howls, short whoops, chattering noises, growling, muttering, angry screams, and imitation of other animals.

Wallace, Ray: In 1958 Ray Wallace was a construction contractor building a road near Bluff Creek, California. One of his employees, Jerry Crew, made the first known plaster cast of a bigfoot print. Wallace claimed to have seen bigfoots many times and said he had photos of them. He also wrote that the creatures were guardians of caves full of gold. Wallace admitted he owned a set of wooden bigfoot feet because, he said, he wanted to use the feet to protect the bigfoots from being killed by hunters. Wallace died of heart failure on November 26, 2002. After his father's death, Michael Wallace told reporters, "Bigfoot just died."

Whoops: A type of bigfoot vocalization tending to be of short duration than howls, but still loud and powerful.

Windigo: Also known as "Wendigo," "Weetigo," and "Witiko." An Algonquin word for a large, malevolent and cannibalistic human-like creature.

Wood Knockers: As used by a sasquatch, any branch, stick, or small log used for wood knocking. Wood knockers used by researchers are often homemade from axe handles, baseball bats, tree limbs, or other stout wooden items.

Wood Knocking: Sounds suspected to be made by bigfoots using a large branch or wooden club to strike trees or logs. The exact purpose of these sounds is unknown, but some researchers believe they may be warning signals to alert other bigfoots of potential danger, or may be used as a "homing signal" so bigfoots can locate each other over long distances.

Wood Knocking Station: Some researchers believe sasquatches may have favorite locations for wood knocking and may stash the branches and limbs used for knocking against a suitable tree for future use. As with many other aspects of the bigfoot mystery, the idea of these wood knocking "stations" is not accepted among all researchers.

Yeti: A local name for bigfoot-like creatures reportedly sighted in the Himalayas of Tibet and Nepal. The word gained worldwide fame in 1951 after mountaineer Eric Shipton found and photographed strange footprints while on a Mt. Everest scouting trip.

Yowie: A local name for bigfoot-like creatures reportedly sighted in Australia.

Zana: A large, hairy, bigfoot-like female creature reportedly captured, tamed, and kept as a curiosity by various owners in Russia in the late 1800's. Zana is said to have had several babies as a result of contact with human males, four of which survived to adulthood. She died and was buried in the 1880's or 1890's. Attempts to locate her grave proved futile, although the body of one of her sons, Kwhit, was recovered and studied. His skull was described by one anthropologist as possessing features that were both modern and ancient.

Appendix
Wood Knock Station Theory
Initiated by Harold Smith
Expanded by Blaine McMillan BC BFRO

It was at the start of the 2006 BC Expedition when I first met Harold and at that time he had approached me with a theory about a possible sasquatch communication point or a wood knock station. A bit of a backgrounder. It is believed that the sasquatch may non-verbally communicate with another sasquatch through the use of knocking sticks against trees and clacking rocks together. Dr. John Bindernagel has described this event in his book, North America's Great Ape: the Sasquatch. Despite being recorded at many locations across the continent this event, to my knowledge, has never been witnessed and the nature of this suspected habit gives rise to several questions.

1. Do sasquatches carry around sticks for the purpose of communication? Or, do they simply pick up any old stick in the forest when they need to whack a tree for the purpose of communication, commonly referred to as tree knocking.

2. Does a sasquatch tree knock from random locations or repeatedly from the same location or a combination of both?

In my experience wood knocks seem emanate from random locations but this does not mean that these locations are in fact random. They could actually be taking place at a location that has been predetermined or established for just this form of communication. If one was to consistently hear wood knocks emanating from a certain direction there is a chance that they may be coming from a very specific position.

While attending the 2006 BC Expedition, Harold took a photo of a suspected wood knock station and in looking at this photo several things appear to be quite evident.

1. There are several sticks leaning in a tepee type formation against a tree. These sticks are roughly 2 to 4 inches in diameter and are 3 to 5 feet in length. The sticks are clean of any protruding branches and the bark has been stripped off. The ends of the branches have not been cut with a tool but do appear to have been forcibly broken.

2. Leaning a stick against a tree means that it is not lying on the forest floor where it would quickly rot with the ever-present dampness and insect activity. To the left of the centre of the sticks is a broken stick that is roughly the same diameter as the ones that are leaning against the tree. It is also free of protruding branches and bark

3. Outside the frame of this particular picture there are several small trees that are also 2 to 4 inches in diameter and are 6 to 12 feet in height. These trees have been stripped of their branches and of their bark, which would eventually kill the tree but would leave it in an intact state. The branches do not appear to have been removed by a deer or an elk rubbing the velvet from its antlers since the braches were on the ground in a rough pile.

The next question that comes to mind is whether or not the sticks in the photo are just another tepee structure? Tepee structures that are thought to be constructed by the sasquatch are usually much larger in size. Some of the larger structures measure more than 20 feet in height while some of the smaller ones have been found securing the end of an arched structure. Once again there seems to be no known rational explanation as to why these structures are being built. However, if you look closely at the sticks in the photo you will see that they are not simply lying against the tree. One end has been securely pushed into the earth so the stick cannot fall over onto the forest floor and rot. It would seem that whoever or whatever placed the sticks in this configuration intended them to stay put until they were needed for a specific purpose.

Those of us who have been lucky enough to actually hear a wood knock can attest to their variety, from the very light tap-tap-tap to the impressive power strike that rings throughout the forest. A blow like this would surely have some effect, leave some kind of mark that could be viewed as evidence. At this point Harold drew my attention back to the photo that he had taken. If you look closely at the cedar tree in the foreground you can clearly see that there are several horizontal marks on the tree. Harold stated that these marks appeared to be bruises on the trunk of the tree and he could actually feel the indentation with his hand.

So what does this theory really imply? To put it simply, this wood knock station is akin to a telephone booth! Take a minute and think about it because if this is true then it is really an amazing discovery. On the evolutionary scale tool use it is a significant benchmark and I believe that this theory puts forward the concept that the Sasquatch may be not only a tool user but also a toolmaker. As defined by Wikipedia, a tool is "a device that provides a mechanical advantage in accomplishing a physical task". This tool, the wood knock stick, does provide a mechanical advantage in announcing the user's location when it is struck against the tree. However, this does not mean that wood knocking will occur only at a station because I am sure that when required a sasquatch could easily improvise a wood knock stick for use while it is on the move. This being said, one thought does come to mind. Do the incidents of rock clacking occur as a result of the lack of a suitable wood knock stick? Are there areas where both wood knocking and rock clacking have been witnessed or recorded? According to the BFRO investigations, the majority of non-vocalization sounds reported from the Chilliwack River Valley have been rock clacking and not wood knocking. Could this be a personal preference for the particular sasquatch residing in the area?

There is yet another significant finding that Harold brought to my attention. In the immediate neighbourhood of this suspected wood knock station there was a well-worn trail and an X formation. Once again it is not known why the sasquatch create these X's but it is believed by many in the field that they are used as an indicator of some unknown purpose.

When there is a study of an unknown phenomenon I believe there is a better chance of validity if the subject can be observed and verified from more than one location. This being said, finding one wood knock station may be very interesting but finding another and another and another would certainly add strength to the theory, would it not?

During the 2006 BC Expedition, Fred and I were monitoring the movement of some of the attendees from a vantage point above their position. To our left there was a path that went down the hill towards a pond. As I was checking out some interestingly large and square fingernail marks on a tree trunk in front of me Fred informed me that he had spotted an X marking the uphill side of the path that was farther to his left. On a closer investigation we discovered another possible wood knock station in close proximity to the X. Unfortunately, it had grown too dark to photograph without the use of a flash and since the operation was still ongoing taking any pictures with a flash unit was out of the question.

A recent discussion with another BFRO investigator yielded some surprising results. Mike Greene, who had attended the first three BC expeditions and many others as well, said that he had a photo of another possible wood knock station from the Sunshine Coast expedition. In the woods, near the other end of the pond, he had discovered a large rotted tree stump, some 4 feet in diameter, and resting inside was a pair of large sticks. The sticks did not look as if they have been used in a while but on the side of the cedar tree behind the stump there are markings similar to those found on the trees near the other two suspected wood knock stations.

The idea of the wood knock station is only a theory. However, I believe that there is some evidence to support it and it is important enough to warrant some additional discussion and further investigation.

Update

Suspected wood knock stations have been found in other locations. Author and sasquatch researcher Chris Noël found a suspected wood knock station near his research area in Vermont. He documented the find in his book *Impossible Visits*.

While investigating the Cowichan Valley prior to the 2007 BFRO expedition on Vancouver Island I was taken out to a site that held numerous secondary sasquatch signs. There were X's, arches; a couple of small tepee structures and…a possible wood knock station.

Located on the edge of a wood line this particular station was a smooth barked arbutus tree. Originally I was taken to this tree to see some very impressive cougar claw marks but once there I found several sticks that were resting innocently against its trunk. A closer inspection revealed corresponding bruise marks suggesting that the sticks had been used to strike the tree. I tested the resonance of the arbutus by doing a couple of wood knocks with startling results.

References

Aviation Ordnance, <u>LUU-2B/B Aircraft Parachute Flare</u>, www.ordnance.org/ luu2bb.htm, 08 March 2012.

Beachcombers, The, Season 2 – Episode 15, (1974), <u>The Sasquatch Walks By Night</u>, www.tvarchive.ca, 08 March 2012.

BFRO, <u>The Skookum Cast</u>, www.bfro.net/NEWS/BODYCAST, 07 January 2010.

BFRO Expedition FAQ: <u>"What's the goal of the expeditions?"</u> www.bfro.net/ news/roundup/exped_faq.asp#purpose.

BFRO Report # 857, (November 2005), <u>Possible sighting around 2:00 AM near Courtenay</u>, www.bfro.net.

BFRO Report # 2113, (April 2001), <u>Daylight sighting by motorist on Hwy 93 about 20 miles East of Radium</u>, www.bfro.net.

BFRO Report # 3945, (February 2002), <u>Possible tracks observed on a frozen lake near Invermere</u>, www.bfro.net.

BFRO Report # 7911, (August, 2000), <u>Possible stalking at Echo Lake near Campbell River</u>, www.bfro.net.

BFRO Report #9876, November, 2003), Sighting by hunters South of Longview, www.bfro.net.

BFRO Report # 11915, (June, 2005), <u>Nighttime sightings outside Duncan: Other incidents mentioned</u>, www.bfro.net.

BFRO Report # 12855, (October 2005), <u>Various Incidents on British Columbia Expedition</u>, www.bfro.net.

BFRO Report # 13390, (September 2005), <u>Possible footprints found in BC Interior</u>, www.bfro.net.

BFRO Report #13800, (October 2005), <u>Possible vocals heard outside of</u>

Duncan, www.bfro.net, 01 March 2010.

BFRO Report #23245, (September 2007), A surprise sighting by a hunter in BC, www.bfro.net, 15 March 2010.

Bigfoot Encounters, Nanoose Bay, BC, Canada, 1982, www.bigfootencounters. com/sbs/nanoose.htm, 19 December 2009.

Bindernagel, Dr. John, (1988) North America's Great Ape: the Sasquatch, Beachcomber Books, Courtenay, BC.

Birkmeyer, Carl, The Get Smart Website, www.wouldyoubelieve.com/cone. html, 16 December 2008.

Burns, Robert, (1785), To a Mouse, http://en.wikipedia.org/wiki/To_a_Mouse, 24 June 2012.

CanWest News Service, (22 May 2007), Tiger turned loose on purpose, police say, http://www.canada.com/victoriatimescolonist/news/story.html, 04 September 2011.

Chadwick, Douglas H, (July 2001), Grizzlies, http://ngm.nationalgeographic. com/ngm/data/2001/07/01/html/fulltext1.html, 26 February 2012.

Conan Doyle, Sir Arthur (1890), Sherlock Holmes: The Sign of Four, Classic Quotes, www.quotationspage.com/quote/24943.html, 15 April 2008.

Cosby, Bill, The Best of Bill Cosby: Street Football, Warner Bros, catalogue# CWX-1798.

Coast Salish History, The Cowichan People gave him the name Thumquas, www.joejack.com/sasquatch.html, 02 February 2010.

Davidson, Robert (2002), Reading Topographic Maps, www.map-reading.com. E-Notes, De Havilland Canada DHC-5D Buffalo, www.enotes.com/topic/ De_Havilland_Canada_DHC-5_Buffalo, 08 March 2012.

Fahrenbach Ph. D., Dr. W. H., (1997), Sasquatch Smell / Aroma / Odor / Scent, Bigfoot Encounters, www.bigfootencounters.com.

Gibbs, Phil, (1996), What is Occam's Razor?, www.physics.adelaide.edu. au/~dkoks/Faq/General/occam.html, 25 March 2008.

Green, John, (2004), The Best of Sasquatch Bigfoot: the latest scientific developments, Hancock House Publishers, Surrey, BC.

Hinterland Who's Who, Animal Fact Sheets, www.hww.ca/en/species/mammals/north-american-elk.html , 18 Dec 2011.

Hinterland Who's Who, Mammal Fact Sheets, www.hww.ca/en/species/mammals/black-bear.html, 18 December 2011.

Hooker, Richard, (1968), M*A*S*H, William Morrow and Company, Inc., New York, NY.

Hunter, Don, and Dahinden, Rene, (1973), Sasquatch, The New American Library of Canada LTD., Scarborough, Ont.

Krantz Ph. D, Grover (1999), Bigfoot Sasquatch Evidence: The Anthropologist Speaks Out, Hancock House, Surrey, BC.

Kruchak, Matthew, Something big afoot, Times Colonist (Section D7), 27 January, 2008.

Lauria, Vince, (1999), Bigfoot-A Primer.

L3 Communications, Infrared Products, Thermal-Eye X200xp, www.thermal-eye.com/products/x200xp.htm, 05 March 2012.

Marner, Doug, (26 May 2007), British Columbia: Neighbor wants tiger declared illegal, Big Cat News, http://bigcatnews.blogspot.com/2007/05/british-columbia-neighbor-wants-tiger.html, 04 September, 2011.

Meldrum, D, Jeffrey. (2004). Midfoot Flexibility, Fossil Footprints, and Sasquatch Steps: New Perspectives on the Evolution of Bipedalism. *Journal of Scientific Exploration*, Vol. 18, No. 1, pp. 65-79, http://www.scientificexploration.org/journal/jse_18_1_meldrum.pdf , 26 February 2011.

Meldrum, Jeff, (2006), Sasquatch: Legend Meets Science, Tom Doherty Associates, LLC, New York, N.Y.

Merriam-Webster Online Dictionary, www.merriam-webster.com, 07 November 2010.

Moneymaker, Matthew, (2007), Deer Kills and Bigfoots, www.bfro.net/avid/mjm/deerkills.asp, 31 October 2007.

Modern Firearms, FN FAL rifle, www.world.guns.ru/assault/be/fn-fal-e.html, 31 October 2009.

Noël, Chris, (2009), Impossible Visits, Xlibris Corporation, 2009.

Paranormal Zone X, Explanations for a Majority of UFO reports-Flares, www.sites.google.com/site/paranormalzonex/UFOs/explanations-for-ufos, 11 March 2012.

Powell, Thom, (2003), The Locals: A Contemporary Investigation of the Bigfoot/Sasquatch Phenomenon, Hancock House Publishers Ltd., Surrey, BC.

Ramis, Harold, (1980), Caddyshack, www.script-o-rama.com/movie_scripts/c/caddyshack-script-transcript-golf-movie.html, 23 July 2009.

Rense.com, (16 June 2003), Bigfoot Tracks in BC Strawberry Field?, www.rense.com/general38/bfoot.htm, 19 December 2009.

Saskatchewan Parks, Blackstrap Provincial Park, www.saskparks.net, 12 November 2011.

Shefferly, N., (2005), "Pan troglodytes" (On-line), Animal Diversity Web. http://animaldiversity.ummz.umich.edu/site/accounts/information/Pan_troglodytes.html, 01 January 2009.

Thomas, Patrice, Boom Car Noise, www.lowertheboom.org/trice/index.htm, 28 December 2008.

Watkins, Thayer, Gestation Periods and Animal Scale, www.sjsu.edu/faculty/watkins/gestation.htm, 05 November 2008.

Wikipedia, Brown Bear, www.en.wikipedia.org/wiki/Brown_Bear, 27 December 2011.

Wikipedia, The Argument Sketch, www.en.wikipedia.org/wiki/Argument_sketch, 15 May 2012.

Wikipedia, To a Mouse, on Turning Her Up in Her Nest with the Plough, http://en.wikipedia.org/wiki/To_a_Mouse, 24 June 2012.

Wikipedia, Vancouver Island, www.en.wikipedia.org/wiki/Vancouver_Island, 29 November 2009.

Wood Knocks & Tossed Rocks

End Notes

Introduction

[1]TV Archives, The Beachcombers – The Sasquatch Walks by Night, (aired on 13 January 1974), www.tvarchive.ca, 16 March 2012.

[2]Hunter and Dahinden, Sasquatch, pg. 100.

[3]Ibid, pg. 101.

[4]Ibid, pg. 102.

[5]BFRO report # 13390.

[6]BFRO report # 2113.

[7]BFRO report # 3945.

[8]BFRO report # 23245.

[9]Dr. W. H. Fahrenbach Ph. D., Sasquatch Smell / Aroma / Odor / Scent, www. bigfootencounters.com/biology/smell.htm.

[10]Dr. W. H. Fahrenbach Ph. D., Sasquatch Smell / Aroma / Odor / Scent, www. bigfootencounters.com/biology/smell.htm.

Chapter One - BFRO Sunshine Coast Expedition, 2005

[11]BFRO expedition faq, www.bfro.net/news/roundup/exped_faq.asp#purpose, 22 Mar, 2008.

[12]Mike has had this thermo-graphic unit for quite some time and it is an early model. The newer units now being utilized by the BFRO are1/5 the size and are capable of so much detail that even depth perception is clearly observable.

[13]John A. Bindernagel, North America's Great Ape: Sasquatch, pg. 197.

[14]Ibid.

[15]Richard Hooker, M*A*S*H, pg. 77.

[16]Thom Powell authored a great book about the sasquatch entitled "The Locals".

[17]Bill Cosby, Street Football, Warner Bros, catalogue# CWX-1798.

[18]Matthew Moneymaker, *Deer Kills and Bigfoots*, www.bfro.net/avid/mjm/deerkills.asp, 15 Feb, 2008.

[19]John A. Bindernagel, North America's Great Ape: Sasquatch, pg. 71.

[20]The idea has been put forward that a sasquatch will even wait until the traffic has passed by him and then step out behind the passing vehicle. If you go to the BFRO website (www.bfro.net) you can read through the posted reports that describe where a sasquatch has been seen on the side of the highway or crossing a road.

[21]BFRO report # 12855.

Chapter Two - BFRO Sunshine Coast Expedition, 2006

[22]Hinterland Who's Who, Animal Fact Sheets- North American Elk, 18 December 2011.

[23]There are several manufacturers of this type of pop-up tent. Look for Outwell, Quechua and Pinnacle.

[24]Navarin is another name for lamb stew and it actually tastes not too bad. But if the words 'lamb stew' were printed on the IMP packaging there would be very few service members who would eat it.

[25]Patrice Thomas, Infrasound, www.lowertheboom.org/trice/index.htm, 28 December 2008.

[26]Quoting from Ty Webb, Chevy Chase's character in the hit comedy *Caddyshack*, Harold Ramis, Caddyshack, www.script-o-rama.com/movie_scripts/c/caddyshack-script-transcript-golf-movie.html, 27 July 2009.

Chapter Three - BFRO Vancouver Island Expedition, 2007

[27]Nanoose Bay, www.bigfootencounters.com/sbs/nanoose.htm, 19 Dec., 2009.

[28]See **Chapter 5 - Tips and Tricks (while on an Expedition).**

[29]Rense.com, www.rense.com/general38/bfoot.htm, 19 December 2009.

[30]BFRO report #11915, 17 June 2005.

[31]BFRO report #13800, 14 October 2006.

[32]Thom Powell, Dance Hall Days, The Locals, pg. 88.

[33]Remote monitoring, www.bfro.net/avevid/remote.

[34]Thom Powell, Dance Hall Days, The Locals, pg. 95.

[35]Salal *(Gaultheria shallon)* is a member of the Ericaceae family. It is an evergreen Pacific Northwest shrub that is picked for use in floral arrangements. The berries were once a major food source for the First Nations people living near the coastal regions of the Pacific Northwest.

[36]CanWest News Service, (22 May 2007), Tiger turned loose on purpose, police say, http://www.canada.com/victoriatimescolonist/news/story.html, 04 September 2011.

[37]Doug Marner, (26 May, 2007), British Columbia: wants tiger declared illegal, http://bigcatnews.blogspot.com/2007/05/british-columbia-neighbor-wants-tiger.html, 04 September 2011.

[38]CanWest News Service, (22 May 2007), Tiger turned loose on purpose, police say, http://www.canada.com/victoriatimescolonist/news/story.html, 04 September 2011.

[39]The model we used was the L3 Thermal-Eye X200xp. According to the manufacturer it is specifically designed for reconnaissance and tactical applications, with the ability to detect human activity out to 450 meters.

[40]The BFRO utilizes several different recordings of what are believed to be sasquatch vocalizations. These recordings were obtained in several different

locations across the US. A comparative spectrographic analysis has revealed that they are from an unknown primate.

41The LUU-2A/B has since been replaced with the LUU-2B/B.

42Designated by the RCAF as the CC-115, the Buffalo was manufactured by De Havilland Canada as the DHC-5D.

43Paranormal Zone X, Explanations for a Majority of UFO Sightings, 11 March 2012.

44The Skookum Cast, www.bfro.net/NEWS/BODYCAST, 07 January 2010.

45The Quotations Page, http://www.quotationspage.com/quotes/Sun-tzu/, 21 April 2012.

46A colloquialism. To "wear many hats" is to be in charge of a number of different areas at the same time with one hat for each different subject.

47See **Chapter 5 - Investigators, Investigations and Questions** for more information on X's and arches.

48Monty Python (1972), The Argument Sketch, http://en.wikipedia.org/wiki/Argument_sketch, 15 May 2012.

49Robert Burns (1785), To a Mouse, http://en.wikipedia.org/wiki/To_a_Mouse, 24 June 2012.

50A video game from the late 1970's and '80s. The object was to maneuver geometric shapes so they fit as a solid mass while the individually fell within a column. The speed of the falling shapes would increase farther you progressed in the game. As a verb, to tetris – to fit random pieces into place like a jigsaw puzzle.

51Jeanne LaCasse attended the 2007 Vancouver Island expedition as a new attendee. She has since become a BFRO Investigator for Washington State.

Chapter Four – Tips and Tricks While on an Expedition

None.

Chapter Five – Investigators, Investigations and Questions

[52]BFRO report # 12855, Various Incidents on British Columbia Expedition.

[53]BFRO report # 7911, Possible Stalking at Echo Lake near Campbell River.

[54]BFRO report # 9876, Sighting by hunters south of Longview.

[55]BFRO report # 857, Possible sighting around 2:00AM near Courtenay.

[56]Thom Powell, The Locals, p. 126.

[57]Sir Arthur Conan Doyle (Sherlock Holmes), The Sign of Four.

[58]Phil Gibbs, (1996), What is Occam's Razor ?, http://math.ucr.edu/home/baez/physics/General/occam.html, 10 December 2008.

[59]Hinterland Who's Who, Mammal Fact Sheets, www.hww.ca/hww2.asp?id=83, 13 December 2008.

[60]Hinterland Who's Who, Mammal Fact Sheets, www.hww.ca/hww2.asp?id=83, 13 December 2008.

[61]Thayer Watkins, Gestation Periods and Animal Scale, www.sjsu.edu/faculty/watkins/gestation.htm, 05 November 2008.

[62]Ibid.

[63]Don Hunter and Rene Dahinden, Sasquatch, pg.117.

[64]Ibid, pg. 46.

[65]John Green, The Best of Sasquatch Bigfoot, pg. 27.

[66]Ibid, pg. 32.

[67]Ibid.

[68]Sea World, Orang-utans, www.seaworld.org/animal-info/info-books/orangutan/physical-characteristics.htm, 29 December 2008.

[69]Sea World, Orang-utans, www.seaworld.org/animal-info/info-books/ orangutan/birth-&-care.htm, 29 December 2008.

[70]Nancy Shefferly, Pan Troglodytes: Chimpanzee, Animal Diversity Web, http://animaldiversity.ummz.umich.edu/site/accounts/information/Pan_ troglodytes.html, 01 January 2009.

[71]Ibid.

[72]Ibid.

[73]Sea World, Gorillas, www.seaworld.org/Animal-info/info-books/gorilla/ reproduction.htm, 03 November 2008.

[74]John A. Bindernagel, North America's Great Ape: the Sasquatch, pg. 71.

[75]John Green, The Best of Sasquatch Bigfoot, pg. 100.

[76]Thom Powell, The Locals, pg. 11.

[77]Dr. George Schaller is the Vice President of the Wildlife Conservation Society's Science and Exploration Program.

[78]Jeff Meldrum, Sasquatch: Legend Meets Science, pg. 32.

[79]Ibid.

[80]Matthew Kruchak, Something big afoot, Times Colonist, Pg. D7, Sunday, 27 January, 2008.

[81]Ibid.

[82]Ibid.

[83]Jeff Meldrum,. (2004). Midfoot Flexibility, Fossil Footprints, and Sasquatch Steps: New Perspectives on the Evolution of Bipedalism. http://www. scientificexploration.org/journal/jse_18_1_meldrum.pdf , 26 February 2011.

[84]Ibid.

[85]Ibid.

[86]Ibid.

[87]Ibid.

[88]Ibid.

[89]Rebuttal to Grading, Appendix.

[90]Chris Nöel, Impossible Visits, pg. 142.

[91]The Blue Forum, http://s2.excoboard.com/BFRO, 10 Aug 2011.

[92]Wikipedia, Brown Bear, http://en.wikipedia.org/wiki/Brown_Bear#Dietary_habits, 27 December 2011.

[93]Douglas H. Chadwick, Grizzlies, National Geographic Magazine, July 2001.

[94]Ibid.

[95]Ibid.

[96]Hunter and Dahinden, Sasquatch, pg.48 and pg.55.

[97]Thom Powell, The Locals – Easy Pickin's, pg. 72 through 87.

[98]Wikipedia, Monster Quest, http://en.wikipedia.org/wiki/Monster_Quest, 03 May 2012.

[99]Wikipedia, Destination Truth, http://en.wikipedia.org/wiki/Destination_Truth, 06 May 2012.

About the Author

Blaine McMillan was born in Saskatoon, Saskatchewan and moved to British Columbia in 1972. After graduating from high school he joined the Canadian Armed Forces and proudly served for 27 years as an Aviation Life Support Equipment Specialist with operational postings to CFB Comox, BC, the MFO Base El Gorah, Egypt and CFB Winnipeg. While in Winnipeg Blaine enrolled in the University of Manitoba where he completed his Bachelor's degree in Criminology. In 2003, Blaine retired from the Canadian Armed Forces and returned to Vancouver Island with his wife Irene and two sons, Bowen and Kamryn.

Blaine's interest in the sasquatch first began in the early 1970's. He has attended numerous expeditions in search of this elusive creature beginning in 2005. In 2006 Blaine began investigating incidents submitted to the BFRO focusing on and completing reports from Canada's four western provinces. In 2007, Blaine was the lead organizer for the first BFRO expedition on Vancouver Island. In the years that followed he directed two more expeditions and has continued to have an active role in researching the sasquatch phenomena in Western Canada.

Made in the USA
Middletown, DE
11 December 2015